Learning to Begin Again:

Daily Reflections on Recovering and Renewal

W. T. Watts, Ph.D.

Order this book online at www.trafford.com
or email orders@trafford.com

Most Trafford titles are also available at major online book retailers.

Printed in the United States of America.

ISBN: 978-1-4669-0736-2 (sc)
ISBN: 978-1-4669-0735-5 (hc)
ISBN: 978-1-4669-0734-8 (e)

Library of Congress Control Number: 2011962186

Trafford rev. 12/20/2011

www.trafford.com

North America & international
toll-free: 1 888 232 4444 (USA & Canada)
phone: 250 383 6864 • fax: 812 355 4082

DEDICATION

For my wife, Kathy and my son, Dan;
my heart and my soul.

TABLE OF CONTENTS

Author Note

The author apologizes for any errors or omissions and has undertaken due diligence to acknowledge all sources. If he has omitted anyone, he apologizes and will, if informed, make corrections to any future editions.

Acknowledgments

I want to thank all of the spiritual teachers and messengers who have endeavored to make this world a better place through their espousal of inclusion, equality and unity. Most especially I would like to thank the following authors who have had the greatest influence on me and are most responsible for my current perspective as reflected in this work: Dr. Wayne Dyer, Ms. Marianne Williamson, Dr. Deepak Chopra, Lama Surya Das, and Ms. M. J. Ryan. Their dedication, insight and discourse have inspired me not only to broaden my viewpoint but also to clarify that viewpoint through writing.

On a more personal level I must express the deepest gratitude to my wife Kathy and my son Dan who have always sustained me with unconditional love and endless enthusiasm.

Introduction

I wrote this work to provide both a sanctuary and a strategy for surmounting substantial stress and emotional turmoil. Whether you have an addiction, a physical ailment, family dysfunction, death or separation from a loved one or any other life event that is causing severe distress, it is vital to create meaning from your pain and to construct a plan that allows you to move forward. It takes hard work and a change in perspective to overcome such distress and to progress but it is necessary if you are to live a satisfying and rewarding life. This book presents such a plan of thought and action.

The attitudes espoused are not new. Humility, gratitude, acceptance and patience are the first line of defense against stress, depression, anger, anxiety and frustration. Eastern and Western philosophers as well as religious leaders have touted these dispositions for years as essential "spiritual" qualities. In my practice as a psychologist, I have found them to be necessary for good mental health. Furthermore, I believe they are the foundations of love, wisdom and courage that, for me, are the paramount personality traits of the "self-actualized" person. These temperaments are crucial, if one is to lead a fulfilling and contented life.

In times of emotional stress and uncertainty, it is an element of our nature to try to maintain hope, control and predictability in our life. The only thing predictable, however, is the control we can exercise over our thoughts (by "framing" or filtering our perspective), our feelings about these thoughts and perspectives, as well as our responses or reactions to these thoughts, perspectives and feelings.

It is my goal to restore hope in the reader by presenting a plan that enables such control (and therefore predictability), as well as a framework to encompass experience so that it becomes more manageable, meaningful and productive. One of the genuine tragedies in life is to suffer pain without creating or learning the meaning. Such a concept is necessary to enhance the future and honor the experience. My desire is to empower readers to confront the "slings and arrows" of daily existence with both the courage and the wisdom that such pain can instill.

This book presents a belief system to assist the reader in times of turmoil, fear and disappointment. My major goal is to promote a mindset that enables the reader to: 1) begin to find meaning in chaos and challenge, 2) to develop a perspective of hope and confidence when faced with stress and uncertainty, 3) to feel sufficiently empowered to confront change and 4) to learn the skills necessary to implement the strategies that promote growth and serenity.

In order to manifest this plan successfully, the reader must be infused with the desire and courage to change. The importance of including awareness and intent in our daily life cannot be overstated. You must want to change and be willing to witness the positive results of this change. If we are to succeed, we must break from the past, conquer fear and generate perseverance so that we purposefully expand mindfulness beyond self-involvement and narcissistic needs. Intent is an act of will that results in a behavioral expression of a perspective and strategy. Intent will concentrate attention and motivation on a specific aspiration and goal. Awareness is tuning into our own consciousness as we sharpen mindfulness to the outside world, in order to perceive the goodness that is in the Universe and in us. As you develop and refine consciousness, you will begin to see the fruits of your labors. We do not want to be as puppets directed by the myths and biases instilled in our past without our consent or cognizance.

My approach is based upon well-researched concepts on information processing. I believe that we choose from among the many aspects of the external environment only those we wish to process. This selection is frequently beyond our awareness. As human beings we tend to select those facets of daily circumstances that confirm our belief system about ourselves, our relationships, our world and ourselves in our world. We must, therefore, sharpen perception so as to acknowledge these predispositions and form an intention to control the information we select to act upon. We are only as powerful as the information we choose to respond to.

With the data filtered through a new awareness, we can begin to develop those personality traits most likely to ease and advance our journey. Humility, gratitude, acceptance and patience are four fundamental attributes that have been advocated throughout the ages by both philosophers and spiritual leaders to improve the quality of life for all. As we evolve in kindness and compassion, these four fundamental dispositions will develop into courage, wisdom and love, providing optimal response to uncertainty, stress and transition. This transformation will generate a new dimension and quality of life-experience and perspective. New possibilities will arise as new solutions to old problems emerge. Truly, "when the student is ready the teacher will appear." The "teacher" is here and "now" is the time to begin.

We were created with an innate drive to nurture all life and to evolve. Unfortunately, the evolutionary necessity of fear has induced an equally powerful drive to remain in the status quo and to resist change and growth. This is our challenge: fear or love, avoidance or approach, unity or isolation. If we are to achieve fulfillment, we must confront the challenge of change. How we choose to do this is our life task.

Ultimately, the choice is ours. We create the reality in which we choose to live. We are responsible for solving our problems and becoming who we were created to be. It is our duty to make our lives meaningful and we are obligated to serve as examples in order to help others find their way to their own destiny.

PART ONE

CONGRATULATIONS AND WELCOME

You are about to embark on a journey that has no end. Personal growth is an ongoing and continual process that requires the personality attributes delineated in each lesson of this work. Your journey is one of truth, growth and courage. You have purchased this book and are reading these words precisely at the time you need them. There are no coincidences.

There are problems in your life now and in the next 366 pages you will learn how to cope with and confront them, master change and thrive. Life is a series of skill sets that can be taught and learned. Chances are that a great deal of your difficulties and impediments are the result of poor choices combined with ineffective, repetitive and self-destructive strategies to overcome those choices. At this point, you may believe that you are helpless and your life is unmanageable. This may be true and this can be a strength because you are now motivated to listen and learn. We develop courage only after all the other alternatives are attempted and abandoned. This is the time to change. Don't minimize the obstacles or the challenge, either now or in the future. These matters forced you to come to this place, so respect them and learn.

Begin with the intent to live compassionately. Cultivate humility, gratitude, acceptance and patience. Follow this by developing awareness in each moment and of your thoughts in the present as well as of the effects of this perspective. This will facilitate your growth and your evolution to become all you were created to be.

This book was written for you. Take the time to read each lesson and to try the activities suggested. Be patient with yourself because you are embarking on a task that is both unique and untested. You are attempting to change a perspective on yourself, your world and your loved ones. This is an enormous but achievable goal. As a result of your efforts, you will also be changing those behavioral habits that sabotaged success in the past. I know it's a lot to venture but you have already taken the first step and no step towards growth is too small. So let's get started!!

Days 1 to 90

DAY 1—HUMILITY

*"Rather to bow than to break is profitable;/
Humility is a thing commendable."*
(Anonymous)

PREMISE

To live effectively, one needs to understand and ultimately accept, boundaries, limits and impediments. Primarily the issue for mental health and wellbeing is to distinguish between what you can and can't control. To be humble is to value yourself and understand your limits. Through humility you view the world realistically and therefore, more effectively. Weaknesses exist as learning opportunities. Each interaction, every thought and feeling, at any moment, can serve as a clue to answer where, when and how we are to proceed. The necessary components to decipher such clues are intent to learn and to do the next best thing as well as awareness of our surroundings and the effects of our thoughts, feelings and actions.

INTENTION

I will begin to realize that I am responsible for my life and my current situation. Humility will guide me in deciding my path. I will ask for help and support. I will learn that there is a power beyond me whether that is in a person, group or philosophy. I am responsible and I can choose. I have the strength to embark on this journey because I now know that true power resides behind my eyes not in front of them.

AWARENESS

Today, I will be aware of what I can and can't control as well as the effects of my behavior and decisions those I love and myself. I can make so I shall choose carefully.

DAY 2—GRATITUDE

"All is beautiful and life is thankfulness."
(Guilin Song)

PREMISE

Gratitude is an essential component to the joy of life. Although it is generally defined as "thankfulness", gratitude comes from the Latin word "pleasing." We become grateful for something that pleases us and it pleases others when we express our thankfulness. Most importantly, gratitude requires an awareness or acknowledgement by one person about the beneficial and beneficent actions of another. Such awareness is propagated by humility. Once we appreciate our need for others and once we begin to trust in the life-affirming plan of the Cosmos, we generate a process wherein we see the gifts and bounty bestowed on us every moment of each day.

INTENTION

I can and will begin my progression towards gratitude. I will start viewing the world and my place in it from a perspective of unity and "we", rather than the narrow self-centered view of my past. I will intend, starting today, to see life as beneficent and fulfilling rather than malevolent and depriving. I have the power to choose to free myself from the self-created chains of regret, despair and resentment that keep me stagnant and filled with self-pity.

AWARENESS

For today, I plan to seek opportunities to express my gratitude to those around me and to my Higher Power for the help and insight offered for my growth. I will be aware of their reactions as well as my own feelings during this new endeavor.

DAY 3—ACCEPTANCE

"All pain comes from a futile search for what you want, insisting that it must be."
A Course in Miracles (1976)

PREMISE

Acceptance guides us and is instrumental in the achievement of growth and contentment. It requires the courage, trust and humility to surrender to what is, so that each skill or trait (humility, gratitude, acceptance and patience) builds upon and reinforces the other. For wisdom, love and courage (our ultimate goals) to operate effectively in daily living, we must choose to accept that which we cannot control. The fact is that despite our wishes to the contrary, we control very little. Exercising the trait of acceptance, therefore, allows us to avoid a great deal of distress caused by our delusion of power.

An integral part of acceptance is forgiveness. Forgiveness frees us from the anger and resentment we choose to live in. This negative force is used as an excuse to avoid the self-responsibility of growth and progress. We often prefer to "romance" negative thoughts of revenge and retaliation rather than to face our obligation to advance and to become the person we were created to be. Acceptance allows us to move on.

INTENTION

I have the strength, courage and endurance, right now, to make a decision to change the course of my life. I choose to trust in the plan of a Higher Power. I may not know either the plan or the source of guidance, at this time, but I do know that my past efforts have only brought me dissatisfaction, distress and depression. Now is the time to change and now is the time to act.

AWARENESS

Today I will focus on what I can change. I can start with my attitude and my acceptance of a new plan.

DAY 4—PATIENCE/TRUST

"How poor are they that have not patience?
What wound did ever heal but by degrees?"
(Othello, Act 2, William Shakespeare)

PREMISE

Patience is one of the four pillars or spiritual traits that sustains love, wisdom and courage. It is a compassionate quality that emanates from and yet reinforces, humility, gratitude and acceptance. As such it helps create a continuing cycle of wellness and spirituality. Patience is the caring, nurturing mother, caressing and reassuring the growing child. It is the feeling of security that soothes the "child-self" and says that no matter the frustration or disappointment all will be well if I just trust in the goodness in life's process. All things work out, maybe not as we expect or would like, but, as they should for the Good of all.

INTENTION

I can generate the imagination and trust to choose patience over anger and frustration in my daily interactions. I now realize that a conflict that frustrates and frightens me is simply something that I wish were different but that I can't control. I can face my fear of uncertainty and ineffectiveness with acceptance. I can trust that things will be okay and that there are lessons to be learned.

AWARENESS

Tonight I will reflect on one instance where I choose patience over anger or frustration. I will begin a journal to note my daily successes and disappointments.

DAY 5—HUMILITY

"Blessed are the meek for they shall inherit the earth."
(Matthew, 5:4-10)

PREMISE

To be humble is to be strong, grounded or solid. Humility is a source of strength because it helps us understand and accept what we can't control. Thus, we can become more effective in achieving our goals because we focus our energy where it is most useful. As we gain wisdom, we begin to see the limits of our power and we are then able to adjust our energy to that perception. Strength and competence is the product of this realization. We develop genuine power because it is born of truth and courage. We prioritize actions as we direct awareness and energize intent to the areas of most significant consequence.

INTENTION

I can do this. I can confront change and the fear that accompanies this challenge. I am strong because my Higher Power is always with me. At any moment, I can connect with my spiritual self that is the source of my courage. I know it is now time for me to move on, grow and evolve. If it were easy, I would have already attained my goals. But I have strength and for today I will persevere.

AWARENESS

Today, I will consider how little control I have over others. I will note one instance where I alter my habit of interfering or managing another and I will observe the consequences of this behavior.

DAY 6—GRATITUDE

"Gratitude is not only the greatest virtue but the parent of all others."
Cicero (21 B.C.E.)

PREMISE

Gratitude stems from humility and adds to the emergence of other spiritual skills and dispositions necessary for contentment and fulfillment. If we take nothing for granted and genuinely understand our role in the unfolding of the Universe, we will develop humility and from this perspective strengthen appreciation for the incredible bounty that infuses our daily life. This is a working definition of gratitude and is the result of persistence, dedication and changed attitudes. It is not easy but the reward is great.

INTENTION

Today I realize that my intent is extremely powerful and for today I will develop the courage to be humble. In this way, I will expand my awareness and be grateful. I will shed the arrogance of independence and embrace the concept of connectedness. I will see the magnitude of the kindness and generosity of others. I am indeed blessed and so appreciative.

AWARENESS

I will make an extra effort today to expand my awareness of the numerous acts of kindness and generosity that surround me. I will increase my gratitude for all things I am and especially for those things that I am not.

DAY 7—ACCEPTANCE

"O God, give us the serenity to accept what can't be changed . . ."
Reinhold Niebuhr (1934)

PREMISE

Genuine "acceptance" is difficult to achieve due to the severe fear and vulnerability that accompany it. To trust that issues will "work out", that moods will pass, that relationships will heal takes a leap of faith that for many is to take a leap off of a cliff. Acceptance acknowledges an establishment of limits, a submission of will, and a discarding of the arrogance of omnipotence. The natural and familiar response of our "child-self" is to scream, protest and tantrum. The truth is that "acceptance" is simply choosing reality and rejecting misconception and self-deceit. It signals a new perspective, a change in problem solving, a life approach that embraces trust and a desire to learn rather than manage. We now understand true "humility", interdependence and helplessness.

INTENTION

I have the strength to comprehend my weaknesses and the trust to progress despite doubt, deficiency and defensiveness. I can choose to face the reality of change, to confront my fears. To know my vulnerability is to know my strength. I have support and I am certain that I can do this one small step at a time.

AWARENESS

Today I will make a sincere effort to allow others to be themselves despite my desire to micro-manage and control. I will be alert to my feelings, especially frustration, but I will become an "observer" rather than CEO.

DAY 8—PATIENCE

"Patience is the best remedy for every trouble."
Titus Maccius Plantus (212 B.C.E.)

PREMISE

Patience allows us the opportunity to pause, reflect and thereby delay or eliminate impulsive reaction to habits, feelings and false needs. When we choose patience, we delay gratification, sharpen judgment and eschew indiscretion. It is truly the "pause that refreshes." Patience serves as a reminder to strive for detachment and objectivity, thereby mitigating unpleasant emotion and revitalizing intellect. Such choice gives us respite to ponder what is and what is not within our power. Patience gives time the space to help us gather the courage to break old habits of instinctive and biased response. It allows us to learn before we repeat mistakes. Through patience we are able to effectively evaluate both our actions and the reactions of others in the present, avoiding resentment, remorse and retribution in the future.

INTENTION

Only I have the power to change me. It is no one's responsibility but my own. I create my life, its problems and it's triumphs. However, I must develop more patience. Change takes time and I have no control over the amount of time needed. It's a long, never ending process of frustration, learning and success. I will improve my awareness and re-energize my intent as needed, but I will never give up. Each day, each opportunity, I will attempt to complete the next good thing and I will move on in acceptance, love and respect.

AWARENESS

Today, I will be extra alert to feelings of frustration. I will describe these feelings in my journal and I will note the circumstances where they were encountered today.

DAY 9—HUMILITY

"I believe that the first test of a really great man is his humility."
John Ruskin (1850)

PREMISE

To realize and to understand how little we really control will initially arouse feelings of fear and vulnerability. We tend to be subject to delusions of control and self-importance, so the child-self does not give up without a fight. We needed these delusions as infants but they are now simply destructive and useless remnants of the past. We can surmount these unpleasant appendages by believing and trusting in a plan greater than ourselves. This includes the presumption that our life is unique and meaningful and everything that happens to us can be an opportunity to learn. This progression is an active, decision-making process that presents a choice. Shall we remain in the perspective of the past or shall we face fear and move forward to fulfill our unique mission in life? Now is the time to begin and only you can choose.

INTENTION

I have the courage to face truth. This is a first step and solely my responsibility. I believe that humility is the perspective of trust and patience in a plan that I can't control. I can control how I view the plan as well as my feelings and reactions to it. I can make it my intention to focus on these issues as I live my daily life. Whatever circumstance I face today will be viewed with the premise that it has a purpose and a lesson specifically for me.

AWARENESS

I will note in my journal tonight two instances where I faced fear and choose acceptance. I will also note my feelings about this change in perspective.

DAY 10—GRATITUDE

"Developing a true sense of gratitude involves taking absolutely nothing for granted."
Albert Schweitzer (1910)

PREMISE

It is exceedingly difficult to genuinely acknowledge the bounty we are given. It is hard to even ascertain. Our child-self asserts that we need nothing and that all we have is due to our control, our efforts. This is another destructive delusion we use to abate our fear of dependence and vulnerability. The child-self hides and denies needing anything that he/she can't provide. As such we live life certain that we "deserve" what we have and oblivious (and therefore unappreciative) of the Good, kind and beneficent powers surrounding us. We don't hear the compliments, we don't see the smiles and we don't feel the touch. The child-self confines us to a lonely, delusional world where we need no one and have no weakness, where everything is delivered on demand with no delay, disruption or distress.

INTENTION

I can listen to Dr. Schweitzer. I can take nothing for granted and realize that all I have has been given through the kindness of others or the beneficence of fate. Where I live, what I own, the state of my health are all unique to me and serve the purpose of enabling me to contribute to life as only I can. My very breath, my life, my friends and my possessions confirm that my Higher Power has blessed me each moment of my existence. I have simply chosen not to see this to protect my ego.

AWARENESS

I will make a special effort to be thankful and I will be more alert to the joys of life and the talents, friends and assets, I have been given.

DAY 11—ACCEPTANCE

"Maturity consists of no longer being deceived by oneself."
Kajetan von Schalaggenberg

PREMISE

It is unlikely that we will attain complete acceptance of either, self, others or our general life circumstance, as we strive to refine and redefine ourselves. As such, we will be tempted to abandon our mission and return to the ways of old. We will feel urges to avoid, deny or minimize the importance of our undertaking and the progress we have made so far. We can, however, avoid this impediment and its accompanying disparagement, depression and demoralization if we stay focused on our daily goals and return to the basic belief that we were created for a reason and our life has a purpose that we can uniquely fill. Our strengths are in our successes And our failures. We must remember how far we've come rather than be discouraged by how far we need to go.

INTENTION

I will choose to persevere as I improve and develop my awareness of my power and my intent to fulfill my destiny. I will not become discouraged when my expectations are not met. Rather, I will view such events as markers to pursue and loving responses from my Higher Power.

AWARENESS

Today, I will strive to become more aware of the propitious occasions that present themselves to help and serve others. I will seize the moment and note in my journal the opportunities presented in my daily routine.

DAY 12—PATIENCE

"Everything comes gradually and at its appointed hour."
Ovid (15 C.E.)

The ability to be patient requires the awareness to pause during times of stress, breathe and reset your attitude to be more in alignment with your goals of gratitude, humility and acceptance. Rather than indulge in the destructive impulse to act on anger and frustration, a few seconds of thoughtful awareness will help us attain both long and short-term goals. Most importantly, through patience we resist an action or thought which distracts us from the moment. Patience quiets the noise so that we may hear the message. When feeling frustrated, angry or resentful, it is likely that we are overcome by self-interest as well as self-deprecating implications and assumptions. In such situations, we need to reestablish our strength and commitment to rationality.

INTENTION

I can chose the self-discipline necessary to restore patience and perspective in a tense and challenging situation. I will also be patient with myself and thoroughly comprehend that I am striving for progress not perfection. Each day in a small way I will improve and so will my life. I will begin to see that I am successful in tasks I was formerly too fearful to even attempt. I will see that trusting in the process and being consistent with my spiritual self yields rewards beyond my expectations.

AWARENESS

I will note the frustrating and distressful situations I encounter, today and I will make a special effort to behave rationally. I will begin to develop a strategy to use in future challenging circumstances.

DAY 13—HUMILITY

"All streams flow to the ocean because it is lower than they are. Humility gives it its power."
Lao-Tzu (6th century B.C.E.)

PREMISE

Humility means understanding and embracing the idea that we, indeed, have a purpose in life and that purpose is beyond our power to ascertain on our own. This purpose is revealed gradually as you begin your life anew dedicating yourself to doing the next good thing as you avoid self-interest, attachment and control. All good comes to you through this dedication and intent. You connect with a life force, a power greater than you imagine and you become united with all life engaged in a similar quest. The perspective of "me-ness" is substituted for "we-ness." As we evolve and develop the capacity to be humble, our role in life and our ultimate destiny come into focus more clearly. Each day we will climb one small step leading to good will and contentment. Each day we will forge a path as we consult our heart and spiritual self.

INTENTION

Each day in every way I'm re-energizing my intent and clarifying my awareness that this is the path to follow. Obstacles remain and I still feel the frustrations that are part of life but I feel stronger and more resolute in my new perspective. I can feel this new power of choice inside of me. I can decide what is necessary and what I can discard. I am not without conflict or distress but these are burdens that I can surmount and questions that I can answer. Life is indeed improving.

AWARENESS

Today I will take notice of the gradual enhancement of my daily life.

DAY 14—GRATITUDE

"You can't appreciate home till you left it, money till it's spent . . ."
W. S. Porter (1909)

PREMISE

Do things really happen for a reason? If we become grateful for what we have, we begin to take little for granted and instead cherish and appreciate what previously would have gone unnoticed. Life gets suddenly better. The air smells fresher, we feel stronger and people seem kinder. As we begin the process of seeing the Good, the bad begins to fade and a cycle of optimistic reciprocity emerges. Consequently, such an attitude of gratitude leads to trust and we begin to look for the positive in all our actions, interactions, feelings and thoughts.

INTENTION

I know it's new but I can learn to accept the goodness and bounty in my life instead of cursing my fate and blaming my circumstances. I can now, gradually, take responsibility for the events, situations and conditions that surround me. I can see the Good and take responsibility to change the bad. I am in control over what is behind my eyes and I can choose to behave with kindness and compassion rather than selfishness, evil, malice and arrogance. I no longer have to hide behind self-pity, blame and resentment.

AWARENESS

I will start a new routine that I will follow each night. I will list three things for which I am grateful.

DAY 15—ACCEPTANCE

"He who does anything because it is the custom makes no choice."
John Stuart Mill (1860)

PREMISE

As we progress, we will begin to think, act and even feel differently. This, in turn, will alter our reactions to change and subsequently, alter the reactions of others to us. Take it slowly because these effects can be quite unsettling. Also understand that others may actively resist such disruption and urge for a return to the status quo. Be aware, persevere and comprehend that if this were an easy task, we would have achieved it, already. At this point trust in yourself and persevere, be more aware of the process than the results. Intend empathy and acceptance and you will note joy and fulfillment.

INTENTION

I can make better choices as I become more aware of my habits and biases. Change is not something to fear and I now know that change can mean growth and choice is empowerment.

AWARENESS

Continue to pray for guidance and try to be in contact with your spiritual-self through relaxation and reflection. Be aware of the choices you have in every moment: love or fear, acceptance or exclusion, progress or status quo etc.

DAY 16—PATIENCE

"Only with winter-patience can we bring/ The deep-desired, long-awaited spring."
Anne Morrow Lindbergh (1956)

PREMISE

Patience puts things in perspective. We begin to understand that most frustration, anger and anxiety are due to transitory situations wherein we have lost appropriate perspective. "I want", "I need", "it must be so" or "I will die" is the voice of the child-self's demanding delusion that it is in control and must have immediate satisfaction. Once we understand this and replace impulsivity with reason, patience covers us with a sense of calm and reassurance that we are, in fact making the choice of self-control over self-indulgence. We embrace the concept that "this too will pass" and we put our trust in the knowledge that things happen for a reason and this situation is an opportunity to learn.

INTENTION

When I feel angry frustrated or impatient, I will pause and reflect, reassessing the situation and restoring appropriate perspective. I can do this and it will substantially improve the joy of life. I will not personalize, project or presume. Reason will rule and I will call upon my spiritual-self to give me compassion and understanding. All is learning. Success is trying and failure is giving up. Each day I learn becomes one more blessed day.

AWARENESS

Today I will write in my journal a brief description of how frustration feels (e.g. heart beating faster, shallow breathing, shaky etc.). I will ponder this and try to identify the circumstances that surround these feelings.

DAY 17—HUMILITY

"Humility is a virtue all preach but none practice . . ."
John Selden (1640)

PREMISE

We compare, we judge and we conclude either that we are "hot stuff" or of no value. Our need to know who we are as compared to who we should be is a constant theme and source of major distress. This is especially relevant when our standards are outside of us and beyond our control. We need to evaluate our goodness and effectiveness as we journey through life but our comparisons must be about ourselves, where we started and where we are now. It's not what we have; it's about who we are. It's not about perfection; it's about progress. Each day presents an opportunity to learn, each day we can intend the next good thing and each day we can serve our Higher Power and "give back" to those who so selflessly help us along the way.

INTENTION

I can be myself and let others be themselves. I don't have to validate my own value by imposing my beliefs, will or needs on someone else. I am perfectly "me" with flaws, strengths and needs. I can achieve my goals in my own way with the resources, virtues and willpower that are part of my essence and experience. I am on a new path and every day I learn more about who I am and more about my destiny. I have erred but I also have succeeded. The path is difficult but also rewarding. Many times I have been tempted to return to past behavior and attitudes but in my heart I know I need to change and going back is the wrong direction. With the help of my Higher Power I will move forward, a step at a time.

AWARENESS

Today I will strive to be positive in all my deeds, thoughts and feelings. I will note occasions of uncertainty and I will write my responses in my journal.

DAY 18—GRATITUDE

"Gratitude is the fairest blossom that springs from the soul."
Harriet Ward Beecher (1862)

PREMISE

Gratitude and acceptance are reciprocal qualities, each reinforcing and promoting the other. If we accept what is given to us by events (in effect, accepting "the hand that we are dealt"), our capacity to cope with and circumvent obstacles increases. This happens because our focus sharpens to what is rather than what should be. Coping with external impediments will significantly improve self-esteem, which, in turn, gives us the courage and honesty to be grateful. Each of the four foundations of contentment (humility, gratitude, acceptance and patience) reinforces and revitalizes the others resulting in a mutually beneficial, life-affirming cycle of growth and hopefulness. The ultimate result of this blessed process is a life of contentment and fulfillment.

INTENTION

I am unique and I have gifts to offer others, which only I can bestow. I will develop the courage to be myself. I know that if I review my character honestly, I will realize all that I am and all that I can be. I will remember that what I have and what I don't have has been given and not earned. With humility, I accept these gifts as well as the responsibility to use such gifts to help others.

AWARENESS

Today I will express my gratitude to another for his or her support, caring and love.

DAY 19—ACCEPTANCE

"Each of us literally chooses, by his way of attending to things, what sort of Universe he shall appear to himself to inhabit."
William James (1884)

PREMISE

Acceptance generates the creativity and power to be aware, face the truth and persevere in our convictions. Through acceptance, we empower ourselves to be whoever we are, absent of comparison, judgment and preconception. We become aware that although we are a work in progress, and always will be, we are perfectly who we were created to be at this moment. We are filled with flaws and faculties that can be used, as we evolve, for the Good of all. Self-denigration, self-pity and self-justification serve only to excuse inaction and victimhood.

INTENTION

I have the strength and honesty to look into my soul and identify the self-destructive rationalization that I use daily to justify inaction. It does not take courage to belittle myself in order to shed responsibility for mistakes but it takes courage to take responsibility and to progress, as I know I should. I can do this. My Higher Power has given me yet another chance to be who I can be and I will embrace this goal and do the next good thing.

AWARENESS

Today I will list in my journal three excuses that immediately come to mind when I think about doing the next good thing. I will also identify what that next thing is.

DAY 20—PATIENCE

"There's only one corner of the Universe you can be certain of improving and that's your own self."
Aldous Huxley (1950)

PREMISE

Patience recognizes that the effects of our behavior are a small part of a more encompassing plan of self-evolution and that we did our best with what we knew. Patience suppresses the "woulds," "shoulds", and "coulds" substituting the "now" and the "is" as the more objective participant-observer perspective begins to suppress the self-critical world-view. We quiet the child-self's insistence on magical wish fulfillment and immediate gratification. Most importantly, patience gives us the power over time. It allows us to pause the present as we consider the future consequences of emotionally driven thoughts, feelings and behaviors. We focus on the moment and what is motivating us as we control the impulse to immediately react.

INTENTION

I can achieve the strength and awareness to pause, breathe and consider consequences during emotionally charged circumstances. I can stop reflexive reactions to distress, discomfort and despair. Rather than blame I will take responsibility for my actions. Rather than make an excuse I will control what I can. Rather than be a victim I will become empowered as I focus on the Good and my objectives. I will gradually change old patterns of reaction and begin new ones that benefit both others and myself. I will sow the seeds of betterment and allow them to grow, as they can.

AWARENESS

Today I will direct my attention to those times when I lose patience and desire immediate results. I will describe the feeling of impatience in my journal.

DAY 21—HUMILITY

"The way to be happy is to make others so."
Robert Ingersoll (1875)

PREMISE

As you embrace humility and self-responsibility, paradoxically, you begin to discover that you are perfectly you and that you have an opportunity to present to others, an individual of substance, consequence and confidence. As such you begin to acknowledge the need to express the courage and compassion that you feel. The most effective and blessed way to do this is to offer your special talents to serve others. Service is the ultimate expression of humility. When offering such kindness it is crucial that it is done willingly and without expectation of recognition, recompense or reward. Do good for itself and for no other motive.

INTENTION

I have the potential to effect change at any time I choose. I have the greatest control over changing myself and since that has become my priority, I have felt responsible, effective and relieved. Relieved in that I no longer feel compelled to blame others or to be rescued. As I take responsibility and I continue to have the humble recognition that I will always need strength, wisdom and kindness from a Higher Power, I will begin to live a more fulfilled and rewarding life. I know that as a result of my experiences and perspective, I have unique contributions to offer others. As I honor and respect them, I show honor and respect for myself.

AWARENESS

I will try to do a random act of kindness today and take special note as to how I feel about it.

DAY 22—GRATITUDE

"You must become the change you wish to see in the world."
Mahatma Gandhi (1895)

PREMISE

We must learn to look inward to manifest the change we wish to see in others. Gratitude is a special gift and stems from humility. We can only become as grateful as we are humble and courageous. We must pray daily for both. It takes courage to open ourselves to new experiences and to find a purpose and lesson in those things that challenge us. It takes courage to become vulnerable and to comprehend that we need others to become ourselves. To confront such truths requires that we silent the child-self's arrogance, fear and hubris. The child-self likes to believe that it is all-powerful, independent and self-sufficient. It wants to return to the womb where need was unknown and satisfaction was immediate. It will never comprehend that the womb indeed belonged to another.

INTENTION

I am becoming more courageous by the day. I am maturing and evolving just as I am supposed to. I am in the right place, at the right time, to fulfill my destiny for today. With the help of my Higher Power, I intend to see and seize the opportunities for achievement that unfold before me.

AWARENESS

I will choose to be more aware of the kindness, respect and compassion I encounter today. I will acquire the resolution to ignore the "slings and arrows" so that I may focus only on the Good.

DAY 23—ACCEPTANCE

"The art of progress is to preserve order amid change, and to preserve change amid order."
Alfred North Whitehead (1912)

PREMISE

If we are to evolve and to fulfill our destiny, we must expose and reject the self-sabotaging thoughts that so frustrate us and lead us to embrace the status quo. There is a part of us that resists change and the growth that accompanies that change, every time an opportunity for progress presents itself. That part of us is called the "child-self" and is a natural (and sometimes useful) aspect of our constitution. To advance is to face the truth through trust in a beneficent plan and through willingness to learn. This, in turn, involves patience and perseverance manifested in the presence of stress and anxiety. We cannot learn without making errors. This is not a moral issue. We must stumble in order to walk.

INTENTION

I am beginning to understand that every fear, anxiety and excuse is a challenge by the Universe to become who I was created to be. My task is to be aware of this challenge and to respond in a manner that propagates peace and acceptance towards others and myself.

AWARENESS

I will accept myself today with the awareness that I am "perfectly" me. Yet, to fulfill my destiny I must utilize my assets and learn from my weaknesses.

DAY 24—PATIENCE

"First, keep the peace within yourself,
then you can bring peace to others."
Thomas A. Kempis (1445)

PREMISE

Patience guides us in listening to the spiritual self as it rescues us from an immediate circumstance of distress. With patience we choose to listen with both ears and heart even to those with whom we disagree. Through patience we gain a new understanding and compassion for our fellow travelers. Patience gives us the opportunity to cherish the challenge of change rather than reflexively reacting with fear, aggression or flight. Our experiences become less personalized and more objective as we confront discomfort and instability with a desire to learn and progress. We begin to impartially observe the noise, clamor and dysfunction surrounding us without becoming a part or participant in that chaos. We maintain focus on the Good, the positive and the eternal and let go the transient, the superficial and the external. Patience is the calm that prevents the storm. It is the pause that refreshes providing reassurance during times of doubt. It is truly an asset worth cultivating.

INTENTION

With my new awareness I can choose patience over impulsivity. In stressful circumstances, I can pause, breathe and assess. My will and my intelligence can surmount my desire to act and escape. I can learn and move on, thereby avoiding the pain, consequence and remorse resulting from unchannelled emotion.

AWARENESS

Today, I will make a special effort to be patient, polite and understanding, despite my anger, annoyance or apprehension. I will choose to put issues in perspective with the knowledge that all things are resolved in time.

DAY 25—HUMILITY

"Humility is the most difficult of all virtues to achieve; nothing dies harder than the desire to think well of oneself."
T. S. Eliot (1922)

PREMISE

To grow, evolve and mature is to expand and utilize those foundations of contentment (humility, gratitude, acceptance and patience) that have proven successful throughout the ages. These attitudes or traits will improve our lives and the lives of those we encounter each day with every interaction. Humility provides a fertile ground for gratitude that in turn fosters acceptance and patience. Each trait in its own way reinforces and is reinforced by another in a cycle of positive reciprocity. Throughout the day, in the course of our routine, we have the power to choose humility over arrogance, gratitude over greed, acceptance over anger and patience over frustration. We have the power of choice to create the world we inhabit. Humility is the beginning, a necessary starting point to expand and advance all that we were created to be.

INTENTION

I can accept the power of choice. With my daily readings, I am increasing awareness and fortifying intent. I know that I am improving and I see my progress as I compare my current attitudes with those of the past. I have been frustrated, I have made mistakes and I have doubted. But each time I prayed and reflected on my goals and each time I found the strength to continue, a step at a time, each instance an improvement over the last. I will continue on this path because I know this is what I was meant to do.

AWARENESS

Today I will be especially aware and I will note in my journal, all the Good I do and all the Good I receive. I will offer a prayer of thanks.

DAY 26—GRATITUDE

"Always look for the friendly intention behind the deed and learn to appreciate it."
Albert Schweitzer (1910)

PREMISE

Can we trust in the future? Are we part of a loving design with a beneficent purpose and power? Without these beliefs, the feeling of gratitude, which is vital for a contented life, will never come into our awareness. With faith in the future and gratitude for the past we can overcome the burdens of negativity and self-hate as we advance at the intended pace. Each day we are provided with everything we need to achieve our goals and fulfill our destiny. We always have the choice, in each action and interaction, to behave in a loving, accepting and compassionate manner or to remain in the fearful, rejecting and competitive cycle of response that brought us to this painful place. The choice is ours and we have the opportunity to be grateful for such options.

INTENTION

I will develop the courage to trust so that gratitude may frame my world-view. This courage will be reached a step at a time and I can choose the patience to move forward in the knowledge that I am unique and that I am blessed. I will resist the familiar blame, regret and resentment of the past that has formerly impeded and obstructed my progress and happiness. I will get out of my own way and flourish according to divine intervention.

AWARENESS

I will open my eyes and allow myself to see the beauty in my life as it is now. I will begin a daily list in my journal noting three things for which I am grateful on that day. I will end the day with a prayer of thanksgiving no matter how bad I feel.

DAY 27—ACCEPTANCE

"Despair is the price one pays for setting oneself an impossible aim."
Graham Greene (1948)

PREMISE

Instead of choosing negative self-talk, we must begin to relish our individuality and our progress over the last few weeks. Each new obstacle and interaction can be viewed from a new vantage point and a new approach. However, this requires that we have the courage to take an honest (possibly painful) self-inventory of our assets, weaknesses, past and future. Each is an essential part of who we are and who we wish to become. Self-deprecation, guilt, regret and resentment play a critical role in our daily decision making process and they must be brought into our awareness if we are to pursue meaningful change. As the scientist (participant-observer) of your life's journey, you must be cognizant of the facts that influence your thoughts, emotions and behavior. Armed with this knowledge, you can begin to move forward and undertake the necessary trial and error learning required for advancement. Acceptance of yourself, your world and your past can facilitate this process. Self-hatred, regret and resentment can only be impediments.

INTENTION

I have the courage to accept, my Higher Power and my current circumstances, as learning experiences. These are opportunities to advance and begin to live a fulfilling life. I will live in the present and watch life unfold as I let go of that which I can't control.

AWARENESS

I will take special notice today of how I sabotage my own success. Negative attitudes, insecurity, resentment and blame will only impede my progress towards fulfillment and contentment.

DAY 28—PATIENCE

"People in a hurry cannot think, cannot grow, nor can they decay. They are preserved in a state of perpetual puerility."
Eric Hoffer (1962)

PREMISE

Patience can take both active and passive expressions. You can "be" patient or you can "allow" patience. It can describe "waiting" or "persisting in the face of impediments." Ultimately, it means accepting what you can't control and persevering in that which you can. You can remain calm in the midst of inner distress and unpredictability or you can confront this turmoil with an abiding trust that all things transpire as they must. It is self-sabotaging to distress, deny or delay over the inevitable. Whether you choose an active or passive strategy, it is vital to remember that patience generates and nurtures courage, wisdom and humility as it channels impulse, irrationality and irresponsibility.

INTENTION

I will choose patience over impulse throughout the day. I will allow time for patience and patience in time. I will become more calm and serene as this process unfolds. As I go through the day, I will accept that I and others will make mistakes and that I will become annoyed, disappointed and frustrated but I do not have to become angry, disrespectful or dismissive. Such control can become my choice and I can also choose to pray for guidance and renewal when the task seems beyond my control. Today I will genuinely "live and let live."

AWARENESS

I will write a brief description of my inner sensations and reactions when I label myself "annoyed", "agitated" or "angry." I will do this to sharpen my awareness of a destructive situation.

DAY 29—HUMILITY

"Really great men have a curious feeling that their 'greatness' is not of them but through them."
Abraham Lincoln (1862)

PREMISE

In order to achieve the goals of fulfillment and contentment, we must first undergo a major transformation in our thinking. We must free ourselves from the child-self propensity towards the "I", "me" and "mine" adopting instead a perspective of "we", "us" and "ours." Humility is the catalyst for this process and relationships are the training grounds. By their nature, relationships create a tension between the need for intimacy and affection with the simultaneous yet conflicting needs to be autonomous and self-sufficient: our need to "connect" conflicts with our fear of connection. How much of "me" do I dedicate to "we"? Humility mitigates this tension because we develop the courage to face the reality that we are not alone and that we need others to survive. We begin to trust sufficiently to ask for help and love sufficiently to accept that help.

INTENTION

I can be tolerant and respectful to those whose perspectives differ from mine. I need not be angry or defensive when my views are challenged. I can reach out to help or be helped and I can give or receive. I don't have to be in control, isolated or detached. I can freely express myself knowing that I am as God made me and I can humbly accept my limitations.

AWARENESS

I will strive to become more compassionate and open in all of my interactions. I will list three ways I'm dependent on others and three gifts/favors that I have recently received. I will thank those people today.

DAY 30—GRATITUDE

"As for him who voluntarily performs a good work, verily God is grateful and knowing."
The Koran (c. 610-632 C.E.)

PREMISE

Being "grateful" includes being both trusting and accepting of circumstances and people over which we have no control. This includes just about everything and everybody. The basic fact is that we do control and therefore are responsible for, our thoughts, subsequent feelings and reactions to those feelings encountered in our daily routines. Although we control virtually nothing outside of ourselves, how we perceive, interpret and react to everyday occurrences is our responsibility. Understanding and truly comprehending our lack of power and control over everything external, can generate gratitude for all that we are, all that we have and all that we will become because so little had to do with us and our attempts at success. Such understanding destroys the arrogance that assumes good things came from our own efforts and the conceit that we deserve such bounty.

INTENTION

I will express my gratitude by giving back to others. Small acts of random kindness as well as behaving respectfully and undertaking community services are among the ways I can express my appreciation for all that I have received. Gratitude does not imply submission or subservience; rather it manifests a confident understanding of both my power and my vulnerability. There is much to be grateful for and I will express this daily.

AWARENESS

Today, I will pray for the gift of gratitude in the morning and in the evening write in my journal three things for which I am grateful.

DAY 31—ACCEPTANCE

"In the adaptability and ease with which we experience change, lie happiness and freedom."
Buddha (c. 510 B.C.E.)

PREMISE

We recreate and rebuild our character by living in the moment, a small step at a time. However, we must intend to be aware of that moment and seek the courage and humility to confront truth and learn rather than to avoid, delay or escape those current circumstances that we find unpleasant. Being aware in the moment requires making brave choices and decisions about the degree of our control. We must then challenge the specter of change and act upon what we can affect leaving the rest to the Power greater than we. In each moment, we create or reinforce who we are and who we will become. Such experiences and possibilities occur throughout our daily routines. It is our obligation to seize these opportunities as steppingstones to our ultimate destiny. In this way, we become responsible and empowered.

INTENTION

I can face and challenge the self-destructive thought patterns mired in the past and immobilizing me in the present. I can free myself from these self-destructive biases and become who I was created to be. I can begin now. I will be more aware of the convenient cycle of blame and excuse that leads to arrogance and rigidity, keeping me in my misery. I will face fear, take responsibility and evolve as I am meant to.

AWARENESS

I will focus on a present moment and sharpen awareness of all the sights, sounds and sense information as they impact on me. I will pause, breathe and move forward with a fortified commitment to behave in a manner more consistent with my ideal self.

DAY 32—PATIENCE

"Patience and diligence, like faith, remove mountains."
William Penn (1693)

PREMISE

Patience is an intentional decision making process. Whether it is expressed passively or actively, patience is a choice we make. This aspect of choice is important because we control our level of awareness every moment. Our choices can be only to act or not. If we chose to act, the choice then becomes to do so out of love or fear. This choice is our responsibility and in every moment we get an opportunity to either affirm or reject the positive values that will contribute to a contented life. However, the outcome of such action is beyond our control and we therefore must frequently cope with disappointment, frustration and unpredictability. This is our challenge and patience will help us cope with these difficult situations. If we are to achieve contentment, our responsibility is to choose with the intent of love, peace and serenity. Patience mitigates the anger arising from judgment and comparison as we concentrate on the present and let go of expectation's prejudicial map filled with "should", "could" and "would."

INTENTION

Despite the trepidation I feel about my inability to control surrounding events, I will step back and trust. I will become an observer rather than a manager, as I learn about the limits of my control. I will accept those limits and trust that the plans of the Universe are wiser and more benevolent than my own. I will get out of the way and let life unfold as I focus on the challenge of changing what I can (me).

AWARENESS

Today, I will observe myself as I participate in life and interact with others. I will take special note of my frustrations and begin to construct a strategy to utilize patience at every opportunity.

DAY 33—HUMILITY

"You will find angling to be like the virtue of humility, which has a calmness of spirit and a world of other blessings attending upon it."
Isaac Walton (1653)

PREMISE

Out of mutual respect, many Eastern cultures acknowledge each other with a bow upon meeting. In some instances the hands are put together with fingers pointing upward. The greeting offered is "Namaste" which loosely translated means: "I honor the place where you and I are one." If we begin all interactions with the perspective of "Namaste," we will create a predisposition towards humility and respect. In this way we take the first steps toward living in a contented, peaceful manner where we don't fear the "other" or attempt control or domination. What we put out to the world comes back to us magnified, love for love, hate for hate. Will we choose inclusion or isolation, acceptance or rejection? This is a choice we make in every interaction.

INTENTION

I can now comprehend that each situation offers me a unique opportunity to transform, to learn about myself and to better understand my role in this evolution. I can and will achieve a new worldview as I peel away the myths that mire me in doubt and fear. I will see my world and myself in a new way. Gradually but ever-changing my perspective, I will achieve a critical mass of confidence and contentment.

AWARENESS

Today I will increase awareness of my power to choose love over hate and acceptance over rejection. I will make an effort to meet someone new and to listen and learn from them as I discard my prejudgments.

DAY 34—GRATITUDE

"Thank God for peace."
Guy Wetmore Carryl (1901)

PREMISE

Gratitude and acceptance guide us to enjoying the moment; we learn to enjoy what "is" rather than what "should" be. Both temperaments promote contentment and decrease the reflex to seek an external cure when we experience unpleasant feelings. We become grateful for the moment because we accept life as it is. The child-self is the voice of the "should". "Should", "would" and "could" are the tools and the chains of judgment and comparison. They are ways we rationalize being a victim and sabotage our growth. Stop them and live your life.

INTENTION

I can do this. I can learn to be grateful. I can learn to see things through different lenses. It starts with realizing that I could have been born anywhere, even in the most dreaded and deprived of circumstances. I could be disabled and impaired. These are the "coulds" I must consider if I am to grow in gratitude. What appears to be a burden or deficit, in reality is an opportunity to learn and affirm my exceptionalism.

AWARENESS

Today I will enlighten myself to the gifts of the Universe and give thanks. I will enter in my journal an action I'm proud of and why I am grateful to have done it.

DAY 35—ACCEPTANCE

"'Enlightenment' is the acceptance of what is."
Dr. Wayne W. Dyer (1998)

PREMISE

Cultivating and generating humility, gratitude, patience and acceptance (especially self-acceptance) is a progression, a slow evolution of growth and maturation. This refinement is built on truth, self-awareness, and self-understanding. We must be open to learn from others. We must consider (not necessarily agree with) their compliments as well as their critiques. We should approach this task by distancing ourselves from judgment and comparison. Pray for the trust and courage to see ourselves as others see us, without the bias of defensiveness. Be a participant/observer and delight as you embrace change and encompass expansion. You are perfectly who you were created to be. Both your talents and your limitations were bestowed on you for a purpose and both will enable you to achieve your destiny.

INTENTION

In order to insure progress and individual growth, I must decide, intend and choose to accept the inevitable. I must surrender my wish to control the uncontrollable and trust in the plan of Providence. In this way, my feelings, thoughts and actions will be guided in the direction of genuine self-fulfillment.

AWARENESS

I will purposefully, that is, with full awareness and intent, make a decision today that I have avoided for too long. I will follow through on that decision and note the progress in my journal. I will especially note my reasons for this particular choice, now. Finally, I will trust that it will lead to positive growth.

DAY 36—PATIENCE

"Be not afraid of growing slowly, be afraid of standing still."
Chinese Proverb (c. 1500 B.C.E.)

PREMISE

Patience reinforces persistence, a necessary quality for progress. It helps us take self-condemnation out of the equation when our attempts don't match our expected outcomes. If we are to grow and serve to our capacity, we must persist and endure with determination, passion and trust. We must be committed to change those areas in ourselves that we control and allow others their own journey of self-discovery and self-growth. As we begin to comprehend that the purpose of any specific task may simply be a lesson in humility and to give us an opportunity to strengthen our frustration tolerance, we will be more able to strategize and persevere.

INTENTION

I will take responsibility for my behavior especially in reaction to frustrating situations. I can learn to reframe my criteria for success and to avoid the self-condemnatory tapes that persuade me to succumb to self-pity. I will choose acceptance over isolation and determination over defeat. I will move forward, learn and choose wisely with love.

AWARENESS

When I get frustrated due to judging or comparing another's behavior to what I think should be done, I will pause and pray briefly for that person and myself.

DAY 37—HUMILITY

"Humility makes great men twice humble."
Benjamin Franklin (1752)

PREMISE

Humility is the center of all that we wish to become. It is the seed that spawns gratitude, patience/trust, love, wisdom, acceptance/forgiveness and courage. Each is necessary to achieve contentment, as they work together to create a life filled with satisfaction and compassion. The focus on humility is the first step of participation in an eternal dance of joy, wonder and love. To embrace this message is to understand the meaning of life as it has been revealed from Eastern and Western scribes, philosophers and holy men. To know this is to understand your place in life. To be humble is to be grateful and satisfied, to accept, to trust and to cherish. It is to be strong and patient, while reflecting upon the all-encompassing benevolence and wisdom of the Universe. It is to live the serenity prayer that for many is the definition of mental health, contentment and gratification.

INTENTION

I can change my thinking and prejudices so that I embrace rather than fear life. I can be humble and understand my role in God's plan. I will become who I was created to be, as I strive to do better; to forgive, as I wish to be forgiven and to love as I wish to be loved.

AWARENESS

Today I will be alert to the signs that I am making a difference. I will watch the expressions and reactions of others as I act kindly. I will make an effort to behave in a way that reflects the Spirit of "Namaste" ("I honor the place where you and I are one").

DAY 38—GRATITUDE

". . . speak of the favors you have received."
Seneca (50 C.E.)

PREMISE

Courage is manifested in many ways; in as many ways as we need, to realize our potential. With gratitude we become even more courageous because we acknowledge all the blessings that the beneficent Universe has bestowed. We trust in others but we also trust in ourselves, that even if our expectations are not met we will still be able to persevere towards our objectives. We will grow and we will learn. We will not become victims; rather, we will become empowered. We will be grateful for courage when we confront change as a meaningful challenge. It takes courage to face daily living without regrets, excuses or criticisms. It takes more courage to live than to die, to love than to hide and to accept than to dismiss. Be grateful for courage because without courage we cannot enjoy all that we have been given.

INTENTION

I am able to develop the necessary inner strength to overcome my fear of rejection or my fear of appearing weak. I can thank those who have helped me. I can comprehend the true nature of my dependence and from that thought I will create a feeling of self-confidence.

AWARENESS

I will be mindful today of my strengths. I will become more aware of my abilities to cope with the unexpected. I will make no excuses today. I will face challenge with the gratitude arising from my certainty that I am never given more than I can overcome.

DAY 39—ACCEPTANCE

"We cannot change anything until we accept it."
Carl Gustav Jung (1910)

PREMISE

Awareness and intent are necessary but not sufficient conditions for any process of change. To make progress and achieve fulfillment we need awareness of our thoughts, feelings and actions both as we enter a situation and as we assess the effects of our strategy on that situation. From humility, and courage, we also need the intent to be honest and to change that, which does not meet our goals. From this perspective we can reassess our strengths and weaknesses as we prepare for the next challenge. Through such awareness and intent we will become knowledgeable of both strengths and weaknesses. This comprehension will help energize and motivate us in those areas we can change; likewise, it will help us accept our vulnerability and dependence. As we accept our weaknesses, so then we can begin to manifest our strengths and create positive change.

INTENTION

I can do this. I can change, a small step at a time. I can advance in my goals of self-improvement. I can learn from my interactions with others and embrace all that is unexpected as an opportunity to experience transition and learn. However, I must first learn to accept what is so that I can construct a strategy to create what can be.

AWARENESS

Today I will observe and not manage. I will accept and not judge, I will trust and not fear. At the end of the day, before I sleep, I will reflect on all that has transpired and give thanks.

DAY 40—PATIENCE

"Patience will lead the snail to Jerusalem."
Irish Proverb (c. 1650 C.E.)

PREMISE

Patience is a function of living in the moment. It is to accept what is placed before you without invoking memories of the past (e.g., "he always does this") or the future (e.g. "if I allow this to continue, I will be doomed, my life will change irrevocably"). Patience is stepping back and accessing the present so as to process mental, physical and emotional reactions. It delays responses and promotes deliberation thereby mitigating desire and impulse. Patience gives us the strength to be aware in the instant. It is the pause that refreshes. It allows us to think, feel and grow in the moment. It is the necessary step that prevents impulse from becoming foolishness.

INTENTION

I can be in the moment. I know how important it is and I can practice anywhere, any time, throughout the day. I only need the intent to pause and be aware of my breathing. As I exhale and inhale, I can focus on the sounds, smells and sensations of my surroundings. As I visualize a serene scene with eyes closed, at this moment, in this time of my life, I realize that these sensations are unique and will never recur just this way again.

AWARENESS

Today I will more attentive in my awareness so as to realize and take advantage of the unique opportunities, challenges and choices presented in the present. Throughout the day, I will pause to take time in order to sense my surroundings and to be alive in the moment.

DAY 41—HUMILITY

"Whatever good you have is all from God,
whatever evil is all from yourself."
(The Koran)

PREMISE

If we are to manifest our destiny in a loving and compassionate way, the first and foremost characteristic that we need to develop is humility. From this center radiates all the supporting traits that contribute to a life of serenity and satisfaction. In order to accomplish this, we must know ourselves (our preferences, our prejudices, our predilections). We must courageously examine our thoughts, feelings and behaviors. We should make a list of strengths and weaknesses of character, then test and validate the list on a continual basis, as we go through daily routines. In this way we become participant/observer's in our lives and we are better able to assess our true nature. We become scientists of the self. A daily journal can be most helpful in this endeavor.

INTENTION

As I come to know myself, I will discover meaning, love and caring on my journey. I will understand that my talents are unique and that only I can give these in service to others. I will see the similarities more than the differences; love more than fear, and acceptance more than rejection. As I move forward in my journey, I will be grateful to be me.

AWARENESS

Today I will search for clues about my resistance to humility as well as my resistance to leading a life of growth and discovery. I will briefly enter my thoughts about each day's meditation in my journal.

DAY 42—GRATITUDE

"An easy thing, O Power Divine,
To thank Thee for these gifts of Things."
Thomas Wentworth Higginson (1890)

PREMISE

What if I found out that I had a fatal disease and only months to live? How would my life change? What would I see differently? Who and what would I miss most? Think of these things today and be grateful for all you are given. This will require courage. It is brave to face your dependency directly and to give thanks without excuses or rationalization. Special people have been put in our life for special reasons. Understand this and treasure them. Treat them with kindness and you will soon appreciate why they are in your life. Listen with love and experience the world's treasures.

INTENTION

I will choose to have the courage to face truth. I can do this. I am able to acknowledge and embrace my interdependence and have the endurance to fight the fear to trust. I will prevail in my gratitude and I will rejoice in my interdependence.

AWARENESS

I will make a special effort today to uncover the treasures that are presented in my everyday existence. At some point, I will pause for a moment to reflect on all the personal gifts I have and all that I have been given. I will give thanks.

DAY 43—ACCEPTANCE

"Be willing to have it so. Acceptance of what has happened is the first step to overcoming the consequences of any misfortune."
William James (1882)

PREMISE

It is important to be in the moment so that we may appropriately assess opportunities and challenges. Fear, judgment, and arrogance are tendencies that impede advancement towards self-acceptance. It is easier to lie in the comfort of self-pity, victimhood and impotence than to take responsibility and persevere, pursue and execute. We must "let go" of the negative but not deny it. See it for what it is, a chain that binds. Self-hate is a chain that we can break with awareness and intent. As we develop humility, trust, courage and love we begin to accept and maybe even embrace ourselves. This is the start of contentment and the beginning of wisdom and trust.

INTENTION

I can set goals, achieve them, assess what I did correctly and observe where I did not meet my expectations. I can step aside, accept and nurture myself, as I would accept and nurture others. While I show compassion, respect and understanding of others, so I will with myself. I will thank my Higher Power as I attempt to evolve in love.

AWARENESS

This morning, I will make a list of three traits that I would use to serve others. I will begin with acceptance, patience and forgiveness. At the end of the day I will review where I succeeded and where I fell short.

DAY 44—PATIENCE

"Our patience will achieve more than our force."
Edmund Burke (1790)

PREMISE

When we intentionally practice patience, we practice awareness, being in the moment, fully feeling and focusing. Similar to meditation, it is a discipline of the mind. It embraces the "now", focuses on the moment and sheds the biases of the past and the fear of the future. It is gratitude, humility and empowerment, all in the same soup, served in an exquisite bowl. Patience connects us with the self, our rhythms and the rhythms of nature. Patience allows us to learn because we control the impulse to react. It gives us time to feel the moment as we assess possibility and potential. It separates us from recklessness and self-indulgence.

INTENTION

As participant/observer, I can more readily practice patience. I can be objective or at least be aware of the emotions aroused during a particular interaction or situation. I will learn that each hindrance is nature's way of telling me to slow down and enjoy the journey. With this approach, the results of my efforts will be successful because I will always learn from my actions and persevere in my convictions. I can reach my goal of not "personalizing." I understand my initial reactions to emotionally charged situations are simply a result of the child-self's certainty that it is the center of the Universe and needs immediate gratification.

AWARENESS

I will practice the age old, "tried and true," ten count. When I feel tense, angry and generally reactive, I will pause, take a breath and count to 10, so that I may more effectively and objectively evaluate a stressful situation.

DAY 45—HUMILITY

"Aren't you ashamed to be concerned so much about making all the money you can and advancing your reputation and prestige while for truth and wisdom and the improvement of your souls you have no thought or care?"
Socrates, (5th century B.C.E.)

PREMISE

On the path to self-knowledge, we will discover previously unknown dimensions of ourselves and thereby dispel the spurious definitions from the past of who we are. We will begin to realize that we are re-creating and re-defining our essence and our identity in each moment. We become empowered because we are no longer at the mercy of self-destructive beliefs and perspectives. If we are to fulfill our fate, we have to see beyond the child-self and become free from false internal and external messages that prevent us from experiencing truth. Be alert to the moment and flexible in your responses, so that you may learn from your actions. In sum, when you are humble, you will learn from all of your encounters because your mind is open and you are willing to extract the lessons from experience.

INTENTION

I can turn negatives into positives as I increasingly acknowledge negative statements. I will control the tendency to say "I can't" and I will develop the habit of saying what I can do, putting it into practical pieces of behavior and acting on them. If I can think it, I can do it and it all starts with small, attainable steps.

AWARENESS

Today I will tune into the self-destructive and self-denigrating thoughts that prevent me from improving. I will face my fear and do something both positive and different for myself in one area.

DAY 46—GRATITUDE

"I thank whatever Gods may be,
For my incomparable soul."
William Ernest Henley (1888)

PREMISE

Gratitude, as it is understood here, is generated from humility. It is also both a potential cause and effect of love. Gratitude embraces the realization that we are special and that we have an incomparable gift to offer everyone we meet. As such, gratitude underscores the importance of service and also has the capability to mitigate, if not eradicate, depression. Once we understand gratitude's importance in our life and that it is truly a gift from a Higher Power, we comprehend the belief that all we have and all that we do is for the purpose of sharing this gift in order to fulfill our destiny. Life has a special meaning for each of us and we can discover that meaning as we discover and accept ourselves.

INTENTION

While I live and celebrate the day, I will remember life's fragility and transience. I can face this and I can prevail. To do so will enhance my joy and gratitude. I have been given generous gifts and the means to implement and bestow them on others. I am grateful for each opportunity to share and expand my awareness of both my limits and strengths.

AWARENESS

I will look to my everyday circumstances for opportunities to empower the seed of gratitude to grow. I will write in my journal about one person I would miss if they were out of my life. I will include three reasons why I would miss them and I will show my gratitude to them today.

DAY 47—ACCEPTANCE

"The best thing to do when it's raining is to let it rain."
Henry Wadsworth Longfellow (1862)

PREMISE

To learn and to grow necessitates perceiving mistakes as learning opportunities, rather than personal failures, defects or deficiencies. This is very difficult. The child-self frequently is heard crying, "I want it now," "you never get it right," "it's always something." Once we learn to accept ourselves, our talents, our weaknesses and our challenges, we will understand that in order to walk we must not fear falling. In truth, we cannot "fail" if we learn from our errors. As many wise men have said: "it's not how many times you fall, it's how many times you get up."

INTENTION

I can fall and get up. I can cope with the extreme frustration of the learning process. I understand that without mistakes, missteps or miscalculations, I cannot learn. Learning is an error-prone process and I can take advantage of my blunders and move forward. I can and I will persevere so that I may be content and fulfilled. I know that I am able to pray and ask for help in times of doubt and need.

AWARENESS

Today, I will note the circumstances and personal beliefs that create frustrations and serve as impediments to growth and progress. I will attempt to learn patience when encountering obstacles and experiencing disappointment. I will employ the participant/observer perspective, as I learn from mistakes and misunderstandings. I will accept my humanity and vulnerability. I will note one example of acceptance in my journal.

DAY 48—PATIENCE

"By learning you will teach, by teaching you will learn."
Confucius (495 B.C.E.)

PREMISE

Patience, with the appropriate intent and awareness, clears the way for learning, as we take the moment to objectively assess a situation and then view it as a learning experience. It now becomes a situation given to us by the Universe rather than a stressful event that is charged with personal involvement and emotional consequences. We create true change by becoming aware of our actions. It is this awareness combined with our intent to be in the moment that frees us from the restrictions of time. Past and future are ignored and our focus becomes the "now". Patience is the personal/spiritual quality that is necessary for this to happen. Each moment gives us a chance to choose and practice patience.

INTENTION

As I look for progress, not perfection, patience will allow me to persevere, despite impediments towards my goals. I will learn that each hindrance is nature's way of telling me to slow down and enjoy the journey. With this approach the result of my efforts will be successful because I will always learn from my actions and persevere in my commitments. It takes patience to develop patience, so I need to be aware of my thoughts, actions and feelings, each step of the way, as I direct my intent to choosing control over impulse.

AWARENESS

I will be aware of my need for immediate gratification today and when I feel that tension, I will pause and determine what I can learn. Sometimes, it will simply be to slow down and allow events to happen as they were meant to, as opposed to how I want them to. I will make a note in my journal as to how successful these attempts have been.

DAY 49—HUMILITY

"Rather to bow than break is profitable;
Humility is a thing commendable."
William Cowper (1773)

PREMISE

To be humble is to be free to accept yourself as perfectly you, flaws and failures, talents and successes. The freedom comes from the emotional distance you create so that another's opinion means little. You listen, assess, evaluate and decide what you want to keep and what you want to let go. You understand that the power is within not without. Your individuality is your legacy; it is that which will contribute to your impact on the world. Your individuality is also that which will make you an agent of change and help you become all you were meant to be. Achieving humility frees you from needing praise and shirking from rebuke. It allows you to go forward. We lose the need to be approved or acknowledged and thus we strive only to do good deeds.

INTENTION

I am strong, I am smart and I am ready to develop and grow. I am at the exact place I should be and if I allow myself, I can see limitless opportunity in the moment. I have all that I need to take advantage of the "Now." It is here and presents itself because I am ready. Everything I have done and everything I have experienced, have prepared me for this opportunity. I will act and I will succeed. I will have courage and I will move ahead. There is no better time than right now to become that which I was created to be.

AWARENESS

Today, I will try to become more aware of my unique gifts. I will watch and observe how I help others. I will make a list of strengths and weaknesses and I will enter it in my journal.

DAY 50—GRATITUDE

"Gratitude creates joy. It gives life meaning and zest.
It is truly a gift from God."
W. T. Watts, Ph.D. (2010)

PREMISE

Again, try to imagine, for just a short time, that you were a soldier and called to serve in a place where you may lose your life. Take the time now to envision this, for it deserves special attention. When you have been able feel the fear, doubt, loss and all other attendant, unpleasant emotions, look around you and understand how precious and fragile your life is. Be grateful for each day and each experience. Everything and everybody who are with you are gifts from the Universe. They will be here only briefly and you will never know when they will depart or be taken from you. Be grateful for all you have been given because so little is due to your own actions. Now, you are beginning to experience the gift of humility and gratitude. Now, you can begin to grow in love and appreciation.

INTENTION

I can overcome my aversion to face truth, the truth of transience, the truth of mortality, the truth of fragility. As I face such foreboding, I become stronger because I comprehend that I am not alone. I am one of many and my fellow travelers are by my side. In each moment, I have all that I need to overcome any impediment or any problem.

AWARENESS

I will have the courage today, to raise my sensitivity to the fragility of life and I will behave with an appreciation for the moment. Each occasion is precious and I will take advantage of the opportunities that are placed before me. I will express love and acceptance and I will be grateful for the opportunity to do so.

DAY 51—ACCEPTANCE

"The cause of happiness comes rarely and many are the seeds of suffering! Yet, if I had no pain, I'd never have pleasure. Therefore, persevere!"
Santideva (8th century, C.E.)

PREMISE

We must learn from mistakes, if we are to ensure progress and accomplishment. If we accept ourselves, we will avoid the arrogance of perfectionism and blame. Acceptance will allow us to take responsibility for missteps and move on. This is the path to knowledge and wisdom. We learn best by accepting both strengths and vulnerabilities. Our child-self fights this. It doesn't want to be strong so it can be cared for and it doesn't want defects because it doesn't trust enough to be vulnerable. Hence, the question becomes should you risk and inevitably make mistakes or should you cling to the status quo and not move forward. In the meantime, the child-self stamps its feet, holds its breath and has a tantrum, moving furiously and going nowhere.

INTENTION

I can become aware of patience today as I accept myself and learn. I can have self-compassion and show the same tolerance for others. I can remind myself (through prayer) of my goals and request the strength to pursue them.

AWARENESS

I will express compassion and caring for someone today, simply to make them feel better, not for any recognition, reward or recompense. Random acts of kindness are the most effective.

DAY 52—PATIENCE

"Courage and perseverance have a magical talisman, before which difficulties disappear and obstacles vanish into the air."
John Quincy Adams (1807)

PREMISE

We can develop the skill of patience throughout the day, during our regular routine. When we are aware that tension, stress, or frustration are causing internal changes, we can intend to pause and readjust the emotional thermostat, rather than letting it run rampant and overheating the whole system. Ultimately, not thinking causes dysfunction, meaning impulse reigns and reason relinquishes control. That's when the stuff happens that we regret or resent. Patience is the magic elixir, which gives us the opportunity to pause, deliberate, and reflect, thereby directing attention to what is impacting at that moment. Furthermore, patience inspires the understanding and interpretation of that impact.

INTENTION

I will increase my determination to reflect on the moment when I begin to feel unpleasant sensations such as, a racing heart, shortness of breath, perspiration etc., not caused by exercise but rather unexpected external conditions. As I grow and evolve, such change, will have significantly less impact both internally and externally. I will learn to cope with the unexpected and conquer my fears and trepidation.

AWARENESS

I will note in my journal one instance today, where I hesitated, reassessed, "held my tongue, "etc. during a situation in which I would have usually responded reflexively. I will ponder and evaluate the outcome of this new strategy.

DAY 53—HUMILITY

"I wish to cultivate such a measure of equanimity as would enable me to bear success with humility, the affection of my friends without pride and to be ready when the day of sorrow and grief came, to meet it with the courage befitting in a man."
Sir William Osler (1905)

PREMISE

Humility is true freedom, freedom from needing the Good opinion of others, freedom from fearing the bad opinions. You can be yourself as you strive to grow in love, compassion and forgiveness. To be humble is to be freed from resentments because you choose to interpret events in a positive way. You no longer judge and compare. Humility is the beginning of this freedom. Arrogance and pride disappear. It is strength and independence, as we begin to understand the true nature of vulnerability and dependence. Humility destroys the masks and pretense of fear and pride. We can now look at ourselves without prejudgment and self-consciousness. Like the toddler running naked after a bath, we can delight in ourselves and be grateful for God's gifts.

INTENTION

I will not allow freedom to frighten me. Rather, I will concentrate on what I can control and what I can achieve. In this small but vitally important area, I will carve a niche. I will use my unique talents to make a better, more pleasant life for others and myself. If I help another even a little it, it is significant; nothing is too small, a smile, a friendly word, a random act of goodwill. Each builds slowly to a significant mass creating change. I can do this.

AWARENESS

Today I will strive to see the superficiality of the external. I will make an extra effort to listen to the judgments of others and determine if they are espousing a message of love or one of fear and rejection.

DAY 54—GRATITUDE

"Gratitude unites us and reminds us that we are all precious as well as contributors to the growth of others. We can learn from anyone and we can be examples to all."
W. T. Watts, Ph.D. (2010)

PREMISE

Gratitude helps us appreciate that success is helping others achieve. It is also accepting help in fulfilling our destiny and attaining our goals. Real satisfaction and contentment resides in giving and not in acquiring external goods or power. To be grateful is to begin to open the door for someone to enter and share our uniqueness. We can offer only who we are and yet it is the greatest gift one can give or receive. When we allow ourselves to be vulnerable, to share and to love, we become an "us". We can then rejoice in all that ensues. To be grateful is to be self-less, while maintaining a firm understanding and cherishing of who we are.

INTENTION

I can do this. I feel confident enough in myself and I trust enough in what I have learned, to choose love and to be grateful. It is scary and it is unknown territory but if I am to progress and fulfill my destiny, I must take this step. I will pray and reach out when in doubt and I will persevere.

AWARENESS

Today, I will make a special effort to be grateful for all my strengths as well as for my flaws. I will attempt to shed the fear of giving and I will do a small favor for no reason other than to serve.

DAY 55—ACCEPTANCE

"What a lightning flash in the gloom it is for this self, cloaked in the darkness of ignorance when awareness is gained even a little bit!"
Atisa (1044 C.E.)

PREMISE

Each event that enters awareness is meaningful because it is an opportunity, to learn. There are no random events, each and every event has a meaning that only we can decipher and understand. However, we must develop the perspective that to discover our path, it is necessary to stay in the moment and surrender our will to the guidance of our Higher Power. We are constantly given directions, hints and indications as to the course we must follow and the attitude to adopt in order to realize our potential. The problem is that we are afraid to follow those directions. We ignore, reject or distract ourselves to avoid the truth. As we accept and trust both our identity and our destiny, we will more clearly find our way.

INTENTION

I can face truth, take responsibility and live my life as I was meant to live it. What I need, I have and I will use it to advance and to help others on their journey. When I am ready, guidance will appear when requested and the means to my objectives will become apparent. I must trust, become more aware and intend love in manifesting all actions, thoughts and feelings.

AWARENESS

I will renew and rewrite one short-term goal so that, for today, I will more clearly focus and pursue what I wish to achieve.

DAY 56—PATIENCE

"Patience and trust go hand in hand."
A Course in Miracles (1976)

PREMISE

Trust is simultaneously knowledge and feeling that the Universe is benign. "Yes, I am here for a good reason and I have all I need to fulfill my destiny." When events become challenging or they don't concur with our plans, trust is manifested by the thought that all will work out, we will learn and the event is part of a larger, grander picture. The truth is that there are no constructive alternatives to this reflection. Is it better to curse the dark or allow the events that we can't control unfold? We must learn to focus our intent on we what we can do, to change those reactions, thoughts and feelings that we control.

INTENTION

I understand that I have choices. I can choose to create my life with courage, wisdom and love as I confront new circumstances and stressful situations. The issue is to choose freely, which is to choose, as much as possible in the present, with compassion and acceptance without fear, bias or whimsy. As I do this, I have the trust that the Universe will guide me. When I am in doubt, I can pray and ask for help.

AWARENESS

Today, I will make a choice with loving intent and then I will surrender the results to God. I will note this event, as well as the feelings, thoughts and actions, in my journal.

DAY 57—HUMILITY

"Before honor is humility."
Proverbs, 15:33

PREMISE

When you are humble, you have no need to control. You allow the world and all the lessons it contains to unfold in its own time. We can give and accept help with no sense of obligation, expectation or reward. We give and accept freely. We do what we can to serve and to help. When you discover that you have ultimate control over a few things and no control over many things, you begin focus on that which you can change. You focus on the present, on the opportunity to express yourself and on taking responsibility for the intent of your choices in the moment.

INTENTION

I have the strength to surrender and trust that what is out of my control is at the discretion of a beneficent Universe. The world has succeeded without me so far, and it will continue to do so after I leave. My humility tells me that I am part of a grand and beautiful plan, which is timeless. My Creator will give me the strength and wisdom to fulfill my role in the best way possible. I simply have to stop self-sabotaging and let it happen.

AWARENESS

Today, I will be aware of how my personality traits can help further love and acceptance. I will focus on what I can change about myself and begin to act on that awareness. I will list in my journal, one aspect of my personality that I wish to alter.

DAY 58—GRATITUDE

"Gratitude is a fruit of great cultivation . . ."
Samuel Johnson (1773)

PREMISE

Gratitude is a gift from God to help us celebrate existence. It transforms living into a work of art that we create, through love and relationships. It destroys, or at least mitigates, depression because it frees us from self-pity and self-involvement, as we become thankful for all that is and all that we are. We then understand, that despite our faults and blemishes, we are perfectly who we are. Such insights are precious. They bolster our self-esteem and help us look beyond ourselves and say: "thank you." We begin to see, feel and comprehend that we are part of a magnificent and beneficent plan. We can bow our heads as we feel the wonder of life and appreciate the magnificence of all that surrounds us.

INTENTION

I can overcome my reluctance to serve. I have been given a chance to ease the suffering, sacrifice and distress of my brothers and sisters. I have the endurance and courage to begin this undertaking and I have the unique opportunity to contribute as no one else can. I can use my talents, imperfections and determination to help others along the journey. I am grateful to contribute to the well-being of others.

AWARENESS

I will cultivate my feelings of gratitude and realize that this is a gift I can receive with a simple prayer/request. Today, I will pray for gratitude throughout the day, and in the evening I will list at least three things for which I am grateful.

DAY 59—ACCEPTANCE

"Obstacles cannot crush me,
Every obstacle yields to stern resolve."
Leonardo Da Vinci (1500 C.E.)

PREMISE

The central challenge to becoming who we were created to be is to transform our thinking, so that we comprehend the distinction between what we can and cannot control in our lives. Unfortunately, due to innate fear and a low self-esteem, we carry with us the delusion that we manage many things and that we are able to regulate most external changes and challenges. This is a significant source of emotional distress and causes most adversarial social interaction. We insist on controlling that over which we have no power and we refuse to trust that without our management, the world would continue to progress.

INTENTION

Nothing can stop me from being me. I simply (it's simple but difficult) will face my fears as a participant/observer and move forward. I will understand that most fears are illogical and have to do with feeling foolish or embarrassed in new situations. That, in turn, is based on unrealistic expectations and a refusal to accept myself for who I am. At times I will be awkward and stumble, but that's okay. I will learn and move forward.

AWARENESS

I will purposely and with intent challenge my comfort zone today in order to behave in an appropriate but novel manner, as I react to others. I will focus on empathy and compassion rather than fear and isolation.

DAY 60—PATIENCE

"Trust man and they will be true to you; treat them greatly and they will show themselves great."
Ralph Waldo Emerson (1841)

PREMISE

If we do not personalize, catastrophize or externalize (project), we will choose or create more efficient and effective solutions. We will become more competent and confident as we confront life's travails. We can empower ourselves by controlling our responses to the unexpected and unwanted. We can assess, take charge and ask ourselves what can we learn. We can trust that whatever is in our life, has a purpose and that purpose is to foster growth and development. We can build our spiritual-selves with any form of change, expected or not. We can choose to meet the unforeseen with love and serenity or fear and distress. We must learn to let go and let the Universe do what is needed.

INTENTION

I will meet the unexpected with equanimity and trust. I know that I will not be given anything that I can't conquer. I have what I need, here and now, for all that I encounter. With acceptance, humility, gratitude and patience my toolbox is full and I am ready for renovation.

AWARENESS

Today, I will make a special effort to delegate some authority or control over a task and allow that person the freedom and respect to manage it as they see fit.

DAY 61—HUMILITY

"Humility must always be the portion of any man who receives his acclaim earned in the blood of his followers and the sacrifices of his friends."
Dwight Eisenhower (1945)

PREMISE

As we accept our natural limitations, we begin to marvel and trust in all that is the wonder of life. We witness the forces of nature that generate all living things despite the most adverse conditions and promote growth in the face of incredible impediments. We start to embrace this awesome and loving, yet frightening and punishing, aspect of creation. We understand that like a flower, we, too, are unfolding and growing according to nature's needs and not our own. We now become observers rather than managers and we lose the inclination to control, as we trust the beneficence and precision of a plan that is beyond our comprehension. We participate in the dance that is life and we experience the unity that exists among all living things. We can experience this, at any moment, if we desire it.

INTENTION

It is scary to let go of the delusions and illusions of personal control and power but I can do it. I can move forward and face doubt and apprehension. I can grow and be everything that I was created to be. The resources are here, right now. They are all around me, if I just seek them and open my eyes. I must allow myself to feel it and act on it. With my Creator at my side, I will evolve as I was meant to.

AWARENESS

Today, I will notice the wonders of nature and how they unfold without any human guidance or intervention. I will let go and let my Higher Power direct my behavior.

DAY 62—GRATITUDE

"I thank the goodness and the grace
Which on my birth have smiled . . ."
Jane Taylor (1810)

PREMISE

Humility is the catalyst for gratitude, just as gratitude is the catalyst for patience, acceptance and love. Each reinforces the other and together they present and offer a synergism, creating contentment and goodwill. To be grateful is to be patient and to trust that our destiny is evolving in a benign manner. Gratitude will enable us to accept the unexpected because we see it as a gift, a message and an opportunity to learn. We embrace life to the degree we are grateful. We understand that life is a journey/process and that we are capable of easing this path or, if we choose, creating obstacles and roadblocks.

INTENTION

I will realize the power of my soul to be grateful for all I have been given. The sun shines, the cup is half full and every day I am better. I have the fortitude and imagination to become more aware and self-disciplined, choosing the positive, life-affirming alternatives presented in my daily life. I understand that this is the only path to growth and that fear, doubt and hesitation will follow me with each vital decision despite my best efforts. This is part of the growth process and I am prepared for such impediments.

AWARENESS

Today, I will focus on the connection between humility and gratitude. As I practice humility in thought and feeling, I will be more able to sense the emergence of gratitude.

DAY 63—ACCEPTANCE

"The great and glorious masterpiece of man is to know how to live to purpose."
Michel Montaigne (1585)

PREMISE

Acceptance is one of the four fundamental, spiritual characteristics that must be developed and applied if we are to achieve the goals of growth and contentment. The other three are humility, gratitude and patience/trust. Taken together, these four provide the bedrock for love, courage and wisdom, the essential spiritual qualities necessary for a life a fulfillment. "The Serenity Prayer" written by Reinhold Niebuhr in 1934, involved "acceptance" as the first spiritual attribute necessary to achieve serenity. Acceptance is a necessary but not sufficient attribute to live life fully with love, compassion, and contentment. If we are to achieve acceptance, we must let go of all fear and doubt, so that we may evolve as we were created to become.

INTENTION

In order to accept, I must understand what I can't control and I must make every effort to control what I can. I must trust in the benevolence of the Universe and comprehend that no obstacle is too great for me to overcome. From this day forward, I will make it my purpose and intent to help others, and to live with love, acceptance and compassion.

AWARENESS

Today, I will plan and follow through on one goal. I will evaluate my progress and re-strategize if necessary. That goal will focus on approaching all circumstances with love and kindness.

DAY 64—PATIENCE

"It is better to suffer wrong than to do it, and happier to be sometimes cheated than not to trust."
Samuel Johnson (1765)

PREMISE

Nothing changes immediately. Everything takes time to grow. "For everything, there is a season." The world is moving without your help and has been for quite a while; the sun, rises, sets and the moon has its cycles. Your body is changing, growing and decaying, all beyond your power to stop or speed up. Allow things to happen, love to grow, children to learn, wounds to heal. Acquire the skill of observation and appreciation. Watch the parade and don't try to direct it. If we can simply observe and limit our need to direct and control, we will become happier more content individuals.

INTENTION

I can view the past differently. I am able to change my perspective and become more inclusive, accepting and compassionate. I can be vulnerable because I can trust. If I allow myself to open my heart and see anew, I will be cleansed of the biases of exclusion, fear, and complacence. I know, now, that I can progress and face my fear. I will move on in trust and confidence. If I have love in my heart my actions have a greater chance of helping others.

AWARENESS

Today, I will try to appreciate how the world around me progresses without my help. I will watch everyone and everything going about their business and comprehend that they are doing so without my advice or management. I will wish all well and focus on my own business, trying to achieve the goals of self-improvement and fulfillment.

DAY 65—HUMILITY

". . . Humility is endless."
T. S. Eliot (1935)

PREMISE

As we accept that which we cannot control and begin to develop a humble perspective, we start to realize, in an epiphany, that in our unique way, we are contributors and essential components of the benevolence that goes well beyond small, idiosyncratic, wants and needs. Again, we experience empowerment and freedom. We begin to love and cherish who we are and shed the need for embellishment or deception. To be humble is to realize that the "I" (as ego and child-self) is minimal and the "them" is non-existent. Our oneness is comprehended and sensed. To be humble and wise is to decide from a perspective of "we" and "us". To be humble, is to realize that "we" are one, of the many, who are one.

INTENTION

Today, I can lose the fear that the child-self uses to imprison me. Today, I can trust in a Grand Plan, a beneficent Universe, and a Power greater than myself. Today, I will comprehend and sense the unity that I have with all my fellow travelers, regardless of race, culture or external appearance. In unity, I will relate to all life as one.

AWARENESS

Today, I will become more aware of the "we" in my interactions and comprehend how precious this factor is in my growth and evolution. I will take special notice and mitigate those self-referential thoughts and feelings that occur as I interact with my fellow journeyman. I will decrease my self-absorption and increase my awareness of others' needs.

DAY 66—GRATITUDE

"For a duration all the ranks of Angels yield eternal thanks . . ."
Christopher Smart (1763)

PREMISE

As we evolve and cultivate humility, gratitude, acceptance/forgiveness and patience/trust, we create a perspective in which every day is challenging yet fun, fulfilling and enlightening. It becomes fun because we are empowered and can master the challenge. It becomes fulfilling because we can use our unique abilities in the service of others and it becomes enlightening because we can comprehend that each day is one part of the journey and each challenge presents a lesson to learn and a path to pursue.

INTENTION

My life is improving each day, one short step, one brief prayer and one compassionate act at a time. By developing and feeling grateful, I will enhance the endurance and imagination to evolve and grow, thereby, fulfilling my destiny. I can understand that in any one moment, I am given and I possess all that I need, physically, spiritually, emotionally and intellectually, to overcome obstacles, face change and accomplish my goals.

AWARENESS

I will be conscious that each is part of the whole and that starting today; I will begin to construct my life anew. I am grateful for this insight. I will tell someone close to me why I am grateful.

DAY 67—ACCEPTANCE

"All is ephemeral, fame and the famous as well."
Marcus Aurelius (second century C.E.)

PREMISE

A significant understanding and insight that we must acquire is the comprehension of what we do and do not control. Acquiring self-acceptance and humility is a crucial aspect of this task. Our child-self will battle the idea that there are things we don't control. It will spit, hold its breath and tantrum at the very notion that it is not the center of the Universe and that it does not manage, manipulate or master all external events and all people whom it encounters.

INTENTION

One aspect of my personality that is within my control is the "child-self." With awareness of its strength, narcissism and magical thinking, I can intend to master it and allow my "higher self" (the internal adult) to determine my behavior and my reactions to that behavior. This is difficult but as I learn and mature, I am noticing the selfishness, greed and jealousy that is part of my self talk. Once I recognize this, I can stop and I can substitute positive, life-affirming statements. I can be in control but I must first be aware and then intend to change.

AWARENESS

I will make an extra effort today, to be aware of and to challenge those aspects of my personality and those reactions that reflect my "child-self." I will note these in my journal at the end of the day.

DAY 68—PATIENCE

"Patience and passage of time accomplish more than strength and fury."
Jean de la Fontaine (1671)

PREMISE

Trust believes that we always have just what we need, just when we need it. Right now is our time, our moment and our opportunity. We must learn to trust our ability to do what is necessary so as to be aligned with destiny. Many dilemmas are caused by a fear, which entices us to manage and supervise a stressful situation with force, hostility and domination. Special problems arise when we try to manage circumstances that are more powerful than our limited abilities. Trying to control the uncontrollable leads to aggression, depression and frustration. To be mentally and emotionally healthy and, therefore, content, know this difference.

INTENTION

I can teach myself to let go. I can know when to surrender and thereby win. I can teach myself to trust the Cosmos when it so clearly tells me that something is not in my domain and not within my ability to change the outcome. External events, other people, and the world situation in general, are examples of "none of my business".

AWARENESS

I will renew my focus on distinguishing between what I can and can't control. I will look inside and begin to control what I can, namely, myself.

DAY 69—HUMILITY

"In peace there is nothing so becomes a man
As modest stillness and humility . . ."
Shakespeare, Henry IV (1597)

PREMISE

Humility teaches us that all of God's creatures are worthy of respect simply because they exist. We are products of God's creation and, as such, are obligated to fulfill our responsibility to make the world a more loving and compassionate place. You are neither more nor less than another. We are all part of a perfect plan and each of us makes a significant contribution. When you are humble, you realize that God has given you all that you need in the moment for contentment and satisfaction. All cravings are illusions created by external forces that wish you to feel deprived, defective and disempowered. You can never get enough of what you don't need. Attempting to satisfy such cravings leads only to frustration, disappointment and humiliation. Be humble and be strong. Realize that by asking for help and acknowledging powerlessness you become empowered. Find the strength within and you will become free.

INTENTION

Change emerges internally and, as we alter our beliefs, we begin to perceive the world differently. As I accept my unity with all life, each experience will change. I will have a different effect on those I encounter and they will have a different effect on me. Today, I have the courage to begin this journey. Today, I will see through lenses of love and compassion.

AWARENESS

I will discern how my needs are being met in each moment. I will act with the confidence that I make a difference and I will intend that difference to be positive.

DAY 70—GRATITUDE

"My mind is hushed into wide and endless light,
my heart a solitude of delight and peace."
Sri Aurobindo (1935)

PREMISE

How can developing gratitude in our daily routine lead to fulfillment? Similar to each of the four pillars of contentment (humility, acceptance/forgiveness and patience/trust), gratitude stands as its own reward. To appreciate what we have, to savor each moment, to marvel at and experience all of life's gifts, is to realize that we are part of a salutary and glorious design. Rejoice in the daily routine, the smiles, the smells, the movement and the magnificence that is life. Practice gratitude as you would a basic physical skill, like tennis or running. Exercise it every day and make it stronger. Gratitude is to happiness what conditioning it is to sports.

INTENTION

I am becoming the power that controls my life, more and more, each and every day. I have the courage to take responsibility for my emotional, intellectual, spiritual and physical responses to all external events. Every day, I see more of what I can and can't control and I am developing the courage of confrontation and the wisdom of surrender.

AWARENESS

I will view life today, through lenses of awe and appreciation. I will choose one aspect of my personality and I will write at least five sentences in my journal as to why this aspect of myself enhances my life and the lives of those I encounter.

DAY 71—ACCEPTANCE

"Every person, no matter who, can be the teacher we need, if instead of judging, we listen, accept, and love."
Buddha (c. 540 B.C.E.)

PREMISE

Unconditional love and unconditional positive regard (Carl Rogers, 1961) are synonymous with acceptance. As it applies to our daily lives, unconditional love is about adopting the notion that we are one of God's creatures and part of the human race, destined to participate in a plan greater than ourselves. We are unique, precious and of unlimited potential. We have a goal, a destiny, to become who we were created to be. We share these qualities with all living things. We are all on a journey and we are all reflections of God's love. If obstacles to our mission are met with patience, trust and courage, they will be overcome for everyone's benefit.

INTENTION

I can begin to see meaning in my life. My sorrows and joys, weaknesses and strengths, fears and hopes all have significance and importance. I can begin to overcome the reluctance to face the responsibility towards myself and others that this thought brings. I can act with compassion and acceptance towards both others and myself.

AWARENESS

I will seek to learn from another today. I will listen to myself when I_begin to isolate, categorize or demonize. I will attend with an open heart and mind. I will try to learn and not compare, take responsibility and not give blame.

DAY 72—PATIENCE

"Life on the farm is a school of patience; you can't hurry the crops or make an ox in two days."
Henri Fournier Alain (1910)

PREMISE

It is essential that we have sufficient humility and trust to comprehend the fact that we will always have what we need, when we need it, as long as we open our hearts to love. This allows change to happen and the unexpected to unfold. Patience is the personal attribute that enables letting go and believing that things will resolve successfully in a manner such that we achieve contentment. Trusting in the moment creates an opportunity to learn and to embrace change. This will gradually give us the wisdom to cope with the accidental and the unanticipated. When we have faith, we develop the power and self-assurance to know what can be changed and what must be turned over and let go. Patience allows this life-affirming process to emerge without our interference. Observe with wonder as you allow the Universe to unfold before your very eyes.

INTENTION

I realize that I am only has strong as the choices I make. Within my choices lies my power. I know that I cannot control external circumstances, challenges and consequences. I can control my behavioral responses and thus my emotional responses to these factors. I can also control how I view and interpret both the initial situation and the outcome of my action. However, I must have patience if this intent is to be successful.

AWARENESS

Today, I will focus on the moment, so that I respond in a manner that reflects the self, I wish to create. I will maximize my awareness by pausing and manifesting patience.

DAY 73—HUMILITY

*"Where there is patience and humility,
there is neither anger nor vexation."*
St. Francis of Assisi (1200)

PREMISE

To be humble is to accept yourself and others. We are all God's perfect creation. You are one of many and if you have more talents, material goods, social power etc., it is not because you are better or more virtuous; rather it is because you are more blessed. Such blessings obligate us to understand that all gifts come from God and those with more, must share. To be humble is to resist that temptation to either embellish or diminish your importance in the Grand Plan. It is to acknowledge, equally, both strengths and weaknesses. It is to always try your best and to be your best as you learn from mistakes. There is no failure, if we are humble, and try to learn lessons from results that did not meet expectations. Get over it! The Universe is not your personal "good fairy." It works in its own time and its own way. Understand this and be grateful.

INTENTION

I can change. I can accept myself and I can accept others as they are. They need not change. Any change I want in others, must start with me. This, I can control. Through intent and awareness, I can evolve into all that I was created to be. It's up to me and the time to start is now. I will become the change I desire in others.

AWARENESS

Today, I will be more alert to my good qualities and their positive effects on those I love. I will perform random and anonymous acts of kindness.

DAY 74—GRATITUDE

"A man in armor is armor's slave."
Robert Browning (1871)

PREMISE

Life is a force that we can resist or embrace. This is our choice. Be grateful for this choice. Pray for the wisdom to decide correctly and constructively. Also, pray for the courage to implement that choice. If we are to achieve our absolute potential, we must be willing to acknowledge, submit to and respect, all that we can't control. To be grateful is to be part of this progression because it simplifies the process of awareness to all possibilities. Gratitude also cushions disappointments because we begin to understand that circumstances happen for the Good. It is foolish to resist change. Have the trust, patience and courage to allow this personal transformation to unfold and to extract the lessons from that process. This will generate gratitude and contentment.

INTENTION

I can succeed in accepting and being grateful for change. I am able to realize that without choice and change, I will become stagnant and depressed. God has endowed me with the desire to grow and evolve. Only fear and immobility will prevent me from realizing my destiny. I can begin today to persevere and to become all that I was meant to be.

AWARENESS

I will be sensitive to my tendency to resist and to fight against that which I can't control. I will list in my journal three personal traits that I like about myself and I will express thanks to another.

DAY 75—ACCEPTANCE

"It is far more important that one's life should be perceived than that it should be transformed; for no sooner has it been perceived, than it transforms itself of its own accord."
Maurice Maeterlinck (1896)

PREMISE

If we believe the premise that God created us and that we are as we should be despite faults and deficits; self-acceptance follows. We start to realize that we are lovable and we begin to appreciate all that we are, as we diminish thoughts of what we are not. Once we achieve this, we will also appreciate how deeply we are loved. As we offer kindness and caring, we receive it and we feel joy and unity. Ultimately, we embrace the idea that we are one with all and that in this moment we have everything we need to achieve satisfaction and respect.

INTENTION

As I risk, I increase my courage and I will grow. As I grow in courage, I become more willing to trust and to venture into new territory. I will be of stout heart because it is here and in service that I will become who I am meant to be. I am frightened at this thought, but I know that I can prevail. If I ask for help, I will receive it. If I pray, my prayers will be answered. All I need is the faith to ask.

AWARENESS

Today, I will write, why I am reluctant to show love, caring, acceptance and trust. I will think hard on this and develop a strategy to master fear.

DAY 76—PATIENCE

"Man needs difficulties; they are necessary for health."
Carl Gustav Jung (1930)

PREMISE

The essence of growth is acceptance (a.k.a. "letting go") and changing our perspective from a place where we have no power, no control, to a place (usually internal) wherein we can confront, challenge and control. The task is to embrace this internal place of power with trust, patience and courage. As we do this, the process begins, where we redefine what can be controlled and what must be surrendered. We delineate and determine our areas of competence and with new resilience, perseverance and determination, begin to build new aptitudes and skills. We become creative and confident as this occurs. Our perspective starts to change as does our recollection of past events and our evaluations of those events.

INTENTION

I must realize that if I think it, I can do it. I can make a change or at least attempt a change and tolerate the inconvenience of disappointment. If "disappointment" means not meeting expectations and this prevents me from making changes, I can easily change expectations and set myself to beginning the long journey with the first, most simple, step. I can do this!!

AWARENESS

I will choose, for today, to respond to the unexpected with love and acceptance. I will note one occurrence in my journal where I confronted fear and acted with courageous love.

DAY 77—HUMILITY

"The sons of Adam are formed from dust; if not humble as the dust, they fall short of being men."
St. Thomas Aquinas (1258)

PREMISE

We are beginning to comprehend that we have a unique and significant responsibility, yet we play a minor role in the greater drama that is the unfolding of the Universe. We have a purpose and we are blessed. All prior events have brought us to this moment and this realization. We are uniquely qualified to fulfill this role. It is why we were created; it is our destiny. Humility is an acknowledgment of this fact. Practicing humility will subjugate the strong power and pull of the child-self who cries that we are supreme and that our needs must be fulfilled above anything else. The child-self is strong and strident. Chances are that we have submitted to this internal critique too much for too long with results of misery and stagnation. Now, since we know better, we can rise above petty self-concerns and move on with our lives.

INTENTION

Change is my responsibility. No one else can do this for me. With help and the four foundational qualities, I can do this and I will do this. I now have the knowledge and determination to fulfill my destiny. I can transform my assumptions, behaviors and emotional responses to the events that impact on my life. As I do this, I will attain the courage to witness the progression of my fellow travelers, as well.

AWARENESS

Today, I will focus on that inner voice of my child-self that says, "Me, Me! Me!!" I will behave in a manner that will put the needs of others ahead of my own.

DAY 78—GRATITUDE

"Developing a true sense of gratitude involves taking absolutely nothing for granted. Rather, always look for the friendly intention behind the deed and learn to appreciate it."
Albert Schweitzer (1945)

PREMISE

Respecting ourselves sufficiently, so that we have the strength to embrace another, should be an objective that infuses each day. When we acknowledge a personal message of love and acceptance, any circumstance or interaction becomes a blessing from the Universe. Be grateful for this insight and our world-view of benevolence, inclusion and acceptance. It is from this point that we begin to grow and evolve into the compassionate beings we were created to become. This is contentment and living a full and complete life. We must practice being grateful each day so that this blessing remains a vibrant aspect of our life. To be grateful for those who choose to share their lives with us and to express this gratitude will improve all aspects of daily living.

INTENTION

I can practice compassion, acceptance and inclusion in all my dealings with others. I will master this for its own sake and not for power, reward, or recognition. I will give freely and anonymously. This is another hard lesson. I usually focus on my own needs and fulfilling my own wishes. Now, with help from God and my friends, I will persevere, move forward and reach my goals.

AWARENESS

I will be attuned today to the positive potential of each interaction. I will speak to a close friend about my goal of living a life full of affirmation and caring. I will also try to see new ways where I can be of service to my fellow traveler.

DAY 79—ACCEPTANCE

"Skills vary with the man. We must tread a straight path and strive by that which is born in us."
Pindar (fifth century B.C.E.)

PREMISE

The primary components of love and wisdom (the foundational qualities) are humility, acceptance, forgiveness, gratitude, trust and patience. Starting with humility, as the fertile soil from which the other traits grow, we blossom into gratitude, acceptance, forgiveness, trust and patience. One leads into the next as it reinforces the prior quality, in a positive life-affirming reciprocity. If we are to attain our destiny's goal of expanding love and joy, we must continually (each day), attempt to honor and accept others. To try to control or change another person is a fool's mission. We must strive to mind our own business, change ourselves rather than someone else, look inward and become the transformation we want to see in others. This difficult goal begins with self-acceptance and the subsequent acceptance of others that results.

INTENTION

I know that I tend to be suspicious and reluctant to accept others. I never want to be vulnerable to hurt or disappointment. I am aware that I tend to compare others and judge them because I want to feel superior. I must admit that I am afraid of being rejected, shunned and isolated, if I'm not in control. I know that if I could master the courage to ask for help, my Higher Power would bless me and I would end the cycle of pushing others away in order to protect myself.

AWARENESS

I will practice being tolerant today. I will make an effort to acknowledge the negative thoughts and harsh judgments I render on to others. I will pause before I judge and catch myself before I reject another.

DAY 80—PATIENCE

"All the strength and solace you need is within you.
Therefore, make your own future."
Swami Vivekananda (1891)

PREMISE

Imperfection is not inadequacy and inadequacy is not incompetence. We are people; we are human. We cannot, nor will we, ever achieve "perfection." We can, however, intend our best, persevere and evaluate as well as, re-assess, re-strategize, re-energize and re-start. We must give ourselves a break. We must be patient, first and foremost with ourselves. Practice self-compassion and understand that patience moves mountains. Small steps to growth do not mean ineffectiveness or inability. Patience will allow us to see progress where, before, arrogance blinded us. We need to open our eyes and comprehend our innate goodness. We will discover talents we have never imagined and we will create the courage to use those talents at every opportunity.

INTENTION

I can allow myself to make mistakes. What choice do I have? I can condemn myself and enable the negative, self-destructive, monologue to play endlessly in my head or I can say, "I am good and getting better." I will not let fear stop me. As I move forward with love and patience, progress will be revealed and contentment will fill my being.

AWARENESS

Today, I will monitor how I handle frustration and I will persevere on a task that I perceive to be difficult and frustrating. I will note my actions and assess my reactions in my journal.

DAY 81—HUMILITY

"We come nearest to the great when we are great in humility."
Rabindranath Tagore (1916)

PREMISE

We are on a journey where we play a small but significant part in a much larger, grander, plan that is beyond comprehension. Our choice is to make the journey with the intent of expanding kindness and compassion or to make it with the intent of acquisition and self-interest. This choice is conscious and purposeful. With awareness, we can observe the results of our choices each day, with each interaction; so that we may determine which course we are on. With such information, we can resume and re-strategize, as well as reassess our goals, so that we may properly move forward. Either way, we will fulfill our mission for the Universe. If we choose the path of selfishness and isolation, our lives will be filled with bitterness and frustration. However, if we choose the enlightened path, we will experience joy beyond our most optimistic expectation. The choice is ours and we can make it now.

INTENTION

I can and will begin this journey immediately. I will accept responsibility and I will begin to pursue growth and maturation. As I become attuned to my inner needs, I understand that I must evolve and move on. Every moment of every day presents opportunities to shed preconceptions and to learn. I can change my life by changing my perspective.

AWARENESS

Today, I will be aware of the effects of my choices on those around me. Am I choosing love or self-interest? I have decided to make the choice of expanding love and compassion in all of my interactions, starting immediately.

DAY 82—GRATITUDE

"All is beautiful, all is more beautiful, and life is thankfulness."
Inuit Song

PREMISE

To be most effective, gratitude, like the other three pillars of virtue and contentment, requires courage. Courage opens our eyes and allows us to be trusting and vulnerable. Courage is saying: "I love you" to ourselves, to others and to life. It is assessing our vulnerabilities and understanding that such an act and intention, in itself, makes us stronger and improves our effectiveness in coping with change and living life. It takes courage to be grateful because we reach that point from a perspective of humility. It also takes courage to comprehend that you have been given more than you have earned. We are grateful when we realize that life isn't fair. If it were fair, we would be far worse off. Think about it.

INTENTION

Through self-talk and introspection, I am able to develop the courage, substance, strength and perseverance of my convictions. I am able to risk because no one can take my spirit or self-esteem. Language is my tool to shape and energize my perspective as I progress, confront change and attain my goals.

AWARENESS

Today, I will be more conscious of my tendency to jump in and manage a situation that is none of my business. I will note in my journal one circumstance or event where I was tempted to take control but I realized I could do little, so I allowed events to unfold. I am grateful to let go of such situations.

DAY 83—ACCEPTANCE

"As rain falls equally on the just and the unjust, do not burden your heart with judgments but rain your kindness equally on all."
The Buddha (c. 533 B.C.E.)

PREMISE

Acceptance is an essential component of The Serenity Prayer because to achieve the contentment and peacefulness that life has to offer, we must appreciate and respect our circumstances and the talents and limitations we bring to any task. It is essential to distinguish between those things that we can change and those that we must surrender. We must feel grateful for who we are and how we came to be at this place. For those of you reading this, you have a special opportunity to become aware and grateful that such a truth has become known. Hopefully, this will serve as an incentive and motivation for you to continue the quest to achieve your goals as you accept the challenge to become who you were created to be.

INTENTION

I find acceptance difficult because I am so judgmental. I believe that I'm special, independent and that my perceptions are unerring. If people are judged "bad", they remain "bad" and don't change. This is also true of the Good. I must step back from these destructive notions of certainty and constancy and face the fact that all is change and all is changing. I am just another person on a special journey that, like all my brethren, is unique to me.

AWARENESS

I will actively be passive today. That is to say, I will decide to be observant and as non-participating as is constructively possible. I will note in my journal one event where I resisted the temptation to manage and instead listened and observed with an open heart and mind.

DAY 84—PATIENCE

"Our entire life . . . consists ultimately in accepting ourselves as we are."
Jean Anouilh (1936)

PREMISE

If we are to achieve all that we were created to achieve, we must accept that we are participating in a marvelous, cosmic dance. Like a small link in a long chain, our role in life is both crucial and secondary to the larger plan. Another paradox! We are vital yet secondary, necessary but not sufficient. Patience and humility allow us to understand this and to trust in a plan, which comprehends that events unfold in God's time and not ours. Ultimately, we let go, observe, learn and move on, all according to an agenda that we can witness and infer but never dictate.

INTENTION

I now understand that happiness and contentment are decisions I make as I navigate through the noise of my daily routine and attempt to focus on the signal that manifests the purpose of my life. I can frame and perceive any event in any manner, to suit any purpose. My choice is whether or not I decide with love or with fear and in a way that can be either successful or destructive. Framed in love or fear, acceptance or exclusion, humility or arrogance, the choice is mine and the power is within. The ball is in my court. I create my reality and I create my emotions, through my thoughts.

AWARENESS

Today, I will attempt to change a situation without becoming a part of that situation. I will do this by altering my perspective from frustration and anger to acceptance and love. I will note how I did this. And I will begin to set up a strategy, so that I will continue to solve external issues by means of internal alterations of perspective as I adapt to change.

DAY 85—HUMILITY

"Humility, a sense of reverence before the sons of heaven . . ."
Euripides (412 B.C.E.)

PREMISE

As we progress in our humility, we emerge from murky helplessness to clear empowerment. Our focus shifts from an external "blame" orientation to an internal, self-control, orientation. With humility, we begin to perceive the changes we can make and we begin to plan and progress as courage and optimism motivate us. We face vulnerability and build patience and trust. We feel resolute and confident knowing that we are guided by our Higher Power. From this perspective, we see the illusory nature of the superficial and we search inward for solutions and truth. We come to embrace the capacity and abilities of the self, the "I". This is generated internally. We resoundingly renounce the power and opinions of the "child-self." These are based on external values relying on the frivolous and shallow. This is the shift in thought, a new perceptual paradigm that we must achieve to attain wellness and contentment.

INTENTION

I want to become empowered and I have the will and wisdom to free myself from the external attachments that try to define who I am. Most of my confusion is generated from these external attachments. Any desire that can be fulfilled only from the outside will destroy me. I will look inward and have the courage to see the strength and power that is within. I realize that I cannot get enough of what I don't need.

AWARENESS

For today, I will focus and feel the internal power that resides in my soul. I will behave in a manner that reflects my new awareness of the strength within. Throughout the day, I will pause, breathe and feel the power that is unity and life.

DAY 86—GRATITUDE

"Each man must look to himself to teach the meaning of life. It is not something discovered; it is something molded."
Antoine de Saint-Exupery (1940)

PREMISE

Gratitude is a gift to the self. Of the four pillars generating and supporting, love, wisdom, and courage, it has special potential to fill us with a sense of appreciation and an affinity for life, as well as all that life has to offer. We begin to feel and to believe that we are just where we should be and that our trials and challenges are unique opportunities given to us by a Higher Power so that we may learn and grow. We feel and believe that we are just as we were created to be, with abilities as well as faults from which we can learn and mature. We understand that strengths are spawned by faults and we know that this can instruct and help us appreciate, as well as, empathize with our fellow travelers.

INTENTION

I am responsible for my choices. This knowledge will give me the awareness of my importance and the mindfulness of my intent so that I may become the person in life I was born to be. It is never too late to start and no step is too small. Constancy is the cornerstone of growth and I will focus and persevere in living with love, acceptance and gratitude.

AWARENESS

I will open my eyes to my strengths, take responsibility for my weaknesses and embrace my potential to expand love. Although I will be active in using my talents for the Good of all, I will assume the position of participant/observer and note the positive effects of my efforts in a manner that reflects respect and humility.

DAY 87—ACCEPTANCE

"When you are good to others, you are best to yourself."
Benjamin Franklin (1759)

PREMISE

If we are to practice The Serenity Prayer, we must be sufficiently humble and courageous to define and face what we can't do and compassionately assume the obligation to change the things we can. In the prayer, we also request, the wisdom to know the difference and the acceptance of those things over which we have no power (the vast majority of people, places and things as well as anything else external to us). In this prayer, Reinhold Niebuhr (1934) offers succinct and profound advice to living a spiritually and emotionally fulfilling life. It is one of the better guides to psychological health and should be recited throughout the day as we encounter new situations and life's travails.

INTENTION

I do believe I am on the right course and that the events of my life occur for a purpose. This is a conscious choice I am making and I will diligently pursue wherever this choice leads me. I will do so with love and compassion. I will pray for guidance and I will accept the impediments that may frustrate me but they will never stop me. I know that I am on the right path and I feel the improvement every day.

AWARENESS

I will make special note today to recite The Serenity Prayer whenever I feel fear or anxiety. I will make a note about the internal effects of this practice.

DAY 88—PATIENCE

"Rejoice in hope and be patient in tribulation."
John F. Kennedy (1961)

PREMISE

Patience is sometimes seen as weakness, fear, passivity and/or lack of passion and commitment. In truth, it is quite the opposite. Patience is living the gift of faith and trust. It is a certainty, a confidence that whatever happens and whenever it happens will be responded to in a way that will appropriately resolve the issue. Patience is also the assumption that the Universe is benevolent and that our trials and tribulations are simply directions and routes to growth. It presents the opportunity to pause and allow thought to slow impulse. Patience prevents us from acting in an inappropriate manner. It is a blessing that permits us to continue persevering towards our goals without regret, resentment or recrimination.

INTENTION

I can feel the strength of patience. I can feel the goodness, acceptance, humility and contentment that comprise the virtue of patience. I must focus on the moment and allow the new and the novel to encompass me as I continue affirming love and acceptance. My child-self yells, screams and throws a tantrum but I am in control and I can stay in control despite impediments, frustrations, and disappointments. If I intend love and contentment, this is what I will be given by the Cosmos.

AWARENESS

Today, I will note one instance where I react differently to one of my many "pet peeves." I will document this incident and the consequent emotions in my journal. I will strive to allow the Universe to unfold as it was meant to, without my opinion, disruption or management skills.

DAY 89—HUMILITY

"Humility like darkness reveals the heavenly lights."
Henry David Thoreau (1854)

PREMISE

As we develop humility, the interactions with others become opportunities to show unconditional love and acceptance. For once, you can love with no hurt because there are no expectations of the other or yourself. Humility allows you to be free, honest and generous. You are not afraid to be who you are. The other is equally free. To compete is to strive for exclusion, to seek superiority, to conquer, to defeat, rather than to accept, include, understand and love. To be humble, is to embrace inclusion, to become the "we" and the "us." You are perfectly you; you are just where you should be in time and place. You are participating in and contributing to a wondrous, universal dance beyond anyone's comprehension. Each day, each second, each encounter is an opportunity to learn and to contribute to this dance that is life.

INTENTION

By controlling my perspective and approaching my brethren with humility and acceptance, I will control those untoward emotions that create such havoc in my life. When my emotional reactions are determined by volatile, unpredictable, extraneous events, I become powerless. I can and will focus on my strong independent, internal core, that place of peace, serenity and satisfaction.

AWARENESS

I will become more alert to the signs that urge me to conform and I will assess and evaluate those signs. I will interact with total honesty but with an honesty born of humility, love and compassion. I will embrace the idea that I am neither more nor less, neither superior nor inferior. I am one with many and I have a unique gift to be used to help others.

DAY 90—GRATITUDE

"Movement and change constantly renew the world."
Marcus Aurelius (160 C.E.)

PREMISE

We are special, with particular talents and we have an opportunity to offer these to all those we meet. Be grateful to give and be grateful that you can acknowledge and enjoy your aptitudes, strengths, potential and abilities. This helps define yourself and eschews the child-self as it clamors for you to pretend to be what you are not. The gift of gratitude encompasses the appreciation and reverence for all life in general and each exquisite component of daily living in particular. This is the best antidote to depression and low self-esteem. It removes us from self-focus and self-involvement and brings us to the wonders of all that lie beyond self-pity and superficiality. Cultivating gratitude makes each day joyful and exceptional.

INTENTION

I am unique. No one was meant to do nor can do what I was created to do. No one has the talents honed from my particular life experience. No one was meant to be me. I am perfectly me and I am developing the courage to follow my destiny in love, humility and gratitude. I realize that who I am changes as time goes on and circumstances impact on my perspective. But my inner core, my true self, is unchanging. It is God's creation and I am as I should be. I give thanks for this knowledge and I accept responsibility for the thoughts, feelings and behaviors that emerge from this awareness.

AWARENESS

I will be especially aware of the unique opportunity offered to me in this moment. There will never be another day like this and I will take every advantage to energize my positive emotions to show my gratitude for this day. I will discuss what my feelings of gratitude are with a friend.

PART TWO

ASSESSING PROGRESS
BEGINNING TO RECOVER

DAYS 91-180

Congratulations! By this time, you have successfully completed 90 lessons based on the wisdom and insight of both Eastern and Western scribes and sages. You may have done this a day at a time, or you may have slipped and had to return to DAY 1. Either way, you've progressed and you deserve credit for your efforts and your determination. You are a miracle.

This is the time to assess your progress. Do not allow what you haven't done to interfere with what you have done. Now you have choice. The act of choosing is sacred but elusive. It is sacred because it signals empowerment and it is elusive because we frequently shun from the responsibility that accompanies choice. On DAY 1, you had little choice; now, you think, you pause, and then you act. When you are in doubt, you know whom to ask, you know to pray, and you know to read this book. Be grateful and understand that you are striving for progress not perfection. Stay the course.

The purpose of these lessons is to instill a world-view and a manner of behaving that promotes individual growth by generating a perspective that confronts the challenge of change, promotes mutual respect and strengthens unselfish thought. You can do this; just look at how far you have come!

DAY 91—ACCEPTANCE

"Chance favors the prepared mind."
Louis Pasteur (1862)

PREMISE

If you want to be accepted and loved, you must accept and love. You must have the courage to be weak and vulnerable. Seize the DAY, seek new opportunities to act with boldness and trust; be open and inclusive of new ideas, new people and new situations. Life and contentment will be yours, only to the degree that you allow it. If you prepare for change, embracing it as a lesson to be learned, an adventure to pursue and a journey to enjoy, life will reward you with unimaginable delight. Free your heart and expand your spirit. Your mind and body will follow.

INTENTION

I will "seize the DAY." I will be grateful for the moments to bare myself to life and all the adventures, challenges and prosperity, awaiting me. I must ask my Higher Power for the courage, trust and openness to begin such a venture. I will intend to be grateful for all the gifts, strengths, and even impediments that are put before me. I can do this, the power is within and the encouragement is all around me. If I allow it, I can succeed beyond my most ambitious dreams but first I must listen and learn.

AWARENESS

For today, I will risk. Starting in the morning, after meditation, I will set my intent on trusting and being vulnerable in at least one circumstance. I will face my fear and note the event in my journal.

DAY 92—PATIENCE

"Genius is only a greater aptitude for patience."
Comte De Buffon (1765)

PREMISE

Both Winston Churchill and Thomas Edison knew the value of patience in generating persistence and in contributing to success. Success is ". . . the ability to go from one failure to another with no loss of enthusiasm," according to Churchill. Edison wrote: "many of life's failures are people who did not realize how close they were to success when they gave up." Patience reflects the confidence we have in ourselves as well as the trust we have in the benevolence of the Universe. Patience urges us to continue towards our goal in the face of doubt, insecurity and the unknown. It tells us to pursue a course and follow a path because we feel it is right and loving. Others may disagree and shout, "get even," "get revenge," and "it's either you or them." However, we can ignore them because we know our path is bringing happiness to others and changing our lives for the better, each day, a step at a time.

INTENTION

Despite the constant change and chaos, the distractions, the distortions and the discord in the world, I can move forward. I can quiet my soul, breathe and pause. I can trust and allow myself to be vulnerable. I can wait and watch the world unfold as it was meant to. In other words, I can be patient. I can then refocus on my commitment to love and compassion, as I move forward in peace and harmony.

AWARENESS

I will take a moment tomorrow morning, upon awakening, to reflect on my goals and to write down one goal that I will pursue.

DAY 93—HUMILITY

"We can't all be heroes because someone has to sit on the curb and clap as they go by."
Will Rogers (1930)

PREMISE

The attitudes of "me first," "I want," and "I deserve", significantly impede the ability to develop humility. In our consumer culture, humility is frequently disparaged, often associated with low self-esteem or self-deprecation. It is also associated with submissive, servile and sycophantic behavior. In short, to be humble is to be a loser. These, sometimes subliminal messages, oppose cultivating humility because it undermines the culture of consumption. We subvert consumerism when, by means of humility, we become empowered and free from external solutions for any real or fabricated, desires and deficiencies. By renouncing the myth that we are inept, inadequate or impaired, we corrode the very core of consumerism. If I am okay, why do I need this product, utensil, or makeover? Such questions destroy the basis of defect, deficiency or deprivation that is essential to the reasoning of such systems.

INTENTION

I've been taught what offends and what soothes, what incites and what dissuades. My perception is my reality. If it's been taught, I can learn it afresh. I can learn to be aware of and rebuke cultural pressures and messages that separate me from my Higher Power and my unique destiny. As I think so shall I be. I can learn my place in the "Grand Plan". I can take my place among the many and I can contribute my unique talents for the Good of all.

AWARENESS

Today, I will act in a manner that maximizes my God-given talents.

DAY 94—GRATITUDE

"We carry within us the wonders we seek outside."
Sir Thomas Browne (1642)

PREMISE

The theory of cognitive dissonance states that you cannot hold two contrary ideas or feelings in your consciousness simultaneously. Therefore, it is impossible to believe and experience that you are deprived, deficient and defective as you also acknowledge and feel gratified for who you are, what you have and for your special talents. As you comprehend and accept this, you will be better able to contribute to the world around you. The gift of gratitude is indeed all-powerful and all-encompassing. It can improve every relationship as well as your quality of life. With the gift of gratitude, depression decreases, isolation diminishes and contentment intensifies.

INTENTION

As I think, so I become. I have this power and I have the intent and awareness to use it for the Good of others. I can channel my energy and the emotions my thoughts generate. The power is in me. I only have to reflect and release it.

AWARENESS

Today, I will be especially alert to signs of self-pity or self-importance. I will immediately replace them with feelings of gratitude and humility. I will thank one person for something they do and express my appreciation to another for their friendship and support.

DAY 95—ACCEPTANCE

"It is in forgiving that we are forgiven,
for it is in giving that we receive."
St. Francis of Assisi (1210)

PREMISE

Acceptance and forgiveness go hand in hand. Forgiveness is crucial to healing our soul. Acceptance is crucial to giving love. The child-self wants to resist this and prefers to resent, hate, and seek vengeance. Resentment simply destroys acceptance in whoever entertains it. To practice forgiveness, we must have compassion, empathy and acceptance, first for ourselves and then for others. When we seek revenge, hold a grudge or harbor hate, dislike or distrust, we are simply projecting our own self-despair, disgust and dissatisfaction. We must, as always: 1. Be aware of these tendencies to dismiss, disparage or disdain and 2. Intend to remediate such weakness and antagonism. "Forgive us our trespasses as we forgive those . . ." If we are to accept others, we must start with ourselves and acknowledge that acceptance is a necessary component of a contented life.

INTENTION

I will be able to forgive myself if I can accept the obvious fact that God made me and therefore I am as I should be. I must have the humility to acknowledge my weaknesses as well as my strengths and I must have the fortitude and self-tolerance to overcome the former and embrace the latter.

AWARENESS

Today, I will simply observe myself in situations and make mental notes for later consideration. I will, especially, notice what feelings proceed and follow a particular interaction.

DAY 96—PATIENCE

"Patience makes lighter/What sorrow may not heal."
Horace (c. 15 B.C.E.)

PREMISE

Maybe we admire the patience we see in others and believe that it is something that we cannot achieve. However, remember that patience requires patience. It is the persistent desire to accept something or someone that previously caused frustration and distress. It is calmly enduring the fabled "slings and arrows of outrageous fortune." Patience is one of the four pillars of contentment. It is a necessary spiritual quality that helps us fulfill our destiny. Patience is the result of having developed humility, gratitude, acceptance and trust. Empowerment embodies patience because empowerment requires self-control. Patience and power are reciprocal qualities, that is, they engage in a dance of mutual reinforcement. In sum, patience encompasses acceptance, self-control and self-possession and it is necessary if we are to mature and achieve our goals.

INTENTION

I know that it is irrational and self-destructive to deny, delay or avoid change. Now I know that patience helps me to confront, reframe and conquer the challenge of change. I will strive to develop the necessary trust, so that the Universe unfolds before me and I seek only to learn the lesson within and the strength to persevere.

AWARENESS

Today, I will practice observing. I will simply watch and resist my tendency to control, manage and alter. I will see how life is moving, growing and creating without my interference, opinion or supervision.

DAY 97—HUMILITY

"A just and reasonable modesty does not only recommend eloquence, but sets off every great talent which a man can be possessed of."
Joseph Addison (1712)

PREMISE

Internally, the "child-self", which must always dominate in order to be satisfied, will not go silently into the night. It is ubiquitously embodied in the cultural ideal of an external solution that is quick, easy and painless. This message permeates the airwaves and drives the economy. If you are flawed, weak, or needy (and you are according to the mass media), there is a simple solution, which can be purchased in easy payments ("even if you have bad credit or no credit at all") or with "a simple phone call." "Get what you deserve and make your life better"; another broadcast bellows, as we try to cope with the frustration of the moment. Here is the promise of easy, no hassle, satisfaction and gratification. No work, no sweat, no bother, all solutions offered from outside. How easy! How illusionary!!

INTENTION

I can do the work necessary to make this change from an external to an internal mindset. Solutions are within my spiritual-self and me. I have the will, courage and wisdom to move forward to self-fulfillment. I am on a sacred path that only I can follow. It will lead me to a special place where I will find serenity and satisfaction. I can and must do this.

AWARENESS

Today, I will be alert to the "easy", "no hassle", solutions for my internal wants and desires. I will make an effort to identify and satisfy these yearnings without resorting to external gimmicks.

DAY 98—GRATITUDE

"For this relief much thanks; 'tis bitter cold, and I am sick at heart."
Shakespeare, Hamlet (1601)

PREMISE

Gratitude is truly a gift from God. If we are integrated with our spirit and have it as our intention, gratitude will arise in our awareness without any other effort. However, we must open our hearts and have the humility, to see the wonder that is before us. With gratitude, we will increasingly treasure each moment, each interaction and each experience. All our senses will rejoice in this precious gift. A sunset, a smiling baby, a familiar song, the touch of silk on your skin and the sweet taste of candy on your tongue; each will become an occasion to rejoice and give thanks. We were created to have joy but we must be willing to allow it.

INTENTION

Change is constant in the physical world and I can change thoughts and their consequent emotions. I can also change those behaviors that follow thoughts and emotions, once I am aware and intend to do so. I thank my Higher Power for this realization and I ask that I may use this knowledge to achieve my destiny by serving others. I now understand that I must give it away to keep it and I must be humble if I am to be grateful, for all true gifts come from my Higher Power.

AWARENESS

I will be more conscious of the joy of living. I will attend to all my sense experience as I go through the day. I will write a personal, brief, thank you note to my Higher Power. I will include at least three things that I am grateful for at that moment.

DAY 99—ACCEPTANCE

"The ineffable joy of forgiving and being forgiven forms an ecstasy that might well arouse the envy of the Gods."
Elbert Hubbard (1927)

PREMISE

By achieving and developing the quality of acceptance, similar feelings and perspectives, such as tolerance and forgiveness are generated. As we allow ourselves to be imperfect a.k.a. human, we accept, tolerate or forgive flaws, imperfections, and weaknesses in others. This is extremely liberating, as we travel through life without creating burdens and boundaries, resentments and aversions. We become free to grow and we allow others the same liberty. We see ourselves as part of a whole, similar yet different, related yet distinct, one of many who are one. It all begins with the acceptance that leads to tolerance, forgiveness and compassion. Fight the fear, muster the courage and begin today.

INTENTION

I can and will do this. I will see beyond, my needs and myself. I will see commonality where before I saw division and difference. I will not compare or judge. I will accept. This raises the fear that I will become lost and that my identity will merge with others. I will counter this thought because I know I was created with unique abilities, honed by singular experience and presented with unparalleled opportunity.

AWARENESS

I will note in my journal the self-destructive thoughts that separate me from others through criticism, stereotyping and dismissiveness.

DAY 100—PATIENCE

"He who knows others is learned;
He who knows himself is wise."
Lao Tzu (6th century, B.C.E.)

PREMISE

As we learn about ourselves, learn to distinguish our wants from our needs and also learn that the world does not revolve around us, we begin to gain the appropriate perspective and distance from the external and we begin to tolerate what caused previous disappointments. We comprehend the concept of choice and individual power. Every moment offers us a choice. Therefore, we are forced to confront what we control despite our fear and resistance. We can choose to become aware of our emotions at any specific time. There is no point in the day that is too late to begin again and to start over. Reframe and grow. Fear, anger, and tension as well as happiness, love, contentment are only simple energy, going through our body due to our interpretation of events.

INTENTION

I fear change because I distrust myself as well as my ability to cope with the unknown. When I trust my destiny and I show faith in myself, I can face uncertainty with the confidence that my experience and unique talents can point to the right path. I can believe in the benevolence of the Cosmos and the relevance of my objectives. I will ignore the noise that shuts out the signal. I am special and I can do things that no one else can. I can serve and I can be fulfilled and content.

AWARENESS

Today, I will note one thing that I believe is unique about me and I will watch how this is expressed in my daily life.

DAY 101—HUMILITY

"Nothing is more amiable than true modesty,
and nothing more contemptible than the false.
The one guards virtue, the other betrays it."
Joseph Addison (1712)

PREMISE

Why do we seek such superficial, external solutions to internal needs? Why is the consumer culture so alluring and so popular? The most obvious answer is that we are persuaded by constant propaganda about our inability to take care of ourselves or satisfy our significant "needs" without some external solution. We constantly hear that we "deserve" to feel better and that we don't feel as good as we "should" or "could." This allows the child-self's arrogance to clamor for immediate satisfaction. Arrogance masks fear and is a perspective that you don't need to tolerate the vulnerability or frustration that accompanies patience, trust and restraint. The child-self rises and rules, craves immediate reward and will accept nothing less. Humility is the only solution to this tension and turmoil.

INTENTION

I will not be afraid of changing. All choices and transitions begin with thought and I know that I can make myself approach change with sufficient humility and gratitude to nullify the demands of the child-self. In any circumstance, at any time, I have the power to frame a problem and to respond in a manner that shows restraint and respect.

AWARENESS

Today, I will delay the reflexive gratification of all impulses for just a moment. I will be aware of "needs", "desires" and impulses as they arise. I will take a moment to pause, breathe and consider. I will show self-control and self-respect.

DAY 102—GRATITUDE

"Gratitude is the most exquisite form of courtesy."
Jacques Maritain (1958)

PREMISE

Gratitude is to life and personal growth what rain is to flowers and what flowers are to spring. We cannot reach the goal of fulfilling our potential of living a contented life, without the spiritual quality of gratitude. Yet our will alone, can never help us capture this feeling. Rather, gratitude is the result of the humility, trust and acceptance that creates both the awareness and the fullness of this sensation. Our Higher Power gives it to us as a reward for our hard work. We must go through the necessary labor and toil of cultivating humility to yield the fruit of gratitude. Dedicated diligence, prayer and acceptance will put you on the path to grateful living and show you the beauty and wonder that is Life.

INTENTION

What I imagine is far worse than what is. I will be able to find the boldness to be thankful for all that I am and all that I receive. I understand and accept that many gifts were beyond my power to generate. I am aware of this every moment and I am grateful for what I receive. I have the courage to face the truth that whatever I have, I have received either through the fortune of my birth or the generosity and benevolence of others. If I am honest with myself this becomes quite apparent. My past has presented me with the opportunities in my present regardless of its pain and adversity.

AWARENESS

I will make a special effort today, to be grateful for all that I am and all that I have. I will be conscious of the gifts of kindness and respect that I both give and receive, throughout the day.

DAY 103—ACCEPTANCE

"Do not spoil what you have by desiring what you have not; but remember that what you now have was once among the things only hoped for."
Epicurus (3rd century, B.C.E.)

PREMISE

By achieving and developing acceptance, we begin to view each event and every encounter as the road to a new, more rewarding life. We stop being defensive, envious, greedy, lustful and arrogant. We allow ourselves to accept i.e., to trust that what is, is as it should be; that who I am is someone who is blest and has meaning and purpose in life. Acceptance says; "this is good" and "I can learn," no matter what the circumstance. Change becomes expected, therefore, less threatening and more manageable. Acceptance allows. It allows us to grow because we acknowledge tribulation as well as triumph, defeat as well as victory. We begin to understand that it all leads to one thing, our evolution and enrichment.

INTENTION

I am able to learn and to accept. I can develop the humility to know what I can't control and the courage to control what I can. Acceptance allows me to look at change, challenge and chaos for what it is, an opportunity to grow and to love.

AWARENESS

Today, I will focus my awareness on allowing events to unfold. I will make a special effort to listen and not interrupt, so that I fully understand what another is telling me. I will respect their thoughts and discover what I can learn.

DAY 104—PATIENCE

"Each of us literally chooses, by his way of attending to things, what sort of Universe he shall appear to himself to inhabit."
William James (1890)

PREMISE

Our intent focuses our awareness and attendance to that which is consistent with our wants, desires and biases. Filters are established early and we rarely know of their existence until we began the journey of self-knowledge. Patience allows us to persevere throughout this journey despite our discovery of contradiction and delusion in many of our primary principles. Patience helps us face this fear so that we may rebuild and form a stronger foundation for our worldview. Patience is a necessary quality for just such awareness.

INTENTION

It is difficult to take responsibility for my actions, thoughts and feelings. However, the truth is that this is all I control. I acknowledge that my preference is to manage anything or anyone outside rather than struggle with these internal conflicts. In the past, I have, to no avail, attempted to control people, places and things because I find it easier and less frightening. I realize that this must change and I can do this. Throughout the day I have an opportunity to assess whether I am in control or not, and when I am, I can act with a loving and compassionate intent.

AWARENESS

I will list in my journal today, an instance where I acted with responsibility and integrity, consistent with my values and goals.

DAY 105—HUMILITY

"He who speaks without modesty will find it difficult to make his words good."
Confucius (6th century, B.C.E.)

PREMISE

Humility is the answer and the counterforce to the incessant cries of the media that there is an external solution which is free from all effort and thought. Achieving and cultivating humility, allows us to tolerate unpleasant feelings of threat (our needs won't be met) and vulnerability (without instant gratification we will surely perish). We acknowledge and accept that a significant part of our lives (primarily the frivolous) is beyond our power to control. As we start to affirm this truth, our life is transformed. Here is the essence of humility. As simple as it sounds, this characteristic is extremely difficult to attain, unlike those external solutions bought in "easy, affordable payments." There are many commercial, economic and cultural impediments to achieving a humble perspective but we can cultivate the courage and persistence to prevail.

INTENTION

I can choose the positive, the forgiving, and the accepting, each moment of every day. As I do this, I will evolve and my life will unfold. I am re-creating myself, each time I change my attitude and respond to the same situation in a different way. I am becoming empowered and designing a destiny of contentment and tranquility.

AWARENESS

Today, I will be alert to the momentary feelings of anxiety that enter my awareness throughout my "daily grind." I will focus my attention and act on one simple thing that I can control. Me.

DAY 106—GRATITUDE

"I give the fight up: let there be an end,
A privacy, an obscure nook for me."
Robert Browning (1835)

PREMISE

Gratitude is the result of surrender to a plan greater than oneself. This requires first, a trust and then an acceptance, of the wisdom and beneficence of a Universe that gives us exactly what we need, precisely when we need it. Similar to each of the four pillars of contentment, gratitude reinforces the others in a reciprocal dance of unity and understanding. To be gratified is to be infused with love and compassion. It is to comprehend, in a small way, the infinite force that resides in us, as part of a power, far greater than ourselves. When we are grateful we can give and receive freely. We can love without fear.

INTENTION

I have choices. I can choose love over fear, inclusion over isolation and compassion over self-interest. Each day, I read, I learn, I think and I grow. My Higher Power guides me when I seek guidance, gives me strength when I am weak and certainty when I waiver. I am strong and able to confront change and I will continue to progress. I have come far and I have far to go. This is a journey not a destination, a process not an objective. Each day I discover more about myself and I become more grateful for the gifts I have and the objectives I have attained.

AWARENESS

During the course of today, I will focus on the moment. I will observe and appreciate those things that authenticate the power and life affirming qualities of nature. I will be grateful for this moment.

DAY 107—ACCEPTANCE

"What is done for you-allow it to be done."
Ibrahim Ibn Al-Khawwas (9th century, C.E.)

PREMISE

Developing and cultivating acceptance gives us an opportunity to more clearly define our goals and ourselves. It allows us to better evaluate what is necessary to fulfill our purpose. As we gradually remove reflexive emotional responses from most situations, we understand that we only witness most events and we are not an integral or necessary part of the event itself. Now, we can begin to distance ourselves and undertake the perspective of a scientist (participant/observer). In this manner, impulsivity is reduced significantly while personal control is expanded and reinforced. We develop the power to hesitate before acting. In this way, we effectively stop the flow of time, as we take control of that moment between thought and action. In so doing, we alter our responses and thereby alter the responses of those we affected. This changes our perspective and we begin to create a new self.

INTENTION

I can generate and shape a new me by responding differently to familiar events and thereby constructing a new perspective. As I change, others change, as does their view of me. If I respond differently, others will experience me differently and consequently modify their behavior. In this way, have I not altered my Universe?

AWARENESS

I will do one thing differently today (be kinder, more thoughtful, more respectful, etc.). I will then observe the changes in another, as well as my emotional reactions to the final result. I will note these in my journal.

DAY 108—PATIENCE

"If there is to be any peace, it will come through being, not having."
Henry Miller (1941)

PREMISE.

Peace, contentment, and serenity all rely on the internal, the soul and the heart. We must strip ourselves of the illusion of the external's power. We must be aware of the misunderstandings and confusion between "wants" and "needs", as well as the predominance of "me" over "thee". Patience helps us hesitate during crucial situations, so that we may evaluate these thoughts. It encourages us to hear the essential information emerging from the Spirit. Patience permits pause and access to the knowledge we need to develop a strategy that resolves the strain and tension caused by external circumstances and our emotional reactions to them. Patience allows us to "be" and to put "become" on hold. Who we are in the moment is a sacred culmination of all the thoughts, feelings and behaviors of our lives up to that instant.

INTENTION

I understand that addictive and self-destructive behaviors, pains and sufferings are caused by avoiding change and that change must come from within. This is my destiny, to shed the self-protective deceptions and fallacies of the past and open myself to a new perspective. I can do this but I need help, I need others and I need my Creator.

AWARENESS

Today, I will note something I learned that would make tomorrow just the slightest bit better. I will attempt to become more aware of all the progress that I have made since I began this program and I will understand that patience will promote even more unfolding and development.

DAY 109—HUMILITY

"Loquacity storms the ear, but modesty takes the heart."
Thomas Fuller, MD (1732)

PREMISE

To resist the basic truth that we control very little of our lives is to subject ourselves to an existence of unnecessary personal and interpersonal strife. It is to pursue power, where it cannot be achieved and to seek satisfaction where it cannot be attained. We become vulnerable to a life of intrapersonal anarchy, where addictions, compulsions, obsessions, harmful moods and/or impulsive behavior reign. As we continue fruitless attempts at control, we create mutually destructive relationships with friends, coworkers, family, lovers, authority figures etc. To find peace, we must surrender and place our trust in a greater power, as we comprehend our role in the greater good.

INTENTION

I now view my existence as meaningful and as having constant opportunity to advance my life and the lives of those I encounter. Because I am unique, I have a singular chance to contribute to the well being of others. I can help through service and by doing this; I will create peace and serenity.

AWARENESS

Today, I will witness as many circumstances as possible, where it is fruitless to attempt control. I will surrender and behave in a more passive, humble and accepting manner when confronted with those outside forces beyond my influence or persuasion.

DAY 110—GRATITUDE

"We, thine unworthy servants, do give the most humble and hearty thanks for all thy goodness and loving kindness to us, and to all men."
Book of Common Prayer

PREMISE

Ultimately, gratitude is granted by a Higher Power to us and reinforces the qualities necessary to achieve tranquility and contentment, namely, love, courage and wisdom. These are generated by and based upon humility, gratitude, acceptance and patience. They are gifts to be cherished, nurtured, accepted and acknowledged. They can be felt and brought to awareness through thought and intention, at any moment we choose. Each interaction, incitement and accomplishment is an occasion to feel and profess gratitude. Gratitude is an opportunity to savor the moment and to realize, with humility, that any particular incident of awareness and benevolence would not have occurred without a confluence of the self with a Higher Power.

INTENTION

I can overcome the shackles of the past and the burden of mythology by focusing and intending to see the Good, the love and the generosity of others. I can intend to acquire the humility to be grateful. I can have the courage to express this gratitude to those around me on a regular basis. I can have the awareness to feel this gratitude so that I enrich my daily living and inspire joy in those I meet.

AWARENESS

I will find, in any random moment I choose, a reason to be grateful. I will write in my journal, what I am grateful for and why I am grateful today and I will silently express thanks for the gifts I have been given through prayer.

DAY 111—ACCEPTANCE

"All things come into being by the conflict of opposites."
Heraclitus (c. 500 B.C.E.)

PREMISE

We are either energized or frightened by the tension created by opposites and paradox. Is it a conflict or merely confusion? Do we avoid or approach? Is this a chance to retreat or grow? These questions and so many more are critical and depend upon our level of acceptance and our trust in a Higher Power. If we accept life, as it is, with all its "slings and arrows", we are more likely to respond to contradiction and conflict, with a desire to understand, to observe and "ride the wave." On the other hand, if we see contradiction and conflict as a threat, a disruption or an impediment, we are more likely to attempt control through force and aggression or to retreat, refusing to see reality and the necessity of a lesson to be learned and a choice to be confronted.

INTENTION

I have all I need to learn from contradiction. I understand that this is the way life presents its opportunities. My instincts have evolved from running or attacking to investigating and choosing. As always, when anxious, my heart still races and my breath sputters, yet I can intend to pause, consider and decide. Contradiction needs to be embraced not conquered, investigated not ignored, confronted not hidden.

AWARENESS

Today, I will look closely at the constant contradictions impacting my life. Do I approach or avoid? Do I accept or reject? There are no simple answers but we can choose the best actions for the moment by intending love and compassion, as we pause to contemplate our lives, our goals and our destiny.

DAY 112—PATIENCE

"Freedom is not procured by a full enjoyment of what is desired, but by controlling the desire."
Epictetus (2nd century, C. E.)

PREMISE

Patience can and will control desire. It can stop the impulse and allow peace and serenity to flow into the Spirit. It tells us to slow down, to think, and to reflect. It prevents us from being pawns of the past, acting in the same manner and feeling the same things under similar circumstances. This split second, this nanosecond, where we pause, makes all the difference between prison and paradise, foolishness and wisdom, the child-self and the ideal-self. Patience says, "wait" while the child-self says, "act."

INTENTION

I will feel more positive about myself and more optimistic about my future as I allow patience to dominate impulse. I can develop the awareness to identify negative and destructive feelings. I can intend to thwart these impulses and substitute patience, pause and optimism. I am in control of such things. With awareness and intent I can generate patience in all my interactions.

AWARENESS

I will note in my journal a "trigger" for frustration. I will describe a situation that arouses annoyance, anger and resentment. I will reinforce my intent to behave differently the next time.

DAY 113—HUMILITY

"True modesty does not consist in an ignorance of merits, but in a due estimate of them."
Augustus William Hare (1827)

PREMISE

Negative emotions, which are reactions to stress or change, such as, anger, frustration, anxiety, fear, envy etc., are reflections of pride and hubris. According to many spiritual guides, for more than 2500 years, our true and only purpose in life is to grow in wisdom and love, as we improve the lives of others through service. By practicing humility, we transform a small part of the Universe (our part) into a place that reflects wisdom, love and acceptance. Once we begin to trust and cultivate humility, we can embrace those circumstances we don't and can't control. We now assuage anxiety and affirm true power by knowing and acting on what can be controlled. We discover that we can only master the attitudes, feelings and actions of the moment.

INTENTION

I have the strength, I have the courage and I have the perseverance to break the restrictive, self-destructive flow of ideas that keeps me from progressing. I accept the challenge of change and each day I will take a small but significant step toward fulfillment. I will develop goals, articulate a plan and initiate a strategy. I will avoid my past habits of self-limitation and self-sabotage. Also, I will avoid doing the same things in the same circumstances with the futile hope of effecting change.

AWARENESS

Today, I will make an effort to notice the negative emotions that arise when I am confronted with a situation that I can't control. I will acknowledge and witness the numerous forces beyond my control.

DAY 114—GRATITUDE

"How often we find ourselves turning our backs on our actual friends, that we may go and meet their 'ideal' cousins."
Henry David Thoreau (1815)

PREMISE

We cannot be grateful without acknowledging the contributions and goodwill of others. At this time, in the consumer culture, we are frequently persuaded by the delusion of independence. We are urged to think of our achievements as self-generated. We are willing to acknowledge things that helped us reach our goals but we are very resistant to recognizing the importance of those close to us both physically and spiritually. We want to take all the praise but we give little credit to those who helped us to get where we are. Gratitude unites us with the understanding that we are all precious and that we all contribute to the growth others. Remember, we can learn from anymore and we can be an example to all.

INTENTION

If I choose to see, I will look in the right direction. I can acknowledge the help from others, as well as the love and support that surrounds me without diminishing my achievements or myself. It may not come from the people I would like but help and assistance has been rendered. I will become more aware so that I may see truth and express gratitude.

AWARENESS

Today, I will focus on those events that prove how vital others are to my well-being, contentment and success. I will thank someone for a specific gift or favor and thereby acknowledge the important role they play in my life.

DAY 115—ACCEPTANCE

"Acceptance of what has happened is the first step to overcoming the consequences of any misfortune."
William James (1879)

PREMISE

When in crisis, the first step is to acknowledge that there is a crisis. Denial, blame or rationalization, serve no purpose at this stage. What we need is the courage to accept, so that such acceptance will lead to understanding and action. Later, we can unravel how the situation evolved and learn from that in order to progress. However, no amount of preparation can shield us from potential disruption, disquiet or discomfort. What we can do and can control is our thoughts. We can be grateful and accept that in every moment we have the tools necessary to cope with any conflict. But the fact is, that conflict, contradiction and confusion are part of life and necessary for growth and fulfillment.

INTENTION

It may seem "wrong", "unjust" or "unfair" but things will not always (or even sometimes) go as I plan, expect or hope for. The Universe does not revolve around me, as the child-self believes. So I will get on with it, move forward and become who I was created to become. Life is beautiful and meant to be lived not hidden from.

AWARENESS

Today, I will write in my journal, one instance where I overcame, the unexpected, the disappointing or the annoying. I will note one instance where I surrendered control and enjoyed the ride. This will be a situation where my expectations were not met, but I viewed it positively, as a happy coincidence, not a horrible mistake or affront.

DAY 116—PATIENCE

"He who conquers others is strong;
He who conquers himself is mighty."
Lao Tzu (6th century, B.C.E.)

PREMISE

Patience reflects and enables self-control and self-discipline. The fact is that, what happens to us externally, does not necessarily dictate how we frame or react to it, emotionally, behaviorally or intellectually. It is our choice. We are in control. Therefore, there are no excuses. Now that we are aware of these facts, it is time to begin planning new responses to familiar situations, in order to create new selves. Each moment, of every day, with any interaction, we have the ability to mold, shape and determine our future. What we offer the world will be rewarded many times.

INTENTION

I am able to summon the energy and motivation to change. If I am to succeed, I must desire it. My choice is to confront change or to remain in the status quo, immobile, helpless and vulnerable. I will take charge of myself and I will take responsibility for all my actions and intentions. I will be aware of my inner monologues and I will be aware of the effects of my behavior and thoughts on those I encounter.

AWARENESS

I will begin to develop an "emergency plan" for situations in which I find myself wanting to react in a negative manner. I will begin to describe, step-by-step, my reactions, as I become aware of this tension. The first step that I will note is the internal feeling of anger, for example, discomfort, edginess, shortened breath, quick heart rate, etc. and my desire to strike out at whomever I perceive to be the cause.

DAY 117—HUMILITY

"Humility is just as much the opposite of self-abasement as it is of self-exaltation."
Dag Hammarskjold (1959)

PREMISE

Humility is not easy to develop. If it were, we would have mastered it. As with all the spiritual traits, we must challenge our early ideas and concepts of the world and of ourselves so that we may evolve to a higher level of awareness. When we focus on the present, we increase awareness of our perspective and accept our internal guide as the center for truth. Therefore, through awareness and intent, we can more easily refine all of the traits we need to advance. While the external influence of culture impedes humility's development, so does the child-self's internal tendency to be arrogant and presumptuous. Dominance by the child-self is simply another way of gaining a false sense of mastery and separating us from our true nature. This is how we create our own prisons. Humility is the key that will unlock our potential, releasing us to become all we were meant to be.

INTENTION

My progress can be variable. Some days will be good, some days not so much, but I can always be moving forward. I will not let my ideas of perfection hamper advancement. I will maintain my focus and my patience. I can always make some positive difference and I can always strive to do so.

AWARENESS

Today, I will concentrate on developing my humility in a deliberate, conscious manner. I will manifest this humility with one act of kindness in the service of love and compassion.

DAY 118—GRATITUDE

"Intimacy requires courage because risk is inescapable. We cannot know at the outset how the relationship will affect us."
Rollo May (1975)

PREMISE

Relationships are scary yet necessary if we are to live fully and prosper. Gratitude mitigates the fear of intimacy and vulnerability because we begin to understand that the opportunities for growth and pleasure far outweigh the risk of pain or disappointment. Gratitude is at the core of good relationships whether they are profound, polite or perfunctory. When we are grateful for those who play a role in our lives, we rise above petty judgments and we fill both our hearts and the hearts of others with love. If we allow ourselves to be humble and vulnerable, we will discover how important certain people are to our fulfillment and emotional health. We must pierce the delusion of independence. We are connected on some level to all and there are special people whom God has put into our lives for particular reasons. Be grateful and humble. These are gifts.

INTENTION

I have the strength, endurance and wisdom to shed my past and to enter relationships without the burdens of fear, projection, defensiveness and resistance. I will confront my vulnerability and I will treat others with trust, respect and appreciation. With the help of my Higher Power and the support of my fellow travelers, I can treasure those who are in my life without diminishing my sense of self or my self-esteem.

AWARENESS

As painful as it may be, I will try to spend a few minutes thinking about life without a specific person. Today, I will enter into my journal the reasons why this person is so important to my life.

DAY 119—ACCEPTANCE

"Set your heart on doing good. Do it over and over, and you will be filled with joy."
Buddha (500 B.C.E.)

PREMISE

As you learn to trust and accept, you find that doing good for another results in a far greater sense of satisfaction and contentment than when you do something for yourself. You'll also discover that most acts of compassion, empathy and generosity involve little sacrifice, certainly far less than you imagined. Self-acceptance is a first step to risking closeness. It is also necessary to free yourself to make mistakes, to feel frustrations, and to commit errors of judgment, in sum, to feel like a fool. If we learn from such missteps they cease becoming mistakes and instead are transformed into life lessons. As we develop the resilience to be human, we find forgiveness and acceptance in the faults, misjudgments and awkwardness of others. Acceptance leads to tolerance, which introduces us to a life of contented living.

INTENTION

I can let go of the fear expressed by isolation, exclusion and bigotry. I can embrace change and diversity, as I move forward with my life and improve the lives of others. I will be trustful, accepting and patient as I encounter contradiction, deviation and incompetence. When overwhelmed, fearful or angry, I will simply focus on doing the next good thing. Through such intent, unpleasant feelings will dissipate and I can progress with my life.

AWARENESS

Today, I will show courage by performing a random act of kindness to a person I fear simply because they are different.

DAY 120—PATIENCE

"Never can true courage dwell with them/
Who, playing tricks with conscience, dare not look/ at their own vices."
Samuel Taylor Coleridge (1798)

PREMISE

The Four Horsemen of self-destructiveness; impulsivity, envy, aggression and frustration, are effectively neutralized when we practice patience and deliberation. Patience energizes us so that we enjoy life and accept what is before us at the moment. Patience allows us to pause before plunging into a situation, so as to remediate an issue that we believe needs remediation. Patience gives thought to action. It overcomes impulsivity before moving forward in the pursuit of our goals and the achievement of our objectives. Patience contributes to progress because it dominates the child-self who needs immediate satisfaction and uncompromising action.

INTENTION

I can cultivate patience. I can persist in the struggle to subdue my child-self, face fear and change my life. I can find meaning in challenge and I can see my strengths and generosity, as opposed to my weaknesses and pettiness. I will seek unity over division, acceptance over rejection and I will become the change I want to see in others.

AWARENESS

Today, when feeling frustrated in a discussion, I will make a point to stop and listen. I will put emphasis on listening rather than being heard. I will cover my mouth and open my ears.

DAY 121—HUMILITY

"The turning point in the process of growing up is when you discover the core of strength within you that survives hurt."
Max Lerner (1959)

PREMISE

Our journey to growth can begin by incorporating humility and trust into our daily routines. In this way we'll initiate empowerment and begin to dominate our own lives. Through such empowerment, we will become more effective managers and we will feel our self-esteem expand. Humility will teach us gratitude, acceptance and patience, as we put the Serenity Prayer into practice. We will comprehend the limits of our control and cultivate the courage to act on our principles and beliefs. Contentment and freedom will blossom and a humble, loving and peaceful person will replace the child-self, with all of its arrogance, narcissism and greed. Interpersonal relations will flourish as love and compassion dominate our perspective.

INTENTION

Maturation is having the humility and wisdom to live, knowing that life does not revolve around us. I am important but I am only one of many. I cannot understand or even comprehend the vastness of the Universe. But I can learn about myself and I can appreciate my strengths and vulnerabilities. I will use this knowledge to advance in my goals.

AWARENESS

I will become more conscious of how humility leads to gratitude, acceptance and trust. Today, I will display courage by standing up for my principles on at least one issue.

DAY 122—GRATITUDE

"Never let the future disturb you. You will meet it, with the same weapons of reason which today are used against the present."
Marcus Aurelius (171 C.E.)

PREMISE

Gratitude allows us to appreciate who we are, where we came from and who helped us get there. If now we are content with our current circumstances, we must be grateful for all that got us here. We must be grateful for those who supported us in bad times and those who encouraged us in good. They are responsible for the blessings and advantages we have. If we cultivate gratitude, we will comprehend that we are exactly where we should be. The characteristic of humility allows us to accept this and to treasure what is. We are aware of the moment; we breathe it in and feel the freedom and power that is our life. We understand that gratitude automatically manifests appreciation. Feeling and expressing gratitude adds passion to our life as well as to the lives of those who have helped us. Gratitude is indeed a gift.

INTENTION

I will resist remembering failure more vividly than remembering success. I will focus on who I am rather than who I am not. I will be grateful for what I have and not resentful for what I lack. I can embrace change as a new challenge and I can resist the status quo. I am grateful for this knowledge and the courage to comprehend and act on it.

AWARENESS

Today, I will think about how some past mistakes have ultimately improved my life; how what I formerly thought were impediments were actually guideposts to my destiny and goals. It's not what has happened but how I respond to what has happened. Thank God.

DAY 123—ACCEPTANCE

"Without Contraries there is no progression. Attraction and Repulsion, Reason and Impulse, Love and Hate, are necessary to human existence."
William Blake (1790)

PREMISE

From Mr. Blake's perceptive comment, we should add that without "Contraries" there is no growth. Yet, conflict alarms us. We run, avoid and deny it but we rarely confront, accept or embrace it. From many perspectives, an essential conflict throughout life is the tension between "Me" versus "We". This is not just related to intimate relationships but applies to all those individuals we encounter in daily living. Understand, cultivating both the "Me" and the "We" are necessary for progress and evolution. Boundaries are as important as acceptance, self-interest as much as compassion, and self-survival as much as group survival. This seeming conflict must not be shunned but understood, as necessary for individual and group growth as well as general advancement.

INTENTION

I will develop the strength to embrace conflict as a necessary step to a contented life. I will understand that with humility, gratitude, acceptance and patience, I can resolve the apparent disparities that life presents and I can actually benefit from the tension aroused when my expectations are not met. Change and challenge are not only good but also necessary for me to attain an abundant life.

AWARENESS

I will carefully look at one incident today that seems unresolvable. I will write it down and I will note the apparent contradictions and conflicts in an attempt to perceive them simply as two extremes of a necessary continuum.

DAY 124—PATIENCE

"Respect yourself if you would have others respect you."
Baltasar Gracian (1647)

PREMISE

Patience will give you self-respect, as you witness mastery, or at least containment, of the most difficult emotions. Patience says that it is more important to delay and control gratification than to succumb to the desire for immediate relief. Patience supplies courage to tolerate the fear of deprivation and supplies the motivation to trust in the future. We must accept the idea that the venture is as important as the destination. Enjoy the moment. Relax in the present without the shackles from the past and future fears. Pause, breathe, feel, and be grateful. Patience is respect; respect for others and most importantly respect for the self. Patience is a knowledge that things will work out no matter how bad we feel at the moment.

INTENTION

Empowerment comes from within. It is the Spirit that unites all of life. I can tap into that spirit at any time simply by turning my will and thoughts over to my Higher Power. Patience creates empowerment. It is control of impulse and reflexive action. It gives us integrity, as mind dominates desire. I will face my fear of empowerment and responsibility as I fortify my intent to identify the sources of frustration in my life. I understand that most frustration arises from unrealistic expectations, as the child-self desires immediate gratification and storybook satisfaction. I will be in control as long as I maintain patience.

AWARENESS

I will take special note today when I delay gratification and control impulse. I will take pride in my emergent empowerment.

DAY 125—HUMILITY

"The sage shuns excess, extravagance, and arrogance."
Lao Tsu (6th century, B.C.E.)

PREMISE

Developing humility is the most important pre-condition to fostering the other spiritual traits (gratitude, patience/trust, acceptance/forgiveness) and achieving a life abounding in growth and contentment. Humility enables us to value our place in life as is. We begin to comprehend the role we play in the unfolding of our small part in the Universe. Through humility, we appreciate all that we were given both internally and externally. We acknowledge who we are and the talents that only we can offer others. We see the gifts and the abundance of goods that have been bestowed and we understand the benevolence of the power that gave us these gifts. Through humility we become grateful and know that we have an obligation to serve and give back for these blessings.

INTENTION

I have the courage and the strength to develop humility. I believe that I am neither greater than nor less than any other. Each traveler has something significant to offer the other. I will learn what I can give and what I can receive. I am simultaneously a teacher and a student. I will move forward in service, giving and receiving love and compassion.

AWARENESS

I will write in my journal one skill and one possession that I can offer others as I serve.

DAY 126—GRATITUDE

"Man is a knot, a web, a mesh, into which relationships are tied. Only those relationships matter."
Antoine De Saint-Exupery (1942)

PREMISE

Creating relationships with compassion, understanding, inclusion and acceptance, is a necessary condition to achieving contentment. Such qualities are reciprocal, that is, they are both cause and effect. Each reinforces and encourages the other in a positive self-perpetuating cycle. As we cultivate the above attitudes, our relationships blossom and multiply. When this happens, we perfect these attributes and promote healthier, more fulfilling affiliations. Our connections to all life become more relevant to daily living and more conducive to growth. Gratitude helps open our hearts and generates courage by reducing fear and thus increases trust, patience and acceptance.

INTENTION

I will resist denying, denigrating and disparaging my qualities and aptitudes in order to be in a relationship. I will not put myself down. I will be grateful for the person who chooses to share part of their life with me but I will see them as equals, neither better nor worse. I will enter all relationships with the courage and honesty to expect mutual caring and respect. I will look to serve and be served, to grow as I teach and to learn as I listen.

AWARENESS

I will increase my awareness of the feelings and bodily effects of gratitude. Today, I will make an extra effort to pray and request that gratitude expands in my life.

DAY 127—ACCEPTANCE

"No one can live happily who has regard for himself alone and transforms everything into a question of his own utility . . ."
Seneca (60 C.E.)

PREMISE

Stepping outside yourself, trusting in your Higher Power and the goodwill of others, is extremely difficult in the midst of the child-self's constant fear. Yet, a step at a time, interaction-by-interaction, we can achieve this trust and therefore grow beyond our greatest expectations. This is not to say that you will never encounter unpleasant feelings or destructive emotions, but the greatest number of encounters will be positive, filled with learning and skill inducing growth. Our child-self cries "Me, Me, Me" as it attempts to continue its control of change and the status quo but we can resist fear and pursue progress.

INTENTION

I will be aware of the temptation to remain in place and I understand that I can be more powerful. I realize that I am my own jailer and am constrained by chains which I reinforce every day as I reject the internal calls of the Spirit for evolution and expansion. I must be constantly aware of these forces. I have the humility to ask for help when necessary and the courage to accept my limitations.

AWARENESS

I will make a conscious effort, to let go of selfish motives, to become more vulnerable and to help another. I will note and record this struggle as well as its outcome in one situation.

DAY 128—PATIENCE

"The greatest mistake you can make in life is to be continually fearing that you will make one."
Elbert Hubbard (1905)

PREMISE

If we are to make the most of our quest for actualization, to be all we can be and to experience this journey to the fullest extent, we must grow from missteps and miscues. This requires both patience and humility. We must first have the humility to acknowledge our frailties and imperfections. Secondly, we must have the patience with ourselves to allow mistakes and to learn from them. When appropriate, an apology is extremely liberating. It does not change the past but it effectively and positively alters the future. Don't be afraid to live life because as many misjudgments as you make, an equal number of miracles are possible. However, we must change our attitude towards ourselves and alter our approach to others as we learn from these oversights. Patience is the key to this process.

INTENTION

I can assume the responsibility for my life as well as the reality I create and the choices I make. I will try not to fear failure; at least not to the extent that it hinders my attempts at growth. I can realize and face the fact that mistakes, missteps, misunderstandings and misjudgments will continue to occur. Such a process must happen if I am to learn and advance. During this progression, I will be patient with others and myself.

AWARENESS

I will think about my beliefs and assumptions regarding what comprises a "good" life and what is the role of patience in achieving that goal.

DAY 129—HUMILITY

"Love grows by giving.
The love we give away is the only love we keep."
Elbert Hubbard (1900)

PREMISE

To be humble is to be grounded, solid and reliable, not passive and humiliated. Humility is not weakness. It is strength and the foundation of a good spiritual life of service and contentment. It takes a good deal of self-esteem to be humble and being humble builds self-esteem. How does this happen? When one understands their position in life, their role in the "greater scheme of things", such a perspective then delineates areas of mastery and areas of weakness. In turn, this permits the concentration of a maximum amount of energy in the areas that will do the most good. Simultaneously, we appreciate our diminished role in areas where we would be least effective. As such, we begin to experience command and empowerment over ourselves as never before.

INTENTION

As I subordinate my needs to the needs of the greater good, I will find that I can be relied upon to follow through on my promises and commitments. This gives me a sense of empowerment because I chose to suppress my wants, as expressed by the child-self, so that I may contribute to others.

AWARENESS

I will be sensitive to the importance of reliably fulfilling my commitments. I will acknowledge that my life affects others. Today, I will demonstrate to someone that I am reliable, responsible and trustworthy. I am important and I can contribute to the Good of all. I will note examples of this in my journal.

DAY 130—GRATITUDE

"There is no hope of joy except in human relationships."
Antoine De Saint-Exupery (1939)

PREMISE

There is so little that we can realistically control when it comes to the behavior of others. This thought can fill a person with paralyzing fear, especially when it relates to those we love. We would like to control them in order to assure that our feelings are reciprocated and that our version of reality and worldview are, at least understood, if not totally accepted. The fact is, we cannot control others in any way. They have their own destiny and it is their responsibility to determine the most positive route to fulfillment. What we can do is be grateful for their presence in our lives and learn as much as possible from them. If we pray for gratitude, on a regular basis, we will receive it and all its benefits to our wellness.

INTENTION

I have fortitude and self-confidence to accept others as they are. I am able to do this because of my progress. I am now able to allow diverse opinions, feelings and perspectives into my awareness without fear, threat or confusion. I can embrace difference and view it as helping me understand myself. I can rejoice in diversity and be grateful for this challenge.

AWARENESS

Today, I will reflect on how previous plans that failed to meet expectations have actually turned out better than anticipated. I will send a card of thanks to someone important to me for no other reason than I am thankful that they are in my life.

DAY 131—ACCEPTANCE

"The struggle between for and against is the mind's worst disease."
Sen-ts'an (8th century, C.E.)

PREMISE

Humility and acceptance teach us that we can learn from anyone during any encounter. There is no "for" or "against", "victory" or "defeat", "them" or "us", there are simply lessons to be learned and progress to be made. When you open your mind and heart to accept the moment "as is" without any equivocation, fear or distraction, you will find your way and a mentor may appear. The Universe and everything therein becomes an instructor for all of life's wonders. As we begin to understand our role in a "Grand Plan", we accept our responsibility in creating our future and we are then empowered and accountable to move forward and progress, as our destiny demands.

INTENTION

I can face fear and summon the courage of self-responsibility. I will ask for and give help when appropriate. I will face change and I will find solutions that are compassionate and effective. Once fear is abated, light shines and growth flourishes.

AWARENESS

Today, I will risk. I will try something I feared before. This act will be motivated by compassion and beneficence. I know that I must "get out of the box." I know that I must challenge the status quo. With this knowledge and the intent for positive growth I will move forward.

DAY 132—PATIENCE

"If thou will make a man happy, add not on to his riches but take away from his desires."
Epicurus (285 B.C.E.)

PREMISE

The consumer culture overwhelms us with messages about what we must acquire in order to be happy, fulfilled and contented. We constantly are inundated with slogans about our deficiencies and deprivations, what we don't have and what we "should" have. Naturally, this is going to lead to dissatisfaction with our selves and frustration with our world as well as those who inhabit it. Patience can mitigate this tension. It can quiet the "wants" by contrasting them with "needs." It can delay impulse and reason can rule. The internal can dominate the external and resist the messages of deficiency, defect and deprivation. The unreasonable "desire" for immediate satisfaction can be put into a more patient perspective of process. Remember H. W. Longfellow (1863); "All good things come to those who wait."

INTENTION

The power of life, of change and of growth is within me, not outside of me or in things, power or popularity. I will have the courage and wisdom to look inside myself for what I need and I will avoid the imprisonment of the consumer culture, which tells me I'm "defective," "deficient" or "deprived." I am as I was made and all growth, change and love come from within.

AWARENESS

Today, I will note one message or one advertisement from the media that tells me how I "need" what they're selling. I will note the message in my journal and think about how often in the past these have affected me and created feelings of need and dissatisfaction.

DAY 133—HUMILITY

"Humility is the ultimate foundation for strength and effectiveness."
W. T. Watts, Ph.D. (2011)

PREMISE

Humility is basic to our wellness. It promotes and reinforces the quality of acceptance. Acceptance, in this context, refers to the issue of control. As newborns, we seemed helpless, yet observe adults when they hear a crying baby. Whether alone or in a crowd, someone will tend to the neonate. Who then is more powerful and more in control, the newborn or the adult? We yearn for such power and control as adults. The child-self wants to be pampered, satisfied and placated. As adults we experience helplessness (lack of control) and tension when we feel frustration, dissatisfaction or isolation. As we attain humility we will focus on areas of strength and dismiss our "weaknesses" as simply opportunities for prayer not personal "failings."

INTENTION

As my trust strengthens the growth of humility, I become confident that I control what I need to control and everything else is harmless and superficial. With this attitude, I will achieve progress and fulfillment. My life will unfold as it was meant to and I will become all that I was created to be. I am as powerful as I need to be.

AWARENESS

I can choose to increase my awareness and accept that I have little control over external events. I will make a conscious choice to let go and trust, today. I will note this event and the effects of this decision in my journal.

DAY 134—GRATITUDE

"A man cannot be comfortable without his own approval."
Mark Twain (1892)

PREMISE

Because we have no control over the actions of others, especially towards us, it is important to note their kindness and compassion, as we interact and communicate. Acts of kindness and friendship are voluntary decisions individuals make on our behalf. Gratitude tells us we are worthy but we must thank them. Gratitude bridges the gap between humility and self-acceptance. We understand that we are worthy of love and as a result we become more loving, grateful and compassionate. Again, this creates a dance of positive reciprocity. As we love, we become more loveable and we cannot love others unless and until we love ourselves. Gratitude energizes and invigorates this process.

INTENTION

I am strong enough and self-confident enough to observe the kindness done to me by others. I can and will be as quick to acknowledge a gift or compliment, as I am to recognize an attack or an insult. Gratitude allows me to appreciate the Good deeds of others and their importance in my life. I can have the courage to be grateful and the awareness to acknowledge it.

AWARENESS

I will intend to be especially aware of my gratitude during those occasions I share with others. I will be more alert to these moments and more attentive to expressing their significance. Today, I will behave in a manner that increases my sense of unity and connection.

DAY 135—ACCEPTANCE

"The beginning of love is to let those we love be perfectly themselves, and not twist them fit our own image."
Thomas Merton (1947)

PREMISE

Acceptance is a necessary condition for love and for any relationship if it is to advance and flourish. Too often, out of fear, we try to mold another, rather than allow them the respect to be perfectly themselves. Acceptance is a sign of strength. It does not mean we are passive, disempowered or submissive. It means that we have the strength and trust to look at another and to help them move forward in their journey. We do this without judgment, self-pity, blame or fear.

INTENTION

I can tolerate intimacy in all its forms and nuances and with the help of my Higher Power, I can also learn when in a close relationship with another. I can give a part of myself, knowing I will get more in return through learning, maturation, compassion and seeing the world through another's eyes. The "we" can grow the "I". I can serve and not be submissive, I can request and not be pleading, and I can love and not lose myself. Indeed, I can flourish with another.

AWARENESS

I will tell one special person how important they are to me. I will note my feelings in my journal before and after events. I will also note the reaction of the person I speak to. This person does not have to be a "love interest" but rather anyone who is meaningful in my daily life.

DAY 136—PATIENCE

"The worst things:/ To be in bed and sleep not, / To want for one who comes not, / To try to please and please not."
Egyptian Proverb

PREMISE

During times of frustration, times that expectations are not met, wants delayed and needs ignored, introspection allows us to step back, reflect, learn and regenerate. All of these are byproducts of patience. Magnifying the importance of a particular moment, desire or person, causing a potentially realistic perspective to become distorted, frequently creates frustration. We see the world through a microscope, intently concentrating on ourselves. Patience is magnanimous, it expands our perspective and in so doing it cools desire and minimizes the importance of a particular moment. As such we can assess, pause and recalculate before going forward.

INTENTION

I can rise above my frustrations and view them as being caused by unrealistic expectations and the desire for instant gratification (impatience). Because I want "It" now and that isn't going to happen, I will see the helplessness and frustration that is generated by such nonsensical suppositions.

AWARENESS

Today, I will pause when frustrated and reflect on the source of my frustration. I will see how I create my own agitation by having unrealistic expectations about others, life in general or my own capabilities.

DAY 137—HUMILITY

"The best way out is always through."
Robert Frost (1947)

PREMISE

Humility is a necessary condition for growth. It will allow us to shed mistaken notions of power and control that cause so many problems in our life. When we force ourselves into situations that are not our business, we get into trouble, yet we continue with this pattern of behavior, foolishly hoping for a different result. It is so important to follow the Serenity Prayer and put our efforts into that which we can control and let go of the rest. Such is the wisdom that we seek. This wisdom will only be achieved after we have mastered humility. It's okay not to be in control. It's okay to trust in a greater power. Let go of your arrogance, face fear and move on with your life. Focus on developing and expressing gratitude, acceptance, forgiveness, trust and patience. Such are the fruits of humility.

INTENTION

Humility has taught me that it's okay to have limits and weaknesses because I can more effectively learn where I must focus my energy and intentions. I must acknowledge a problem to solve it. I must admit my imperfections, if I am to change and overcome the status quo. With humility, I can have the insight and the inspiration to be better tomorrow than I am today. Each day I can move forward.

AWARENESS

Today, I will be more aware of my efforts to gain control over situations where I am powerless. In one instance, I will surrender and become an observer rather than a manager. I will then evaluate and assess the consequences. I will note lessons from this in my journal.

DAY 138—GRATITUDE

"Pride is the mask of one's own faults."
Anonymous

PREMISE

Gratitude allows us to give and receive without shame or false pride. Whether materially, emotionally or behaviorally, we can share and rejoice in our connection with others. We shed the veneer of rugged individuality and revel in mutuality and trust. We celebrate our commonalities and reject our differences. Each day, each action, becomes a gift that we both give and receive. With gratitude, love freely flows between and among all who participate. Gratitude connects us and fosters respect, understanding and empathy. We listen without the barriers of self-protection and we become open to the Spirit of love. Gratitude propagates such thoughts, feelings and behavior. It is the gift that keeps on giving.

INTENTION

Only I can make the decision to permit myself the freedom and confidence to be grateful. I am not a victim and I am not deprived. I have been given all I need to succeed and I am surrounded by love and support. With the help of my Higher Power, I will acknowledge this and I will move forward in gratitude, to become who I was meant to be.

AWARENESS

Today, I will focus on the effects my gratitude has on my general outlook and worldview. I plan to express my thanks through behavior rather than words. This will be a challenge.

DAY 139—ACCEPTANCE

"Best is to know all things; good is to listen when you hear what is right; worst is to be ignorant and deaf to the wisdom of another."
Hesiod (8th century, B.C.E.)

PREMISE

If we are to grow, we must learn from others and if we are to learn from others, we must respect and accept their perspective. "When the student is ready the teacher appears." We can learn from anyone, much to our humility, contentment and joy. Acceptance acknowledges what we cannot master and helps us shed obsessive doubt. It strengthens us because we become focused on those areas that can be changed. It takes determination, courage and trust to surrender the delusion of mastery and to place our faith in the unknown and uncontrollable. However, once we comprehend and accept our limits, we can move forward with confidence.

INTENTION

I must learn to let go. I must learn that it is okay to let another be who they are and trust in the wisdom of the process. I can do this, one step and one interaction at a time. My intent is firm and my resolve is clear. I will let go and watch in wonder as the Universe unfolds.

AWARENESS

Today I will be as "self less" as possible, so that I may listen and learn, love and live, accept and be accepted. I will pray that I gain the strength to trust and the courage to step aside.

DAY 140—PATIENCE

"Self-reverence, self-knowledge, self-control, / These three alone lead life to sovereign power."
Lord Tennyson (1842)

PREMISE

Patience is both a cause and an effect of self-respect and self-acceptance. Patience is antithetical to the self-absorbed mindset that can be so destructive to our relationships. As we get out of our own way and quiet the "child-self", we learn that life unfolds very well without our meddling or management skills. We let go and allow the Universe to take over as the 12 Step programs recommend. This cognitive/behavioral strategy instills the capacity to step back and channel our participant/observer, so that we learn to cherish the moment.

INTENTION

I can and will teach myself not only to accept change but also to embrace it. I can visualize the child-self crying out in fear, yet being powerful and demanding, always striving to retain the status quo. I can use the visualized parent to soothe that child and confront my fears.

AWARENESS

I will write down in my journal, what I would say to that fearful yet demanding child, so that I would comfort it and enable myself to get on with growth. I will focus on this visualization of the child-self having a tantrum, red-faced and out of control as the parent intervenes with both reassurance and limit setting.

DAY 141—HUMILITY

"No one can hurt me without my permission."
Gandhi (1937)

PREMISE

How can I allow myself to be vulnerable and trusting in a world that is threatening and overpowering? As we grow and mature, we learn that we can only be as threatened as we allow. Therefore, we cannot be overpowered and we are not vulnerable. Our spirit is eternal and everything external is transient, given to us for a few short seconds of distraction. Strength is within. We become empowered, as we comprehend our place in the greater scheme of things. We perceive that we are small but we are strong. We play a significant but minor role in life similar to a link in a chain composed of other links. Our choice is to fulfill our mission with joy and compassion or fear and isolation. Either way we will fulfill our mission as we are destined to. As we become humble, we understand that it is okay to surrender and trust. Joy and satisfaction will follow from such humility.

INTENTION

I accept and recognize that the change I seek, internal change, does not occur quickly or dramatically. Rather, such evolution and advancement is incremental, building upon itself and slowly reinforced by each step. This is difficult and requires courage, persistence and self-acceptance. If I have the humility to acknowledge that I cannot do this alone, I will ask for and receive my Creator's help.

AWARENESS

I will be aware of the anxiety that accompanies trust. Today, I will record one instance of surrender and my assessment and evaluation of the results.

DAY 142—GRATITUDE

"Evidence of trust begets trust, and love is reciprocated by love."
Plutarch (100 C.E.)

PREMISE

The art of giving and receiving is an essential aspect of all relationships and it begs the question; how much of "me" do I offer to create and enhance the "we"? It is important to remember that just as much love is expressed in gracious acceptance as in deliberate donation. Both parties share in this joyous and selfless dynamic, an all-at-once circumstance of benevolence rewarding each. Any type of gift will do: an object, a favor, a compliment, or a kind thought. Forgiveness, acceptance and inclusion, may be the greatest remittance with the most extensive and expansive effects. Love requires such simultaneous active and passive efforts. Such reciprocity is engendered by gratitude.

INTENTION

I can have the humility to receive with gratitude. I am able to discover love that is given freely because I can give love freely. I can give with graciousness and magnanimity and I can receive with gratitude and modesty.

AWARENESS

Today, I will be sensitive to those gifts, favors and compliments offered by others. I intend to interpret actions towards me as benevolent and caring rather than mean-spirited and dismissive. I will lower my guard in the name of vulnerability and acceptance. I will be grateful for all I am given.

DAY 143—ACCEPTANCE

"Enjoy when you can, and endure when you must."
Johann Von Goethe (1798)

PREMISE

When we accept our role in the Universe and the limits of our control, we also accept our responsibility to become the individual we were created to be. We are responsible and we have power over our actions and our emotional reactions, but we cannot necessarily affect all of the results of our behavior nor can we necessarily control that which preceded our behavior. We develop mastery over the manner in which we view things and how we react to those views. If we focus on love, compassion and acceptance, our sole intent can be for the Good of others and we will find that solutions are more apparent and wellness more easily attained.

INTENTION

I can be in the moment and employ the participant/observer perspective, so that I do not become emotionally part of a negative event, in my life or the life of others. I realize that I am asking a difficult thing of myself namely, to stand back and not control. I can allow and not direct. With the help of my Higher Power, I will come to an understanding and acceptance of my limits. I can make an extra effort and demonstrate the courage to act upon those things that I do control, namely, my interpretation of the moment and my reactions to that interpretation.

AWARENESS

I will pray for the strength to be passive and the courage to observe. I will avoid situations where I'm tempted to take control. For today, I can accept what I am given and play the hand that is before me.

DAY 144—PATIENCE

"Those tormented by the pain of anger will never know tranquility of mind. They will never rest."
Santideva (c. 750 C.E.)

PREMISE

Patience will mitigate anger and prevent all the aftereffects such as guilt, shame and yes, even jail. Anger is fear gone awry. Its expression is the result of deficient self-respect and compassion. It is frequently the aftermath of misunderstanding and self-absorption. Anger is the "child-self" crying out for attention, wanting things one way and one way only, absolutely and immediately. The fear is based on the belief that we must control external events or we will be destroyed. It is a desperate attempt to gain power through physical means. Anger is the behavioral expression of a hidden belief that we are weak, vulnerable and powerless. The results of these assumptions create panic and impulsivity. Patience reinforces trust and empowerment, soothes the savage breast and allows us to listen with the intent of learning and understanding.

INTENTION

My power lies within my ability to choose and my ability to choose lovingly. This strength can be expanded by compassionate awareness and persistent intent. I can aspire to love, forgiveness and acceptance, as I observe the changes in my attitudes, behaviors and interactions.

AWARENESS

I will examine my anger to discover the fear generating it. I will begin to compose a list of my most disabling apprehensions, for example, assaults to my self-esteem, rejection, the frustration of not meeting expectations etc. I will note these in my journal and think about them throughout the day.

DAY 145—HUMILITY

"Our daily existence requires both closeness and distance, the wholeness of self, the wholeness of intimacy."
Judith Viorst (1986)

PREMISE

When we allow a sense of vulnerability and trust to enter our soul, we open the way to constructing meaningful and loving interpersonal relationships. Trust and acceptance destroy the child-self and it is this child-self that rejects others because to be intimate is to increase vulnerability and dependence. Humility gives us the strength to allow another into our heart. It permits compassion to enter our perspective and inspires service to dominate our behavior. With humility, relationships become about mutual growth and giving. Such relationships reject the status quo and the need to conquer and acquire, dominate and accumulate. We begin to see others as equals, equally flawed yet equally lovable. We are one with all, at the perfect time in the perfect place.

INTENTION

Each person I encounter is sacred. To help one is to help all. Each small act in each brief moment can result in a critical mass leading to contentment, love and serenity. We are all connected by God's love. I understand that I am here to serve, to offer my unique gifts to others. In this way, I will be fulfilled and complete.

AWARENESS

Today, I will be more aware of indications that someone is offering kindness and compassion. I will give up control and trust another. I will note this behavior and its effects in my journal.

DAY 146—GRATITUDE

"You life is but a day;
A fragile dewdrop on its perilous way
From the tree's summit."
John Keats (1816)

PREMISE

In every moment, we can renew our life by renewing awareness. Everyday actions can be undertaken with fresh intent and an innovative perspective. In each moment, there is an opportunity to both give and receive. This is a simultaneous INTENTION of acceptance, love and inclusion. It is a celebration of a relationship, a bonding of humanity. By giving and receiving, we create an occasion to mature (expand our perspective), as well as to better understand and accept our world and ourselves. Gratitude is also an act of courage because we acknowledge our interdependence and are therefore vulnerable to rejection.

INTENTION

I can celebrate the day by having the strength to be vulnerable. I can comprehend helplessness and the importance of my partnerships, as well as my dependence on others. I am grateful to those who have chosen to share part of their lives with me and I treasure their contributions to my well-being.

AWARENESS

I will focus on things that are special in my life and that are given to me freely (the sun, friendship, kindness etc.). I will make a special effort to thank someone who has supported me. I will choose the means (letter, card, phone etc.) or just say "Thank You".

DAY 147—ACCEPTANCE

"It is within our power not to make a judgment about something, and so not to disturb our minds . . ."
Marcus Aurelius (161 C.E.)

PREMISE

There are many ways to manifest and advance acceptance as we face the daily challenges of life. One way is to demonstrate compassion for others by listening and loving them without judgment or comparison. Just to be with the person in the present, listening, understanding and learning will liberate the mind from refurbished history, ingrained prejudice and selective attention. Let it happen. Cease blaming, categorizing and denying, rather attempt to serve and understand. Remember: "I honor the place where you and I are one" ("Namaste"). Adhere to this, accept what you see and embrace rather than manage or control.

INTENTION

The judge and critic are strong. It is our nature to evaluate, opine and decide frequently before facts can hamper our fixed mindset. I can be strong and resist the temptation of simplifying. I am aware of the "judge" and critic that lies within. The bias and the distortion that such predilections impact on my perspective impede love, compassion and forgiveness. If I can identify and challenge these thoughts, I can be less dismissive and more loving. As such, my truth will be more objective and my life less filled with rancor, resentment and victimization.

AWARENESS

Today, I will be aware of how harshly I judge and compare others. When I feel particularly resentful, angry or hurt by an individual, I will stop and offer a prayer.

DAY 148—PATIENCE

"Have patience and endure: this unhappiness will one day be beneficial."
Ovid (12 B.C.E.)

PREMISE

Don't give up in your quest to develop patience! You are on a mission that no one else can accomplish. Ask for and you will receive all of the spiritual help and encouragement you need to successfully complete that mission. Be focused, be determined and you will succeed. Give patience time, allow it to develop and expand. Reflect and unfold the will of the Spirit. Patience expresses our strength and reflects our integrity and self-control. It is the prelude to compassion and gratitude and it must be developed slowly, as the mind dominates the primitive impulses that are based on fear and self-absorption.

INTENTION

I have the strength, the wisdom and the necessary intent to allow patience to enter my life and play a role in my destiny. Lack of patience is simply a fear expressed by the child-self as it dominates the parent-self. I can visualize quieting and comforting that never-pleased child and I can visualize myself slowly tolerating those actions in others that previously angered or annoyed me.

AWARENESS

I will list two phrases I use to quiet and calm myself when I feel irritated. I will review those phrases and note them in my journal. I intend to increase my awareness of those incidents, actions and habits of others that tempt me to relinquish my self-control and indulge in my angry, immature impulses.

DAY 149—HUMILITY

"The spiritual seeker ultimately finds that he was already at the destination, that he himself IS what he had been seeking and he WAS, in fact, already home."
Ramesh S. Balsekar (1947)

PREMISE

What we need is all around us. When we are ready, the teacher will appear. Seek and you shall find. Believing is seeing. Each statement points to the same truth and when we are humble, this truth is no longer hidden. It becomes obvious. Our Higher Power is with us at all times, helping us through bad times and making good times better. We are never alone. All we have to do is pause, focus on the present and be willing to have God enter our soul. When we intend goodness and love, we become aware of the presence of our Higher Power. Be humble, be aware, and be prepared.

INTENTION

As I achieve a humble perspective, I will learn to honor myself and to be grateful for all that I have. This occurs because I clearly understand that my Creator cherishes me. I have an obligation to be all that I can and I will achieve this, as I comprehend that with my Creator's help, I can do anything. However, I must have the humility to ask for assistance.

AWARENESS

Today, I will focus on the signs of a power greater than myself. I will have the humility to be vulnerable and to look and wonder at the miracles that surround me. Today, I will pause in the middle of my busy schedule and, for a moment; focus on God's presence.

DAY 150—GRATITUDE

"When I give, I give myself."
Walt Whitman (1880)

PREMISE

Every day, we can offer those we meet, the unique gift of our individuality, our history, our perspective and ourselves. We can open ourselves and share, in an effort to reach out and understand another. In turn, we create a circumstance where we can receive their singularity and good will. Such a perspective, coupled with the courage to try, will enable us to make every interaction an opportunity for mutual discovery, understanding and empathy. Simply intending it to be so can generate such a celebration of life. We are indeed the creators of our future and designers of our destiny.

INTENTION

"I" can manage to give freely without expectation of reward, influence or recompense. I can give myself to others freely and require nothing in return. I can do this because I know that I can achieve what I seek only by giving it away. I become whole and satisfied by hoarding nothing and sharing everything.

AWARENESS

Today, I will be aware of my fear of risk especially as it relates to relationships whether they are casual or intimate. I will have the courage to face rejection and attempt acceptance and compassion for another.

DAY 151—ACCEPTANCE

". . . our life is the creation of our mind . . ."
Buddha (c. 500 B.C.E.)

PREMISE

The act and intent of totally integrating humility into daily living and into each social interaction, enables us to realize that we can be our best selves without being perfect. This is an important step to growth and contentment because it mitigates the fear of failure. We feel and comprehend that we are cherished by others and, more importantly, by our Higher Power, despite our flaws, foibles and frailties. In fact, we begin to see that we can be embraced especially for our faults and lack of perfection because they are part of what defines us. We no longer need to blame, compare or judge. We can "be" and so can others. When we achieve this mind-set, we will feel a gratification with intensity beyond imagination.

INTENTION

There is so much to be gained from letting go, surrendering and trusting. Yet, I fear making this decision and adapting to this new viewpoint. Like every hurdle that I've encountered, I know that it can be overcome. If I just let go of my pride and fear, embedded in my child-self, I can then decide to move forward with the intent of loving and serving.

AWARENESS

I will take a risk today. I will engage in one act of random kindness with no expectation of reward and simply focus on the process of serving another.

DAY 152—PATIENCE

"To persevere, trusting in what hopes he has, is courage in a man. The coward despairs."
Euripides (c. 422 B.C.E.)

PREMISE

Patience, humility, gratitude and acceptance are assets in our quest for growth and fulfillment. While it is frequently seen as weakness in our culture, in actuality, patience arises from a deep certainty in the self that all stress, crises and conflicts can and will be resolved. Patience promotes and facilitates success because it generates persistence. In turn, persistence is born of trust in ourselves and in our Higher Power. Despite doubt, insecurity and change, persistence keeps us focused and motivated. With patience and persistence, we can reach any goal and achieve any aim.

INTENTION

I have the ability and will to change my perspective such that I view humility, gratitude, acceptance and patience as positive traits that will help me lead a life of contentment. I will not view them as passive, submissive or servile. In this way, I will facilitate my goals to become all that I am created to be.

AWARENESS

During the next four days I will begin each morning with a prayer, requesting that I increase my patience. I will take a note each evening of one event that shows my prayer was answered. I will be grateful for this.

DAY 153—HUMILITY

"Remember that what you have now was once among the things you only hoped for."
Epicurus (300 B.C.E.)

PREMISE

Why are we here? What is life all about? Why am I writing this at this time in this place for you to read at another time in another place? We all have a connection and humility helps us accept and embrace the perspective that our lives have a unique purpose and that we are part of a plan, a process, which is far greater than we could ever imagine. We are only one part. Yet, we play a critical role. Every event in our lives and every event in the lives of those relatives, who came before us, brought us to this place. Despite the odds and the distance between us, we are here, the result of many and varied circumstances that we neither planned nor even imagined. Think about that and embrace the beauty that is existence and connectedness.

INTENTION

I can do this. I can discover my purpose and my unique talents. I now know that every thought causes an emotional response. I also know that I am capable of controlling my thoughts and, therefore, my emotions. My Higher Power has given me this insight and I will use it to improve my life and the lives of those around me.

AWARENESS

Today, I will open myself to the events in life and respond with the knowledge that all is purposeful and that there are no coincidences. I will act on the premise that I am here to serve. I have the humility to understand that I am only one and I have the pride to comprehend that I am one who can make a difference.

DAY 154—GRATITUDE

"Sweet is the breath of vernal shower,
The bee's collected treasures sweet,
Sweet music's melting fall, but sweeter yet
This still small voice of gratitude."
Thomas Gray (1769)

PREMISE

Gratitude is necessary for happiness, satisfaction and progression. Each day, the opportunity to initiate and enhance this attitude presents itself, if only we open our hearts and allow ourselves to experience this new perspective. Gratitude increases self-esteem because we are enabled to see the Good in our selves and our actions. We begin to understand that we are as we should be and our flaws present possibilities for growth, as they enhance our individuality. These "flaws" can be used as an incentive to direct our lives on a path of compassion and contentment.

INTENTION

"I" can acknowledge my defects with courage and truth. I can do this without condemning my past, my present circumstances or myself. My imperfections will allow me to see, accept and even cherish, the humanity of others. As I strive to improve, I need not condemn, compare or criticize anyone. I will move forward in love and compassion. In this way I can reach my destiny and manifest my purpose.

AWARENESS

I will be more aware of my faults today and how they hamper my progress. I will enter, in my journal, one event where I met a personal goal.

DAY 155—ACCEPTANCE

"The secret of health for both mind and body is not to mourn for the past, worry about the future, or anticipate troubles, but to live in the present moment wisely and earnestly."
Buddha (c. 500 B.C.E.)

PREMISE

The future is a projection, a fantasy, a construct of imagination, while the past is distorted by memory, falsehoods and revisionism. This leads to fear, isolation and inertia. Both projection and fear will hamper any attempt at change or growth and therefore, are significant impediments to contentment. Fear of the unknown (especially of change), lack of trust as well as lack of focus and intent, all contribute to immobility and the feelings of misery we experience in the "Now."

INTENTION

I will live in the present and confront the fear of change. Each day, I have an opportunity to begin again, to apply what I have learned yesterday and to renew intent, sharpen awareness and continue my goal of becoming and being who I was created to be. It scary and I'm afraid, but if I pray for help and listen for guidance, I can succeed.

AWARENESS

At least five times today, I will purposely stop what I am doing and focus for about a minute, on the present. I will quiet my thoughts, attend to my breathing and begin relaxing each major muscle from head to foot. I will then say to myself: "I am exactly where I should be and right now I have all that I need to succeed."

DAY 156—PATIENCE

"I am, indeed, a king, because I know how to rule myself."
Pietro Ariteno (1537 C.E.)

PREMISE

Patience enhances our awareness of the moment and counters the tendency to immediately react to unpleasant emotions. It promotes stillness and reflection, allowing us to put an event into perspective. We become empowered, able to access self-power, so that we choose, strengthen and reinforce integrity while bolstering self-esteem. Patience reminds us that we are in control and that ultimate power resides within us, not outside of us. We make more effective and loving decisions when we choose to allow patience to rule impulse and emotion.

INTENTION

I firmly believe, now, that my motivation is unwavering, focused and unshakable. I am aware of my biases and weaknesses. They are part of me and can be controlled, altered and tempered. I can change any destructive pattern of behavior including impatience, irritability and intolerance. With renewed awareness and energized intent, I can evolve into the person I was created to become.

AWARENESS

This morning I will begin the day with a prayer for patience. I will ponder on how I will show my patience in predictable situations of stress. I will plan my strategy and note the results in my journal.

DAY 157—HUMILITY

"Is there any one maxim which ought to be acted upon throughout one's whole life? Surely, the maxim of loving kindness is such."
Confucius (c. 510 B.C.E.)

PREMISE

As you achieve humility, you will notice that you become more genuinely interested in the welfare of others. This is due to the child-self decreasing and relinquishing control of your apprehensive perspective. This is marvelously liberating. We evolve from "me-ness" (meanness?) to "we-ness." Selfish interests wane, as we become strong enough to look inward for satisfaction. We are now becoming more spiritual and more unified as well as empowered and self-possessed. Integrity (wholeness) encompasses others, their needs, interests and welfare. Our reflexive response ceases being "what's in it for me?" and becomes, "how can I help?"

INTENTION

I have the power, the patience and the humility to fulfill my mission. Humility has taught me that others have needs that I must respect, if I am to mature and develop. I understand that thoughts are filtered, judged and reconciled with the past before I am even aware of the thought. This knowledge puts me on alert, increases awareness of my thought processes and empowers me. I will exercise the diligence necessary to monitor and master myself. I accept that humility allows such strength, unselfishness and realization. I have the courage and trust to be tolerant, charitable and inclusive. As such, I begin a positive and life-affirming cycle of mental health and stability.

AWARENESS

Today, I will focus on the needs of my brethren rather than my own needs and wants. I will undertake an anonymous act of kindness.

DAY 158—GRATITUDE

"If you see no reason for giving thanks, the fault lies in yourself."
American Indian proverb

PREMISE

Gratitude is the nectar of humility. It is both sweet and pleasant. It banishes self-interest and self-destruction. It is vital to cultivate this delicate fruit, that we may be strengthened against the child-self. Our narrow, narcissistic nature, leads us to arrogantly isolate and disdainfully dismiss the Good that surrounds us. Gratitude prevents, or at least mitigates, this tendency. It is indeed a gift. Seek reasons to be grateful and discover a new satisfaction in your life.

INTENTION

If I intend to be grateful, I will find gratitude. If I seek goodness and beneficence in my life, I will find them. If I let go of resentment, distrust and fear, I will open my soul and see the wonder of life and the blessings bestowed on me. I can be grateful for what I have and what I have not, for what I found and what I lost, for what I did and for what I did not do. But I must search, I must intend to uncover this or it will remain hidden. In sum, the reasons to be grateful surround me and with intent and awareness, I can discover this gift.

AWARENESS

I will focus on my inner reactions, sensations and feelings, as I think about one thing for which I am grateful. I will actively search to see all the reasons to be grateful and all the wonders that comprise my life. I will start with those closest to me, those I love.

DAY 159—ACCEPTANCE

"Where there is charity and wisdom,
there is neither fear nor ignorance."
St. Francis of Assisi (1215 C.E.)

PREMISE

The child-self wants the status quo. It is afraid of change. It is afraid of acceptance, inclusion and any fact that contradicts its worldview. Our adult-selves cry "go away", "be quiet", as we try to move forward. All the while, the conflict remains, as the child-self kicks, screams and tantrums not only to keep things as they are but also to proliferate the prejudice, delusion and deceit that have justified inaction. When faced with this struggle as well as the anxiety and despair it brings, we minimize the distress and dysfunction. "If it ain't broke, don't fix it", becomes our motto but in our heart we know that things are badly broken. Acceptance isn't complacency and it isn't sitting around, accomplishing nothing while marinating in self-satisfaction. Instead, acceptance is confronting change and rising to the challenge of growing. AFTER, this process, we are then in a position of strength so that we know our limits and we can chose to accept what we can't change and change what we can.

INTENTION

I was created for a purpose and standing still is not learning or growing. Hiding from life, due to fear of change, prevents me from becoming all that I can be. I am meant to be more than a pawn of my history, of old bigotry and myth. I will seek truth, I will face fear and I will grow.

AWARENESS

I will perform one act of charity to dispel my fear of vulnerability. I will ignore projection, prejudice and past denials to focus on engendering compassion in the moment and acceptance in the long term.

DAY 160—PATIENCE

"Patience is needed with everyone, but most of all ourselves."
St. Francis de Sales

PREMISE

Throughout life, the child-self in its destructive capacity, combats and resists the positive forces of spirit, patience and growth, to protect the status quo. The child-self hates change. Therefore, it hates inclusion, acceptance and compassion. It knows no gratitude because it credits itself with all successes and satisfactions. The child-self resists growth so that we stay dormant and we retain the fictitious security of bygone days. It is very clever and insidious, yet it demands immediate satisfaction. We must constantly be aware of its presence, especially as it manifests itself in helplessness, apathy, paralysis, victimization and rationalization. We have not failed because our requests and expectations were not immediately satisfied, it may be that we simply haven't allowed enough time for resolution. That is, we were impatient.

INTENTION

I will make it my business to be aware of the power of apathy and complacency. I know that I can resist the temptation to "not do." If I choose to have reason dominate impulse, I will recognize this negative force and I will plan to begin taking just one small step in the direction of change, knowing that with each step the power of inertia becomes less.

AWARENESS

I will write in my journal at least one paragraph about how I feel when I want to do nothing while knowing I must do something.

DAY 161—HUMILITY

"What we have done for ourselves alone dies with us; what we have done for others and the world remains and is immortal."
Albert Pike (1878)

PREMISE

Previously, the concept of "service" was misunderstood by many of us. It was restricted and self-centered. We would help others only if it profited us or when we expected some type of reward, recognition or repayment. As we have evolved and served others, we have realized that to give with compassion, love and understanding is really to receive. We now know the meaning and value of genuine service. We feel it, we know it, and we do it. To free ourselves, through kindness and generosity, from the needy, demanding, and insecure child-self, will help us evolve and become the person we were created to be.

INTENTION

As I give, so shall I receive. I will give freely, today, and therefore, I will be free. The process of self-sacrifice, self-control and self-love is arduous but possible. I, and my fellow journeyman, have been given this task and the means to accomplish it. We cannot do it alone but we are strong enough to humbly ask for help and to give thanks when help is received.

AWARENESS

I will be more conscious of others' needs and how I address them through the actions of service and compassion. Today, I will be generous and loving in my behaviors.

DAY 162—GRATITUDE

"If the only prayer you ever said in your life was 'thank you', that would suffice."
Meister Eckert (1297)

PREMISE

It is as important to remember the disruption, discomfort and devastation, as it is to remember the wonders of life and the successes of action. We can use misfortune to remind ourselves that we are strong and we are survivors. As we become grateful for the moment, we find that resenting past events makes no sense because these are precisely the events and circumstances that we have used to create and become who we are. If we strive with acceptance, love and humility to be the best we can be, we will succeed one-step and one day at a time. This is a reason for celebration and true pride. We have survived and possibly thrived; now it is time to grow in love and acceptance. Leave the past and enter the future. Pursue your newfound insight and give thanks!

INTENTION

I can endure and actually succeed from the stress that accompanies change, if I focus on the Good, the love and the support that surrounds me. The uncertainty, fear and vulnerability that comprise stress can be diminished or discarded by giving thanks for what is.

AWARENESS

Gratitude can be felt and brought into awareness at any moment we choose. Today, I will substitute my destructive thoughts for those of gratitude.

DAY 163—ACCEPTANCE

"When one door closes, another opens, but we often look so long and so regretfully upon the closed door, that we do not see the one which has opened for us."
Alexander Graham Bell (1900)

PREMISE

Projection is the great "what if?" Projection generates and justifies fear while reinforcing inaction. The child-self blasts "I will die if you move in that direction!"; "What if . . . ?" You fill in the blanks because the child-self knows you and your vulnerabilities better than anyone, including you. The child-self is so subtle, so insidious and so powerful that it is elusive. Catching, confronting or even defining it, is extremely difficult. If you feel vaguely bad, dissatisfied, unfulfilled, fearful or angry, chances are that your child-self is there, behind the bushes in the mind, calling the shots. This is why awareness, intent and acceptance are so important. Acceptance fills us with trust and certainty that what is, is exactly what we should be given. Our task is to define within that reality what we can and can't control. With acceptance the natural yet destructive propensity towards projection is conquered or at least diminished.

INTENTION

I can identify thoughts or feelings that intrude on my behavior and alter my prospective of change and growth. I will follow the suggestions below to increase my awareness and fortify my intent to progress on my journey in a loving, accepting manner.

AWARENESS

I will increase awareness of destructive thoughts and list five of them in my journal. I will begin with "I can't . . ."

DAY 164—PATIENCE

"Teach me to feel another's woe /To hide the fault I see; /That mercy I to others show, /That mercy show to me."
Alexander Pope (1738)

PREMISE

We make more effective and loving decisions when we have patience because it helps us control our child-self, as it bolsters and fortifies empathy and self-respect. Again, this creates an all-important, self-reinforcing cycle of positive energy, as hate, judgment and comparison are negated and understanding, forgiveness and acceptance take their place. Consequently, we can more readily tolerate the "slings and arrows" of life's whims. We begin to view those who annoy us most as those from whom we can learn most. Here is an opportunity to grow.

INTENTION

I will embrace this opportunity and I will move forward in accepting the faults of others with loving understanding. I will avoid the temptation to believe I am superior in this intent, rather I will see the similarities of my own annoying behavior to that of others.

AWARENESS

I will write in my journal one paragraph about the exasperating traits of the first person that comes to mind. I will then write a second paragraph about my similar behaviors.

DAY 165—HUMILITY

"As soon as you trust yourself, you will know how to live."
Johann Von Goethe (1829)

PREMISE

To progress in our lives is to grow, to evolve into being that person we were created to be. Unfortunately, the human condition is such that there appears to be an equal and opposite force, the child-self, that is dedicated to not moving on and instead to preserve the status quo. This is the force behind fear, hesitation and insecurity. It resists looking at the past so as to motivate progress. Rather, it looks at the past so as to preserve the "good" tradition or it looks at the past as an excuse for inaction. It seems easier to accept "failure" than attempt success. It seems easier to remain in our self-made prisons than to move on and discover all that life has to offer. Through the cultivation of humility, we become able to trust enough so that we acknowledge our vulnerability and, as such, we can move beyond the "myth of me" constructed by others.

INTENTION

In each moment, I am given the means necessary to achieve what I must. Through humility, I am able to acknowledge this. I also accept that I can't achieve my goals alone. With this "knowing", my world opens to all that I can be. I now feel the courage and trust to persevere and to ceaselessly move my mission forward. If I allow my Higher Power to direct me, my way will be revealed. However I must listen and open my heart with humility.

AWARENESS

I will be alert to the signs of self-imposed restrictions based on fear. Today, I will face my fear and begin my journey of growth in at least one instance.

DAY 166—GRATITUDE

"Appreciation is a wonderful thing: it makes what is excellent in others belong to us as well."
Voltaire (1763)

PREMISE

Gratitude is all-inclusive in its bounty. It brings light to all the dark crevices of our soul. It embraces empathy, compassion and acceptance as it shuns fear, competition and rejection. It inspires intimacy, trust and patience. With an infusion of gratitude, our perspective evolves from a narrow view of wants, needs and resentments, to a more encompassing perspective of satisfaction, fulfillment and forgiveness. We see abundance, joy and love in more aspects of our lives.

INTENTION

I can embrace change because I know my strength and I can remember all those times that change was scary but conquered. I can remember my positive traits, my courage and my progress. These times have made me stronger and more certain of my abilities. I have a reservoir of fortitude and resources ready to help, if I just ask. For every challenge, in each moment, all that I need is around me. I must remember this and seek help when I feel helpless.

AWARENESS

I will focus on what I have, not on what I want to have or what I lack. I will concentrate on who I am, not on who I'm not. Today, I will pray for gratitude and the gift of appreciation, upon waking.

DAY 167—ACCEPTANCE

"Do not seek to have events happen as you want them to, but instead want them to happen as they do happen, and your life will go well."
Epictetus (c. 1st century, C.E.)

PREMISE

When we try to take control of too many issues, we lose our focus and become overwhelmed. It becomes easy to despair and abandon our objective as being too difficult or too burdensome to fulfill. Yet fear propels us to attempt control rather than acknowledge our need for guidance and support. Projection is used to justify this fear. With projection, we don't have to identify or articulate our fear; rather it incites us to hide behind "caution." Before we begin any new action, fear intrudes and blocks the thoughts or inclinations of growth by asking a variety of "what if" questions, the answer to which will always portend doom or failure. There are times when such caution is appropriate and we must carefully evaluate our thinking. But more often, such reflexive hesitance is an excuse for inaction and a significant impediment to development.

INTENTION

To identify and change years of destructive thought patterns is extremely difficult but I can do it. My life has meaning and I need to change. I am reading this book and thinking about this lesson for a reason. Let me have the knowledge of that reason and the courage to carry it through.

AWARENESS

Today, I will pray for the knowledge and the strength to fulfill my destiny and before bed I will write down three goals to achieve in the near future.

DAY 168—PATIENCE

"The person who makes a success of living is the one who sees his goal steadily and aims for it unswervingly. That is dedication."
Cecil B. De Mille (1955)

PREMISE

Projection is a terrible habit we all have, in which we wonder "what if?" before we even attempt to achieve an objective. We frequently imagine the worst consequences of a particular course of action to such a degree that we stop trying and simply justify stagnation. The fearful child-self will tell us that we are being "cautious." However, if we are honest and courageous, we will often discover that "caution" is frequently a rationale for immobility, due to fear. Projection can be a significant barrier to persistence (striving to become who we were meant to be) and patience (foregoing immediate gratification and resisting the frustration and sense of helplessness that accompanies an expectation of instant satisfaction). We must limit our propensity for projection so that patience may rule and dominate our approach to fulfillment.

INTENTION

I can trust and be patient in my pursuit of growth. I understand that each new path involves new skills that can only be acquired through persistence (trial and error). I can learn to accept the frustration and disappointment that occurs when I consider the amount of effort necessary to grow. If it were easy, I would have already done it. All flowers blossom in their own time, so I can be patient.

AWARENESS

Today, I will take special notice when I'm frustrated. I will attempt to acknowledge this and distance myself from the situation by using my participant/observer skills. I will pray for patience when I falter.

DAY 169—HUMILITY

"To conquer fear is the beginning of wisdom."
Bertrand Russell (1950)

PREMISE

What does freedom mean? How do we learn to move beyond our past and into the present? How can we redefine ourselves if we don't know what that means? Where do I begin? These are all relevant questions, as we pursue our unique odyssey to growth and development. We can start by looking honestly and with humility at where we are in a particular area. How do we evaluate our physical health, wellness, growth and rate of progress? How do we perceive the current condition of our intellectual, social, spiritual, and financial progress? Choose an area to focus on. How would you like to change? What stops you from making that change? Make a decision, construct a strategy, be honest and humble and then proceed, one small step at a time. How will you start today? Now begin! You're on your way!

INTENTION

I will control my level of fear by adjusting my perspective about change. Thoughts and judgments produce feelings that can be positive or negative. I must choose which. I have the tenacity, humility and wisdom to nurture the positive and shed the negative. I will set life-affirming, achievable, goals for myself each day. Each evening I will give thanks for all that I have learned and I will humbly request that my Higher Power show me the way.

AWARENESS

Today, I will decide on the area and the behavior I want to change. Today, I will begin my journey to growth and competence.

DAY 170—GRATITUDE

"The gift of gratitude will either prevent or mitigate depression."
W. T. Watts, Ph.D. (2010)

PREMISE

One of the most significant impediments to gratitude is an attachment to a life story of deprivation and hardship. Such an obsession with victimhood will become a self-fulfilling prophecy. Often we prefer to find fault in our past in order to blame the shortcomings and frustrations that are part of our present. This keeps us prisoner to the status quo and enslaved by a negative self-image. The pay-off is an alleviation of self-responsibility. As we bathe in self-pity, we absolve ourselves from any need to go beyond where we are. We indulge in proactive protectionism i.e. we conjure up all the reasons why we can't, instead of implementing a plan for the future and enumerating all the reasons why we can.

INTENTION

I have the ability, the resolve and the resourcefulness to move forward and create a new me. I am not a victim of my past. Any problems, real or imagined, have been endured. With courage and creativity, I can use lessons from these events to be stronger and more effective. I create my own reality and it does not have to be determined by past events or the opinions of others. I am grateful for the trials of the past because they have made me stronger and better able to face the present and the future.

AWARENESS

I will focus on the thoughts that keep me enmeshed in the status quo. These destructive thoughts will be noted in my journal. They usually begin with "I can't" or "It's too hard." I will try one new thing and confront any fear or frustration that attends this pursuit.

DAY 171—ACCEPTANCE

"*. . . our thoughts today build our life of tomorrow . . .*"
Buddha (c. 500 B.C.E.)

PREMISE

Note well the words of the Buddha. Our present thoughts, those in the moment, not prejudiced by the past or restricted by self-limiting fear and immobility are the keys to achieving future goals and fulfillment. Be aware of this moment, feel the life and feel the gratitude that awareness engenders. Most importantly, feel the freedom and then move on. Therefore, don't project. As you move forward, you will be presented with new facts and new challenges. Each requires a "nip and a tuck", a small but critical adjustment as you, leave the past and create the future. Invoking the Serenity Prayer as needed, moment-to-moment, is a good approach. Accepting that which you can't control is a necessary part of this process.

INTENTION

The challenge is to be in the moment. I can do this just as I can conquer all of the other challenges. When I stay in the moment, I allow myself to feel the strength of the Spirit, the expansive fortitude and goodness of the non-physical. I accept what is and I don't attend to what "could" or should" be. This spirit is the source of all strength and is available at any time, simply by focusing my awareness.

AWARENESS

I will practice stopping during the day, just for a moment, to pause, breathe, and sharpen awareness of my surroundings. This will reinforce my intent to let go and to proceed with a renewed commitment to do the next good thing. I accept what is because it is good.

DAY 172—PATIENCE

"Fear is stronger than arms."
Aeschylus (467 B.C.E.)

Projection is the great "what if?" that keeps us immobilized and satisfied with the status quo. It is subtle and insidious, frequently disguising itself as "wisdom" and "caution." Make no mistake, projection is often masked as fear and when you're feeling tense, "wound up" etc., it may indicate that your caution is preventing you from moving forward in a productive, growth enriching way. You must think and be aware. Be aware of the feeling of immobility and the contradictory restlessness and impatience. Also, be aware of your justification for not moving. If you fear failure, think of what that means to you. How do you define "failure"? Are you just afraid to try? Are you in your own way and creating your own impediments to success? Think! Then move forward and evolve, a step at a time.

INTENTION

I can proceed with caution when fearful and I can, therefore, develop and mature. I will face my demons because I know that fear of fear is fueling my hesitation. This is why it is so difficult to forge a new path. It takes motivation, trust in my Higher Power and disgust not satisfaction, with the status quo. If I feel complacent, justified or resentful, forward movement becomes extremely difficult and immobility comes to rule the day.

AWARENESS

Today, I will try something new and I will note all the "what if's" and doubts. I will observe carefully the result of my attempts. Today I will confront my hesitation and fears. Today will become another day of growth as I confront change and choice with patience and trust.

DAY 173—HUMILITY

"Men do not care how nobly they live, but only how long, although it is within the reach of every man to live nobly, but within no man's power to live long."
Seneca (32 C.E.)

PREMISE

To be humble is to be empowered and to be empowered is to be free. How can we be truly free when so many of our biological needs are dependent upon others for gratification? Surely we need others for our physical, social and spiritual wellness. To be free does not mean being isolated. While we strive for unity and inclusion, we must also strive for boundaries and a strong, independent self. While love, inclusion and acceptance are necessary traits for a contented life, so are self-confidence and self-reliance. This is the quandary and tension that is life. We face this each day with each interaction. Our choice must not be made from fear but rather, from love of self and love of others.

INTENTION

Each day, as I follow this program, I feel stronger and more confident. I am more certain of my ability to cope with change and more certain that the help I need is all around me. I am empowered and I reflect the strength of my Creator and the certainty that I am finally on the right path. I am strong enough to ask for help and confident enough to pursue my goals. This is what it means to be humble.

AWARENESS

I will increase awareness of my needs for intimacy and how they conflict with my needs for independence. Today, I will make a point to express my compassion. I will then closely watch the effect on the other and myself.

DAY 174—GRATITUDE

"The absurd man is he who never changes."
Auguste Barthelemy (1830)

PREMISE

Gratitude promotes a perspective that engenders courage and trust. With a grateful heart, we can move forward because our focus becomes what we have and what we have achieved. We do not become burdened by thoughts of scarcity and deficiency. We begin to recognize the goodness and support that surrounds and encourages us. We actively recreate ourselves by embracing a new realization and engaging in new behaviors. We attempt additional roles in our daily interactions and find ourselves implementing acts of kindness and goodwill. As others respond to our new identity, our new roles are reinforced and we continue to develop and evolve. In this manner, with every action and interaction in our daily routine, we recreate our reality and ourselves.

INTENTION

I can break the chains of fear and stagnation. I will develop the determination to appreciate myself and I will embrace the responsibility that this entails. I have the courage to change and grow, to alter the negative to the positive, to turn hate to love and detachment to attraction. I can live and I can give, as I confront my impediments and achieve my destiny.

AWARENESS

Today, I will be more aware of my inner responses to change. I will allow myself to feel the fear, constriction and hesitance when encountering the stress of the unknown and the unpredictable. I will grow. I will grow by confronting reluctance, embarrassment, shame and stagnation.

DAY 175—ACCEPTANCE

"As a boat on the water can be swept off course by a strong wind, so the intelligence may be carried away like any of the roaming senses on which the mind alights."
Bhagavad Gita (c. 2nd century, C.E.)

PREMISE

As with many of the traits that are necessary in order to achieve growth and contentment, acceptance is hampered and vilified by the consumer culture. The credo of consumerism is that you are "defective," "deficient" or "deprived" and something outside of you is the solution. You are broken but you can be fixed ("in 5 easy payments", "cash or charge", "everyone gets credit" etc.). Acquisitions then become solutions and you continually search in the external, extrinsic and superficial for the "fix" that will magically make everything better. Consumerism wants you to be an "addict of consumption." Addiction starts by a craving for something you don't need until it controls and directs the healthy mind to destroy the body that follows. We must cease looking outside to repair what is broken inside.

INTENTION

As difficult as it may become, I will attempt to pierce the delusion of the superficial. I am not what I own. I am just as I was created to be and I can transform weaknesses into strengths and use these strengths to serve others as I enhance myself and learn. I will not be deceived by the fallacy of a superficial solution.

AWARENESS

Today, I will review what are my favorite things and I will think about how they define me and if they hamper my effort towards improvement.

DAY 176—PATIENCE

"The worst troubles I've had in my life are the ones that never happened."
Mark Twain (1885)

PREMISE

Mark Twain spoke to the essence of projection. It is the cause of our persistent use of the same strategy only to receive the same results. We act rashly, with little consideration or reassessment then become frustrated and perplexed. We wonder how can this be? Why us? Yet we fear the different and embrace the familiar in order to avoid the anxiety of assertiveness as well as the contrived and imagined repercussions from the unknown. The predominant thought is that: "the devil you know is better than the devil you don't." This justifies both our immobility and our impulsivity; our biases and the status quo. We stop thinking, assessing and strategizing because they take too much effort. We marinate in self-satisfaction as self-hatred looms. We hide from what we know is real and refuse to take responsibility for our cowardice and inaction. We forego patience for instant gratification. This must stop and patience must rule, if we are to become content.

INTENTION

I can generate courage and patience to be who I am. I can tolerate the frustration arising out of impatience. I accept the fact that there are events which are beyond my control and that the Universe has its own wisdom and plan.

AWARENESS

Today, I will be courageous, ignore my fear of ridicule or rejection and compliment one person randomly and unexpectedly. I will cultivate patience. I will breathe, pause and assess when I feel frustration.

DAY 177—HUMILITY

"True modesty does not consist in an ignorance of our merits, but in a due estimate of them."
Augustus William Hare (1827)

PREMISE

How can I be self-reliant and independent, while simultaneously needing others socially, spiritually and physically? Humility is the answer. While this does not appear to be a contradiction; yet, the tension generated from this question affects us each day. It is the fear of transition, dependence and uncertainty. We want and need to have a sense of control, yet we can and do control so little. We avoid taking responsibility for issues over which we can exercise some dominance, yet we magically wish to manage so many things that are beyond us. Faced with this fact, we obfuscate, deny and hide. There is no greater fear than lack of control. How is this resolved? We need to regulate that small but significant, area of our life where we can actually make a difference. That needs to be our focus and our "business."

INTENTION

I will cease self-sabotage and I will escape the grips of the child-self. I realize that I will never be totally free from false "needs" and distressing sensations. I understand that even though I may experience one moment of contentment, the next moment could be one of challenge and discomfort. Acknowledging this as the "human condition" and accepting it, allows me to move forward with a minimum of malaise.

AWARENESS

Today, I will be attuned to things that grow, flourish and evolve with absolutely no help from me. I will mind my own business and bow my head to the wonder that is existence.

DAY 178—GRATITUDE

"Regrets and recriminations only hurt your soul."
Armand Hammer (1987)

PREMISE

The events and the people who are part of our history are the primary powers that defined who we are and where we are in the quest to fulfill our destiny. As we cultivate gratitude and appreciation for today, we inevitably become grateful for yesterday and thereby release ourselves from regret, resentment and reproach. We move on with our lives, liberated from the obligation of pleasing others. We gain respect for our emotions, memories, predispositions, abilities and ourselves. We become grateful for who we are and what we have. There is no greater contentment.

INTENTION

I will realize the love that is around me as I begin to love myself. I am God's creation and from that I can grow and realize my potential in all areas of action, feeling and thought. God loves me and I will love others by showing acceptance, compassion and understanding. This will improve my life beyond measure.

AWARENESS

I will be extra vigilant today so as to notice the numerous acts of kindness bestowed on me. Today, I will tell someone special how grateful I am for their participation in my life.

DAY 179—ACCEPTANCE

"Open your eyes, and you will have plenty of bread."
Proverbs 20:13

PREMISE

The consumer culture dictates our "wants" and transforms them to "needs". It indoctrinates the "perfect" you to become dependent and damaged. In reality, consumerism creates, amplifies and disguises wants as needs. Similar to the difference between lust and love, we blindly move forward with a fixation on "more" and, as a result, we mortgage our true nature in order to have immediate satisfaction from the newest gadget. Acceptance changes this self-destructive dance. It constructs a barrier between the consumer culture's messages of inadequacy and the truth that we are as God created us with everything we need to fulfill our purpose at this time, in this moment.

INTENTION

I will work to get past the superficial, so as to see my own desire for acceptance, love and compassion actualized. I will search for good intentions rather than to criticize my fellow journeymen. If I allow myself, I will find the courage to trust.

AWARENESS

Today, I will refocus and re-energize my intent to see goodness rather than negativity in others. I will strive to be the person I want to see in others.

DAY 180—PATIENCE

"Audacity augments courage; hesitation, fear."
Publius Syrus (1st century, B.C.E.)

PREMISE

A core self-destructive tendency is to do nothing rather than something. To limit options to such a degree that we become immobile leads to helplessness, low self-esteem and depression. To persevere in this confining perspective, when we are inflicting pain upon ourselves simply because we fear change and uncertainty, is to hinder growth and to reject the natural maturational cycle that will lead to wisdom and contentment. To bask and marinate in the familiar and to limit our options to the status quo, is to cover our eyes from future promise and achievement. If we are to become content, to prosper and to grow, we must move forward, risk and change behavior.

INTENTION

I can do rather than simply consider, act rather than cogitate, love rather than fantasize. I am able to move forward, one foot in front of the other, baby steps before giant steps, crawling before walking, but ever forward.

AWARENESS

I will take note in my journal of one goal that I want to accomplish but have been neglecting, delaying, and evading. I will document a first, simple step and today I will attempt that step. This will be the beginning of a new effort to become all that I was created to be.

PART THREE

REASSESSMENT, REEVALUATION AND RECOMMITTING: APPRECIATING PROGRESS AND CONSOLIDATING GAINS

DAYS 181-203

Let's pause for a second and consider your progress, your struggles and your significant strengths. You are a miracle. This understanding is so important, if you are to continue on the road to growth, maturation and evolution. If you are to become all you were created to be, you must appreciate your progress. Think about where and who you were just a few short months ago. Think and always remember: it is never too late to begin the journey you were created to undertake.

A reason that you stumbled in the past when pursuing change is that you may have become despondent due to ignoring or acknowledging just how far you have advanced. An unrealistic expectation of perfection or the concept that there is some (arbitrary) endpoint to these goals will stunt your progress. You have chosen a "life-style". By definition this will not end until you do. You are at the early stages, where you are constructing a solid foundation (seeking to integrate humility, gratitude, acceptance and patience into daily living) to help conquer future circumstances of distress and dismay. You started this journey with the awareness that you were tired of being miserable. Remember that, and revel in your success.

For the next 90 days try to appreciate yourself and all you've achieved as you focus on your goals. Begin to consolidate your gains and assimilate the personality traits that you have been practicing into your everyday routines. Most of all, be grateful for all that you have become. Appreciate life and understand that the best is yet to be. Again, congratulations on your progress to this point and on your persistence and perseverance.

DAY 181—HUMILITY

*"There speaks the man of truly noble ways/
Who will not listen to words of praise."*
Johann von Goethe (1815)

PREMISE

As we evolve and our humility expands, we comprehend that we are neither greater nor less than our fellow travelers. We have been given profound gifts, the gift of life and the gift of ourselves. We are loved by our Creator simply because we are. This love can neither be added to, nor detracted from, regardless of the rewards, praise or blame heaped upon us from others. God's love remains, while the Good and bad opinions of others rise and fall like the temperature. Therefore, we are genuinely free, as we chose to manifest our humility and gratitude, acceptance and patience in our daily routines. We can now prevent impulsive, behavioral responses to external seduction. We can now pursue our destiny, and determine our fate, regardless of praise or disparagement.

INTENTION

As I affirm my humanity, I gain strength derived from my unity and connection with all life. This is the force of the Universe, always moving, always changing and always improving. When I began this journey I combined my energy with all of existence and I continue to believe in this power. The power of "we."

AWARENESS

Today, I will focus on how I become influenced by outside opinion. I will determine my own fate and rate of progress as I trust in myself yet seek guidance from my Higher Power.

DAY 182—GRATITUDE

"Gratitude is the antidote to bitterness and resentment."
MJ Ryan (1999)

PREMISE

By reducing regret and resentment in the present moment, gratitude helps us appreciate the past, despite our sordid and destructive memory of its adverse effects. How we love to blame our past for the state of our present, yet if we comprehend that, at the least, we survived these events, we realize that we must have powerful skills enabling us to progress and move on. By cultivating gratitude, we begin to cherish who we are now and we begin to see the flower that has grown from the decay. If we cherish who we are, we cannot simultaneously denigrate our past, rather we accept that we have become stronger because of it.

INTENTION

I will become strong. I am able to see the fruit of my struggles and I am able to understand that despite the hardship, I remember that things could have been worse. I can adapt an attitude that will see the Good in others and myself, as I treasure all that is and has been.

AWARENESS

I will be sensitive to my positive, life-affirming habits today. I will be more aware of my strengths, those emotional, behavioral and mental reactions that increase my awareness and tendency towards compassion, tolerance and positive resolution. Today I intend to avoid, at least once, doing the same thing as a reaction to the same problem. I will note this in my journal.

DAY 183—ACCEPTANCE

"To seek all your applause from outside yourself, is to have your happiness in another's keeping."
Claudius Claudianus (370 C.E.)

PREMISE

Self-acceptance resists, in each day and with every interaction, the false belief that if we will acquire a specific object, we will become content, satisfied and respected. This cultural message is unceasing and we must consciously intend to receive the opposite message that all power and fulfillment comes from within. Our initial response to such a challenge is distress, fear and uncertainty. We must have the courage to trust in ourselves and the beneficent Universe in which we reside. Acceptance of this challenge, trust in the outcome and faith in the future, will foster contentment and mitigate torment. Accept the new as a challenge to learn. Trust that learning, despite its pain and frustration, will make the future better.

INTENTION

It is frightening to grow, to evolve, to progress; if it were easy we would have already done it. To challenge uncertainty, to trust when confronted with the unknown, and to align with the Spirit is the only way to reach fulfillment and contentment. I know I can move forward, progress and evolve as I was created to do. Just as in the dark, feeling my way, cautious but continuous through one step at a time, progress happens. When I feel weak, uncertain and anxious I will pray and seek support.

AWARENESS

Today, I will challenge one long held stereotype about others or myself. I will first identify this belief and I will make a conscious effort to confront my fear and face my self-made wall of deception.

DAY 184—PATIENCE

"Patience is the companion of wisdom."
St. Augus*tine* (410 C.E.)

PREMISE

Patience and indignant disparagement cannot coexist. They are cognitively inconsistent and create stress and mental dissonance. At any time, when in the moment, we can choose (therefore intend) to have either judgment or patience. Do we want dissidence and judgment or harmony and compassion? Impatience is a judgment. It is impulse driven. We're annoyed, so we condemn rather than understand, curse rather than bless and exclude rather than empathize. Impatience is a disease of "should." "He 'should' know better." "Life 'should' be different." Get over it! It is, what it is, and no amount of whining, wishing or wanting is going to change that.

INTENTION

I can conquer my impulses, if I just intend to and become aware of my feelings during stressful situations. A brief prayer, requesting that the feeling and situation pass, should suffice to soften the cruel effects of destructive emotions.

AWARENESS

Today, I will attempt to allow impatience, frustration, and intolerance etc., just flow through me by taking slow, deliberate and deep breaths. I will give thanks for this ability and having a choice. I will ponder the results of my new behavior and try to increase the frequency of this practice.

DAY 185—HUMILITY

"Love conquers all things; let us to surrender to Love."
Virgil (31 B.C.E.)

PREMISE

We must constantly focus on a goal of cultivating humility, if we are to be totally successful in our quest for personal growth. While establishing humility is only the first step to contentment, it is probably the most difficult, due to a selfish and fear based orientation added to the effects of the consumer culture and advertising indoctrination. Humility contradicts the arrogance of acquisition. It tells us that our gifts and bounty come from our Higher Power. We have all we need, and we can never have enough of what we don't need. The idea that "more is better" leads to addiction, dissatisfaction and destruction. Humility will ground us and help us understand our place in the Universe. Humility is not humiliation; rather it is a strength that allows us to be in better contact with our spiritual selves as well as the Spirit of others. Humility leads to compassion, acceptance and contentment. It is the necessary first step on our journey to our destiny.

INTENTION

I will surrender the battle so that I may win the war. I am able to do this because humility teaches me to choose those conflicts that I can alter and to focus my energy on the goals I can realistically achieve. Material things will not satisfy me; instead it is knowing and dwelling in that place where I am in contact with my spirit that will lead me to peace.

AWARENESS

Today, I will increase my awareness of needing only my Higher Power for fulfillment. I will listen, assess and act with the intention of increasing mutual respect, love and acceptance.

DAY 186—GRATITUDE

"Life will bring you pain all by itself. Your responsibility is to create joy."
Milton Erickson, M. D. (1961)

PREMISE

Another significant obstacle to fostering gratitude is the tendency to wallow in self-pity. Such whining can be quite tempting because of our tendency to create a shield of helplessness in order to avoid the sword of self-responsibility and empowerment. "I can't . . ." "I would but . . ." "If only . . ." etc., are phrases which justify and rationalize mediocrity and debilitation. We're comfortable inhabiting this Universe. Here we can wallow in stagnation and obsess over what could have been. Gratitude for what is and whom we are, as well as the motivation to move forward are enhanced and energized when we choose to view our world in a grateful rather than an arrogant perspective.

INTENTION

I have the endurance and fortitude to fight the child-self's absorption with entitlement and conceit. I can see through my tendency to strive for self-glory and to demean, diminish and deny all the blessings bestowed on me. This is fear-based and I will have courage and humility to be appreciative and courteous for all the bounty that surrounds me.

AWARENESS

I will search for kindness in all my interactions today. I will write a brief note of thanks to someone who, long ago, helped me through a difficult time.

DAY 187—ACCEPTANCE

We are fools whether we dance or not; so we might as well dance."
Japanese Proverb

PREMISE

Dependency can be a form of self-destruction. It can reflect an innate tendency to resist empowerment. There appears to be a natural, inborn clash of identity, between the "I" that is "me" and the "I" that is "we", exclusion versus inclusion, self-sufficiency versus reliance. The simultaneous desire to return to the womb (to be totally cared for and to avoid all stress), strongly conflicts with the desire to be in control, to have total power i.e. to be physically and emotionally independent. We fear vulnerability and we fear isolation. Each interaction presents a choice. Will I walk farther with another or will I walk faster alone? Do I trust or do I doubt? Am I one or one of many?

INTENTION

I will have the strength and courage to be vulnerable and trusting. I will have the self-assurance to reach out for help or to offer help. I will connect yet I will be separate. I will have the self-confidence and self-love to place a portion of my well being into the care of another. I can trust and I can question.

AWARENESS

Today, I will focus on developing the courage to trust. I will allow myself to be vulnerable. I will note, in my journal, the circumstances and the effects of this new approach. I will be an objective recorder and a "participant/observer."

DAY 188—PATIENCE

"Do not be a harsh judge of yourself. Without kindness towards ourselves we cannot love the world."
Buddha (490 B.C.E.)

PREMISE

Patience is trust and acceptance. Criticism nullifies these, as the child-self strives to regain control and savor superiority. Faultfinding attempts to mitigate the unpleasant feeling of vulnerability by assigning blame and responsibility to others. Patience is a confidence generated by a belief that we are blessed and eventually all will be well. Therefore, it is inconsistent with condemnation, exclusion or resentment. With patience, we persist and endure in the face of challenge because we reason and listen instead of renouncing and rebuking. We know that a flower will blossom, the wind will blow and people will be who they are regardless of what we do. We know that life is good and patience allows us to accept this.

INTENTION

I am as God made me. My imperfections are opportunities to learn and grow, if I just accept them and don't become defensive or angry. I can use my parent-self to reassure the demanding child-self, that it is okay to want and not receive. Many "wants" are false and what we need is all around us each and every moment of the day. Patience affirms this.

AWARENESS

I will write down five things that I now have for which I am grateful. I will further note, how long it has taken me to get these things. I will contemplate the role patience had in attaining these objects, talents, friends etc.

DAY 189—HUMILITY

"He who loves only for himself is truly dead to others."
Publius Syrus (1st century B.C.E.)

PREMISE

Yes, there are numerous, varied and insidious, external forces, constantly at work to make us discontented, dissatisfied and distressed. There are as many outside forces as there are outside remedies. However, even more intense is the persistence, tenacity and endurance of the child-self. Without prompting, from the superficial, the child-self will assert and demand priority as it valiantly struggles to remain a constant in our consciousness. The lure of the safe, immediate, and secure is palpable with every decision we make. Once we attune ourselves, we hear it loudly and clearly, declaring our superiority and primacy. But we know in our spirit, it is afraid. We also know that it must be silenced, if we are to grow and progress. Humility will help us through these times.

INTENTION

I must shed the skin of complacency, of unwillingness to risk, and then, move forward. I will embrace the fact that to live is to change. I will embrace the fact that I have little control over this process but I have significant control over how I perceive it. Humility will teach me that trust, patience, gratitude and acceptance are the paths to expansion and fulfillment.

AWARENESS

Today, I will listen for that inner voice of the child-self crying out for immediate satisfaction. I will silence it through service and compassion.

DAY 190—GRATITUDE

"Be content with you have; rejoice in the way things are. When you realize there is nothing lacking, the whole world belongs to you."
Lao Tzu (6th century B.C.E.)

PREMISE

How can we be grateful for today, if we are hungry, alone, broke and tired? The truth is that we have a choice regarding what we focus on. We make a decision as to our fixation point, depending on our self-concept, our view of the world and our desire to either move forward or stagnate. When we make this decision, we can easily find someone who is better or worse off, in more or less pain, poorer or richer. Therefore, we can be emancipated from toxic thoughts and feelings by having the courage to confront them and change perspective. In this way, we also open our minds and free our spirit so that we may discover new solutions.

INTENTION

I can conquer my need to be pessimistic and victimized. I can move forward, focus on the positive and find resolutions to all current problems. I am unable to create solutions when chained to negativity, injury and resentment but with a positive attitude and a realistic view of my challenges, and myself I can progress with love, courage and wisdom.

AWARENESS

I will search for reasons to be grateful. I will list, in my journal, three of today's blessings.

DAY 191—ACCEPTANCE

"Reality is a construction of what we remember."
Fred Alan Wolf (2006)

PREMISE

To love ourselves, ultimately we must accept our history, even as we review, revise and restructure it with each new experience. We must shed our delusions of lack and debilitation. Ultimately, if we accept and appreciate who we are, there is no logical choice but to accept and appreciate from whence we came. We must eventually reconcile our early memories, flawed yet refurbished, with current circumstances and conclude that through it all, our decisions and reactions to those decisions determine our identity and have brought us to this place at this time. It serves no purpose to become a victim or slave to resentment. Blame and regret only reinforce misconceptions and imprison you with your past. If you allow thought of defect, defeat or disability dominate your past, they will seep into your perspective of the present and chain you to the status quo.

INTENTION

I am special and I deserve my place at the table of life. Where I came from, all the trial and tribulation, joy and jubilation, are parts of me. Most importantly, I can choose what memories I will use for growth and those I will leave behind in the attic of my personal history.

AWARENESS

If possible, I will reach out to a relative and contact them through a letter, e-mail or phone. I will honor that part of me which is from them.

DAY 192—PATIENCE

"If you believed more in life, you would pace yourself and trust in the beneficence of the Universe."
Frederick Nietzsche (1890)

PREMISE

Culture militates against serenity and maturation, so it is an uphill battle to delay gratification and to consider the repercussions of becoming a cog of consumerism. The culture caters to our child-self, with the message that all good things must come immediately and to wait is the equivalent of being rejected. We are told through the media that if we are loved it must be demonstrated by an expensive purchase and that we "deserve" to have immediate gratification. The distinction between needs and desires is purposely blurred and we become immersed in an atmosphere of urgency, disappointment, dissatisfaction and deprivation.

INTENTION

I will keep focus on the "now." I am more than my impulses and I have the strength, courage and perseverance to step back from desire, whimsy and passion. In this way, my rational parent takes control and I can move forward towards my goals.

AWARENESS

I will note three occasions today where I stopped, relaxed and took notice of my surroundings. I will then readjust, as needed, and pray for patience and guidance.

DAY 193—HUMILITY

"Delay is a decision we make."
Theodore Sorensen (1963)

PREMISE

The child-self wants control every minute of every day. It is fearful of trust and fearful of transformation. It wants immediate satisfaction, certainty and stagnation. When you have the urge to do something else, to challenge yourself, to start a new project etc. that fear of failure in your belly, those doubts that disturb you, that voice, that screams "No"; that is your child-self, whining, crying, demanding that things stay the same. It fights to control you and keep you dependent, distrustful, and immobile. No matter how bad things are, no matter how desperate and despairing the situation, your child-self proclaims, "nothing is as bad as change."

INTENTION

I can face the truth. I am capable of accepting that change is necessary to achieve my destiny. To fight change is to be contrary to the will of my Creator and contrary to my internal imperative to grow and prosper. I will cease running, avoiding and delaying. Today I will say, "Yes." I will look life in the face, I will pray for guidance and I will move forward with love and compassion.

AWARENESS

I will focus on my fears and my reluctance to do something different and to try something new. Today, I will face my fear of change and growth. I will approach an habitual problem in a new way.

DAY 194—GRATITUDE

"Our greatest foes, and whom we must chiefly combat, are within."
Miguel De Cervantes (1610)

PREMISE

Through a lens of gratitude, we can accomplish our role and responsibility in promoting compassion and service, rather than indulging in a narrow focus of judgment, comparison and impatience. There will always be occasions when we encounter a self-imposed wall that is too towering to surmount and too expansive to circumvent. If we instead, focus on abundance and gratitude, we will create the courage to change our perspective to one of competence and fulfillment. This is what gratitude generates and this is how we succeed. We must remind ourselves daily that we always have what we need but we rarely have the trust and confidence to seek and find it.

INTENTION

I am strong enough and smart enough to recognize and overcome the negative self-talk that has plagued me for so long. Each day, I learn and each day I can improve by identifying and combating those times when a self-sabotaging soliloquy asserts itself. I was created to be happy and fulfilled. This can happen when I confront those time worn clichés that say I am not worthy of happiness and contentment.

AWARENESS

I will take notice of the frequent messages that say "I can't", "I'm unable", "I'm defective", etc. Today, I will perform one act that is positive but which I've resisted for a long time. I will note this in my journal.

DAY 195—ACCEPTANCE

"Of all the dangerous energies that can breed inside our minds, one of the most harmful to our contentment is the wish that things were otherwise."
James Hoover (1977)

PREMISE

Acceptance is one of the four spiritual qualities that we must cultivate in order to live a peaceful and fulfilled life. It is one of the four personal qualities that supports love, wisdom and courage, the primary components of contentment. The central challenge in developing the attitude of acceptance is to temper arrogance, anger, jealousy and greed, so that our spiritual path is clear and our focus becomes humility, acceptance and love. As we grow, our goal becomes service, self-discovery and self-awareness. We begin to learn who we really are, as we gather the courage to face truth and destroy the myths and delusions from our past. This creates a new identity and understanding of our purpose in life as well as a renewed viewpoint of the world we inhabit.

INTENTION

I can control the child-self, so that its arrogance and self-indulgence does not interfere with the development of my spiritual goals. I will identify the frequent intrusive incidents where I hear the child-self demand, "Me! Me! Me!" and I will humbly ask for the strength to focus on another thought, person or circumstance.

AWARENESS

I will become acutely aware of what is and I will intend to avoid the "should", "would" and "could", which prevent contentment and fuel dissatisfaction.

DAY 196—PATIENCE

"Seek not to change the world, but choose to change your mind about the world."
A Course in Miracles (1976)

PREMISE

Humility begets gratitude that then generates patience and acceptance. Be in the moment. Question the difference between "needs" and "wants". Hear the message you are given and ask: "Do I really need this right now?" Listen to your inner wisdom, enjoy the Universe and give thanks not cash. Treasure what is and you won't need to purchase what may be. We must lose the arrogance of self-importance: the illogic of: "if I want it, I must need it and I must have it now because I deserve it." We must cease to be an automaton of acquisition, placing our self-worth and identity on the price and the number of objects that we own.

INTENTION

I can separate "needs" from "wants", the present from the past and impulse from rationality. All I have to do is stop, breathe and ask my Higher Power to reposition my position as needed in order to fulfill the needs of the Universe.

AWARENESS

I will note one effort, one act, wherein I attempt to view another in a kinder, gentler manner and resist judgment, comparison and disapproval.

DAY 197—HUMILITY

"The absurd man is he who never changes."
Auguste Barthelemy (1830)

PREMISE

The beauty and blessing of humility is that it enables us to feel the vulnerability that arises when we realize what we can't control. Once, we have the strength to be humble, we have the strength to face the truth. The truth does set us free and humility gives us that truth. Now we begin to understand how little we control. Are we therefore powerless? How do we proceed? The Serenity Prayer gives us the answer. We begin to focus on those few things we can control. Our thoughts, our perspective and the consequent emotions these sensations arouse are the areas of potential effectiveness. This is our new domain and the starting point for growth and evolution. We can choose to observe, assess, consider and then act. In these things, we have control. We can also make the choice to trust and believe in a force greater than ourselves. Herein lies the wonder of humility.

INTENTION

I am strong because I know where I am weak. I am perfectly me, with blemishes and weaknesses. I am capable of working to improve the lives and perspectives of those I encounter. I can do this. I can and will break from the past, as I comprehend that my humanity is the bridge to my true spiritual self and service is the vehicle I can utilize towards a contented and serene life.

AWARENESS

Today, I will watch how events unfold without my help. I will accept my lack of control over most external things and I will trust in the benevolence of my Higher Power.

DAY 198—GRATITUDE

"Every man supposes himself not to be fully understood or appreciated."
Ralph Waldo Emerson (1840)

PREMISE

In any moment, we can choose to appreciate what we have and we will find that it is all that we need to achieve our goals and to overcome adversity. However, we must avoid the pitfalls and imprisonment of self-pity, in order to acknowledge the abundance surrounding us. By staying focused, separating from the past and our preconceived notions of failure, we can become filled with joy and gratitude. When all else fails, if we serve others, our spirit will soar.

INTENTION

I can see beyond myself. I can make myself see opulence instead of scarcity, possibility instead of limit, love instead of fear. As I trust in the beneficence of both my spirit and that of others, I will attain that courage necessary to see the positive potential and the effectiveness of every act that spreads gentleness and joy. I am grateful for this insight.

AWARENESS

I will seek the Good in all acts and discern the lessons of all errors. I will review the Good deeds of the day and write two examples in my journal. I will ponder my progress and be grateful for the advancement I have made. I will say a prayer of gratitude for not being the center of the Universe.

DAY 199—ACCEPTANCE

"Every man is a piece of the continent, a part of the main."
John Donne (1623)

PREMISE

To accept and forgive our self is to embrace all that is human. It is to see in others, kinship and kindness. It is to derive strength and greater self-acceptance from the unity and closeness we feel with our fellow journeyer's. Thus, through acceptance, a mutually reinforcing cycle develops, increasing our spirituality and contentment. True self-acceptance is a gift to others and our self. It requires honesty and integrity to face our shortcomings with caring and our strengths with skepticism as well as obligation. Acceptance is the ability to perceive our self and others both as we are and as we can be. The result is a more loving and tolerant person as well as a more compassionate and inclusive life.

INTENTION

I can focus on unity rather than uniqueness, acceptance rather than exclusion, love rather than fear. I have the strength and endurance to overcome the constant needs of my impulses (child-self). I can free myself from this self-imposed confinement, move into the light and choose the unity of spirit over the isolation of narcissism. I understand that condemning another or myself is a futile act that serves only to reinforce a false sense of control. If I live and give others the same right, I have no need to vilify, judge or compare.

AWARENESS

Today, I will focus on my kinship with others, even those whom I don't like. I will pick one person who is a particular irritant, say a prayer for them and write in my journal five ways in which we are similar.

DAY 200—PATIENCE

"All things come round to him who will but wait."
Henry Wadsworth Longfellow (1857)

PREMISE

Fear significantly impedes the cultivation of patience. Patience requires trust. We must trust in our ability to cope with change and in the benevolence of that cosmos which demands such change. Without this trust, we will easily become irritable, intolerant and impetuous. Ultimately, patience reinforces acceptance so that we can now tolerate those people, places and things that would ordinarily cause stress, anger and anxiety. The issue is to reframe and reinterpret the circumstance (change our perspective and the way we consider a stressful situation) so that we do not allow the inner stress (uncomfortable emotion) to distort judgment and thereby influence response. In essence, we cope with and neutralize fear by interpreting the situation differently.

INTENTION

What I need is always around me. I can choose to simply stop and pray for the knowledge of my goal and my role in attaining that goal. I will have the intent and perseverance to follow through on that awareness and to move forward with courage, compassion, and persistence.

AWARENESS

Today, I will note one instance where I observe my fear, anxiety or discomfort to interfere with my patience. I will attempt to identify and note the object of my distress and how it made me irritable, intolerant and indignant.

DAY 201—GRATITUDE

"The desire for imaginary benefits often involves the loss of present blessings."
Aesop (c. 550 B.C.E.)

PREMISE

The purpose of media advertising is to create "wants" and conflate these with "needs." Thus begins, a cycle of useless consumption, leading to constant disappointment, frustration, resentment, and fear. We are robbed of gratitude, of savoring what we have and we are left with dissatisfaction and desire, helplessness and hopelessness. We can't understand that what we seek is what we already possess. Instead, we focus on what we don't have, how we are lacking, and what others have. Thus, we feel depressed, deficient, defective and destitute.

INTENTION

I have a choice and I do not need to submit to pessimism and helplessness. I can look to a fulfilling future and make the present pleasant. I can go beyond the child-self, take control and responsibility as I achieve my goals, one by one, and a day at a time. I have the power to take the first step, small as it might be and to remember that no step is so small that it doesn't signal a new beginning.

AWARENESS

Today, I will focus on the small steps to growth and achievement. I will make a special effort to face the unknown, the uncomfortable, and the untested. I will realize and act on the fact that no effort towards growth goes unrewarded. I will move forward in love and compassion and I will be grateful for each step I take.

DAY 202—ACCEPTANCE

"What we are today comes from our thoughts of yesterday . . ."
Buddha (c. 500 B.C.E.)

PREMISE

You are perfectly you and the result of an imperfect life story. If you are content with whom you are now, no matter what happened then, no matter how painful or destructive the circumstances, you survived and you learned skills that led to growth. The lessons may have been difficult but they helped determine how you view yourself and how you respond to the world, at this time. You are here, now, and this is exactly where you should be. Extract the gift of growth, gratitude and learning from the past. In this moment, as you read these words, your thoughts merge the past, present and future. It is your responsibility to recreate yourself and fulfill your destiny. You have all you need to be successful right here, right now.

INTENTION

If I focus on being grateful both for what I have and what I don't have, and accepting my current circumstances, I can better comprehend my special place in the world and the Good that I can bring to others. I will succeed in developing the courage to see the positive, to accept my responsibility in creating my reality and in bringing this message to others.

AWARENESS

Today, I will again write down three things in my journal for which I am grateful. I will try not to duplicate my past effort but I will revisit that entry and ponder the contents. The gift of gratitude must be earned and pursued on a daily basis.

DAY 203—PATIENCE

"There is nothing so bitter that the patient mind can not find some solace from it."
Seneca (60 C.E.)

PREMISE

Impatience arises when we feel immobilized, vulnerable and powerless. It originates from beliefs such as; "I'll never get this done in time," or "This is too much" etc. Usually the child-self chimes in with something like: "You'll be doomed if you don't succeed." During such disturbances, patience helps us regain composure, as we step back, reframe perspective and dissect the current impediment into smaller, more manageable pieces. In this way, we begin to focus on what we can control as the disorder and distress subsides. As we improve in this skill, we began to gain confidence in our ability to cope with the stressful and the unpredictable. We become empowered and disciplined as our confidence grows and we confront change and surprise with tolerance and reflection.

INTENTION

I will uncover the assumptions, prejudices and distortions behind my impatience, once I get into the habit of pausing and reflecting on my thinking. Impatience is simply unrealistic expectations combined with arrogance ("things must be as I wish") and impulsivity ("I must have my way, NOW"). With humility, empathy and compassion, I can dominate and overcome such unpleasantness. I can infuse patience with reason in order to master intolerance and recklessness.

AWARENESS

I will write about the aspects of a situation that I can change. I will clarify how I can choose to view one facet of a familiar but challenging circumstance differently. I will note that feature in my journal.

PART FOUR

LOVE, WISDOM, COURAGE THE ULTIMATE GOAL

DAYS 204—302

Spiritual leaders and influential philosophers of both Eastern and Western traditions have stressed the necessity of a life ruled by love, wisdom and courage. This is the ultimate achievement of self-actualization and is the result of continual practice in humility, gratitude, patience and acceptance, in every aspect of our lives. At this point you have done that and it is now time to move on.

While love is the emotional expression of wisdom and wisdom the intellectual expression of love, courage is the attribute that triggers action, energizes behavior and propels us to interact with the outside world. Each day with each relationship we are presented with obstacles and opportunities to either grow or to regress. Relationships provide us with the occasion to behave differently, to learn and to advance, through interaction with another. Judgment and comparison will quickly destroy a relationship and, therefore, must be avoided each moment that this temptation arises. At the life-affirming end of the spectrum, acceptance/forgiveness, patience/trust, humility and gratitude will facilitate the development of all relationships. Furthermore, these are the qualities that constitute love and wisdom and are traits that we need to express each day if we are to move to the next level and achieve contentment.

At this point you have accepted that you have a problem. You have also dedicated yourself through the last 203 lessons to solving that problem and changing the basic personality traits that led to that problem. You are now ready to move on in your recovery and to reassess, reevaluate and restart your quest. You are entering a new and more exciting dimension of change. All my goodwill, thoughts and prayers are with you.

DAY 204—LOVE

". . . the greatest loss I had known was the loss of my heart."
Tin Man, The Wizard of Oz (1900)

PREMISE

Love has many different meanings, from friendship or social love, to passion and sexual love, to a general feeling of goodwill or unity with all. For the purposes of this work, each form of love is considered to consist of humility, gratitude, patience and acceptance. Variations of love are described in numerous texts, often dependent upon the level of Eros or desire (sexual love). However, the author believes that all forms of positive, mutually affirming love consist of the aforementioned four qualities, each separate, yet each working with the other to form a synergism which alters thought, emotion, behavior, and therefore, life perspective. Love is also trust and respect. Above all, such a metamorphosis of self requires awareness, intention, self-discipline and most importantly, self-regard and self-love.

INTENTION

This is scary but I can do this. I can allow myself to love and be loved, to give and to receive. However, I will move slowly, always respecting others and myself. To love is to be vulnerable and courageous. Despite my past history and my current anxiety, with God's help, guidance and support, I can do this.

AWARENESS

I will list five thoughts about the concept of love. I will list three aspects that make me afraid.

DAY 205—WISDOM

"Wisdom is a virtue that pervades the Universe and is innate within each of us."
Lama Surya Das (2007)

PREMISE

If wisdom pervades the Universe and is innate, why are so many people, including us, doing so many stupid things? This is a question that many ask but few answer. The author believes that we must work to become aware of and then to utilize, the many attributes that are part of our natural heritage. Once we become enlightened, we can then access those qualities and put them into action as we intend the "good." Wisdom is the intellectual and cognitive expression of love. It is a "knowing" that looks through the lenses of forgiveness and compassion and is shaped by experience. It is making selfless decisions based on benevolence and empathy, not solely for our own benefit. Wisdom is a combination of love and experience, not simply a conglomeration of facts.

INTENTION

My life has meaning and my actions have effects. I am able to think and assess before I act. I have the strength, courage, awareness and intent, to evaluate a situation and to gauge my emotional reactions in the present. When in doubt, I can choose to pause, breathe and assess before responding.

AWARENESS

Today, I will be mindful of the impulses to act without thinking. I will make a point to pause before moving forward.

DAY 206—COURAGE

"Then, if you don't mind, I'll go with you," said the Lion, "for my life is simply unbearable without a bit of courage."
The Wizard of Oz (1900)

PREMISE

Without courage everyone's life is unbearable. We become slaves of fear and vulnerable to any impulse which will relieve our distress. Courage helps us face the truth. It allows us to state our beliefs and behave in a manner consistent with those beliefs. With courage, we live a life of integrity and healthy self-esteem. Integrity is living consistent with our ideals yet accepting with honesty our foibles and imperfections. We become enabled to move in a loving direction despite fear and resistance. Courage gives us the candor and freedom that fear impedes. Courage gives us a life perspective in which we participate effectively, honestly and with love. Courage is the behavioral manifestation of our ideas and ideals expressed in love and wisdom.

INTENTION

I realize that I have, I had and always will have a choice. I just ignored or delayed it. Now I know the choice is to live as I was created to live, in contentment, gratitude, acceptance and trust. I need courage to do this and I must work towards courage and choose courage with each and every interaction. I can succeed in this task. I will live a life of courage and freedom and today the journey will begin.

AWARENESS

I will define "courage" and write down how I believe I can express it. I will look, today, at every opportunity to embody courage and to feel the freedom that it bestows.

DAY 207—LOVE

"The supreme happiness of life is the conviction that we are loved; loved for ourselves, or rather in spite of ourselves."
Victor Hugo (1862)

PREMISE

We cannot love others until we can love ourselves. How did we learn about our deficiencies? Why do we know more about who we are not rather than who we are? As infants we had impressionable and docile minds and we needed approval, so we listened and followed those who would tell us about the world and our place and duty. They were not "bad"; they had their own agendas and their own role in to play, taught by previous generations and delivered daily to their willing ears. We could not question, we could only believe. Now is the time to question, now is the time to face the fear that is aroused by inquiring and searching. Now is the time to change and embrace ourselves for the magnificent creation that we are.

INTENTION

I understand that as I face my choices, I have an opportunity to re-create myself. I know that with turmoil, chaos and change I have a chance to challenge false views about love and myself and how they are expressed. With support, guidance and prayer, I can develop the courage to face old fears, challenge established perspectives and confront the uncertainty that accompanies change.

AWARENESS

I will list in my journal three feelings I have when thinking about love. I will ponder my history and state my story regarding experiences with love and loss.

DAY 208—WISDOM

"There are two things to aim at in life; first get what you want and after that enjoy it. Only the wisest of mankind achieve the second."
Langdon Smith (1901)

PREMISE

Wisdom promotes our ability to enjoy life, to moderate impulse and to temper expectations. Wisdom lets us enjoy the "now," refuses to regret the past or project our present difficulties into the future. Wisdom helps us both realize and accept that life is change and both the difficult and the easy will look and indeed, be different, tomorrow. Wisdom says: "tomorrow is another day;" while the child-self says "I want it now and if I don't get it now, I'll die."

INTENTION

I am able to enjoy life. My Higher Power has made life beautiful and it is only my self-destructive tendencies that change this process. I know that I am part of a plan greater than myself and I know that my Higher Power has given me all that I need in this moment to circumvent and conquer any obstacle. I can cultivate the courage to accept happiness, free myself from blame as well as resentment and proceed in pursuit of my destiny.

AWARENESS

Today I will list what I have and why I am grateful. I will list five things in my journal that I have been given.

DAY 209—COURAGE

"True courage is in facing danger when you are afraid and that kind of courage you have plenty."
Oz to Lion, The Wizard of Oz (1900)

PREMISE

Are courage and humility opposites? Is there any relationship between the two at all? Is there a conflict as I try to enhance both humility and courage? Are they mutually exclusive? The truth is that humility is the ground, the fertile soil, from which all the other virtues are generated. Gratitude, patience, acceptance, courage, wisdom and love, all stem from humility. Each relies on humility to transform their essence into unique patterns of behavior that combine and synergistically contribute to our growth and evolution. Humility enhances courage that, in turn, promotes action. It helps you acknowledge both physical limits and emotional weaknesses. Only with humility and courage working together can you be genuinely strong.

INTENTION

I understand and I accept the task before me. Too often, I have avoided the courage necessary to affirm myself. I must choose to take the necessary actions for self-affirmation because no one else has that power. I am accountable for all I create as well as my responses to these creations. Each moment I make decisions and I have choices. The effects of these decisions and choices are my responsibility. I will not shirk from this. I can and will accept that I have control over my life and that I determine the level my happiness.

AWARENESS

I will choose to be responsible for the actions necessary to create happiness and contentment in my life and in the lives of those I love.

DAY 210—LOVE

"No, 'my head is quite empty', answered the Woodman; 'but once I had brains and a heart also; so, having tried them both, I should much rather have a heart.'"
The Wizard of Oz (1900)

PREMISE

Every day with each interaction, we can choose to advance love or reinforce fear. According to many spiritual teachers, love consists of, but is not limited to, the four essential traits of spirituality namely; humility, gratitude, acceptance/forgiveness and patience/ trust. Every expression of these is an act of love. In turn, each act will generate kindness, compassion, tenderness and mercy. Such is our choice made each day with each interaction. We decide which we will express and when.

INTENTION

I can develop the courage to express love and the courage to receive love as well. I can shed my mask and become more vulnerable because I will trust in my ability to cope with disappointment and to embrace success.

AWARENESS

I will list in my journal three loving thoughts.

DAY 211—WISDOM

". . . but you will come to me tomorrow morning and I will stuff your head with brains. I cannot tell you how to use them, however; you must find that out for yourself."
The Wizard of Oz (1900)

PREMISE

Although wisdom appears to mean a variety of things depending on one's perspective, it seems to be universally agreed that wisdom is a transformative quality to which all should aspire. But like all the characteristics espoused in this writing, it is a process and not an end point. Wisdom evolves as we do. It is experience plus knowledge, viewed through the lens of compassion and acceptance. Wisdom constantly grows with love and reinforces itself. It knows that it doesn't know and it has the humility to ask, listen and learn.

INTENTION

I know that wisdom leads to gratitude and gratitude reinforces wisdom. I am able to use and enhance the intelligence that God has given me so as to create wisdom. I will see the world through "wise" eyes by intending love towards others and improving self-awareness of my blessings.

AWARENESS

Today, I will make a "gratitude" list of five things that I do not have and for which I am grateful.

DAY 212—COURAGE

"Courage is. . . . the foundation that underlies and gives reality to all other virtues and personal values."
Rollo May (1975)

PREMISE

Dictionary definitions generally agree that courage requires "facing danger." What "danger" is, how it is defined and how "facing" is defined, in many cases, is idiosyncratic and relative. For some, facing intense fear of snakes by venturing into the desert is equal to the courage of a soldier facing enemy fire. Every day requires courage, hope and perseverance, from each of us, to face tasks which others may deem easy, useless or mindless. The point is that frequently the "average" person underestimates their courage, tenacity and determination, because we compare, judge and undervalue the self while overvaluing others. Let's appreciate us!

INTENTION

I have the courage to trust in myself and in the goodness that is united with all life. I am aware of the constant self-critic that arises, unbidden, out of fear, that "I can't," "I shouldn't", "I am less than". I can hear those cries from the child-self, fearful of the adult taking charge. I can say . . ."No more!" as I move forward to reach my objectives.

AWARENESS

I will note two specific negative thoughts that occur to me when confronted with change. I will put these in my journal and counter them with thoughts of courage and love.

DAY 213—LOVE

"Love cannot attack."
A Course in Miracles (1976)

PREMISE

Fear attacks. Fear excludes. Fear is the child-self demanding yet vulnerable, powerful yet frightened, aware yet in denial. We must counter this force from bygone days and embrace inclusion, love and acceptance, if we are to grow and become content. We must question biases based on the past that urge hate, stereotyping and arrogance. Our identity and world-view have been taught and bequeathed, before we could question, without our awareness, consent or understanding. Now is the time to look inward, to conquer fear and acrimony, to question those ideas that would demean, diminish or destroy the different, the displaced and the vulnerable. We can progress but we must shed the imposed deprecation from the past and embrace all that we are and all that we have.

INTENTION

I know that I have made much progress and have come far. I know that I always have the power of choice and that the choice can always be growth rather than stagnation, love rather than fear, acceptance rather than isolation. I must act on what I can control and I can control my actions, thoughts and feelings. I will do so with the help of my Higher Power.

AWARENESS

I will document a situation that offers a choice between avoiding someone and confronting them. I will list why I choose to master rather than to succumb to my fear. I will give a brief sentence about the outcome of my efforts and my current feelings about my choices.

DAY 214—WISDOM

"You are wise when you live in harmony with yourself and with all of creation."
Don Miguel Ruiz (2005)

PREMISE

We frequently mistake knowledge for wisdom but wisdom is far more elusive and requires the emotional components of acceptance, humility, gratitude and patience. Although the Scarecrow said he wanted "a brain", as one reads The Wizard of Oz, it is ascertained that wisdom is the requested quality and "brain" is the means to acquire that. Wisdom is unique among the aforementioned traits (humility etc.) because it emerges from the others, with experience as a necessary component. Wisdom is the culmination of these interdependent traits as they are lived and assimilated during our journey to self-growth. Wisdom is the pinnacle of cognitive achievement.

INTENTION

I am aware that wisdom is more than facts, more than knowledge and more than intelligence. It is a head/heart combination that I can attain by cultivating the first four personal qualities advocated in this book. I am able with my current knowledge, intelligence and experience, to manifest these qualities in my daily life so as to approach the world with wise eyes.

AWARENESS

I will note one experience today where I can demonstrate a new, mature and wise response capability, in a relatively difficult, yet familiar, situation. In effect, I will respond differently to achieve different results. That is a sign of wisdom.

DAY 215—COURAGE

"Life shrinks or expands in proportion to one's courage."
Anais Nin (1964)

PREMISE

Courage requires both internal (emotional) and external (behavioral) components. Courage is as much, moral fortitude and perseverance in the face of adversity, as any physical action such as challenging an overpowering enemy or putting oneself in danger to save another. It sometimes takes as much courage to walk away as to confront. Courage incorporates and expresses humility in situations where we surrender control and manifest the strength to trust in a power greater than we. Furthermore, without courage our minds and hearts contract. Courage requires daily practice without which we create a very small jail where no one has the key but us. Frequently, it requires far more courage to live than to die.

INTENTION

I know my life has meaning and that I was created for a purpose. But fear and doubt combined with love for comfort and predictability, have created a mindset that resists change and advancement. Each decision away from the security of the status quo is similar to being in mud and moving forward only with great resistance and enormous effort. Today, I will try to move forward with the grace, integrity and certainty intended by my Higher Power. That is courage and I will begin to express it, now!!

AWARENESS

I will ponder how I resist change and growth and I will attempt to develop a strategy and approach so that I confront, rather than avoid, fear.

DAY 216—LOVE

"Love grows by giving."
Elbert Hubbard (1910)

PREMISE

Our power, our future and our contentment emerge from and depend upon, consistently choosing love over fear, acceptance over isolation, the "we" over the "I." Awareness of the effects of such choices, and the intent to focus on and to always do "the next right thing," will help us choose correctly. It is so important to feel the power of choice and to acknowledge the responsibility to exercise this blessing. We will lead a contented life when we are predisposed to act on our loving inclinations, instead of the aggression and narcissism fueled by the child-self's avoidance and ignorance. Love is learning, it is the greatest learning of the soul.

INTENTION

I have learned that I always have the power of choice. As I hone my awareness, I discover that every moment of every interaction is a choice. My intent is to choose growth over stagnation, love over fear and acceptance over isolation. I will feel my inner spirit so that I make these choices from the perspective of love, inclusion, acceptance and compassion.

AWARENESS

I will speak to a close friend today and reveal my plans to change my focus and perspective to love, inclusion and compassion.

DAY 217—WISDOM

"Where is the wisdom we have lost on knowledge?"
T. S. Elliott (1947)

PREMISE

Wisdom requires a peaceful and contented approach to existence that extends beyond self-interest and accepts a more inclusive, holistic view of cause and effect. With wisdom comes the understanding that we are not the center of the Universe. The child-self becomes somewhat mute and we are able to see more clearly the difference between that which we can control and that which we must surrender to God. Wisdom, therefore, is an ever-changing combination of humility, gratitude, acceptance and patience. All of these qualities result from self-mastery and self-awareness. They are interdependent and equally necessary in wisdom's development.

INTENTION

I have learned to look beyond myself as I view others, my world and myself in my world. I can see another point of view and I am learning that such a perspective advances not only my evolution, but also the evolution of those I encounter.

AWARENESS

I will write one attitude that has changed recently and I will cite an example of that in my journal, noting especially the positive contrast between past and present. I am making progress despite impediments and frustration. I will continue with this good fight and pray for courage as I seek support.

DAY 218—COURAGE

"There is no living thing that is not afraid when it faces danger."
Oz to Lion, The Wizard of Oz (1900)

PREMISE

The response to the danger that can come from without is frequently called "fear." The state of having fear is called "afraid." Danger also comes from within. It can be physical pain signaling the body is under internal attack or it can be imagined danger also known as "anxiety." Each limits our functioning and each feels real. It is crucial that we heed and respond to the signals from either state. We can then delineate and execute a strategy or plan of action. Courage is required in each and every stage. It is necessary to face the "danger" or "painful" signal as something that must be acknowledged. We must be aware, intend growth and be proactive so that life patterns may resume and we can move forward with our progress and goal seeking.

INTENTION

I am aware of my fears and my anxieties. I will work to create the courage and to choose the actions that will confront these impediments and allow me to move forward. I will no longer hide in the status quo and then bask in complacence. I will be alert to signs that make me want to remain "as is."

AWARENESS

Today, I will be especially aware of my power to choose. I will feel it, I will think of it, and I will act on it with the intent to expand love and kindness. I am empowered and I can choose, action over inaction, growth over stagnation. I will note in my journal one step that I take today to confront fear, hesitation or inertia.

DAY 219—LOVE

"An authentically empowered person lives in love."
Gary Zukov (1999)

PREMISE

When we do attain love, fear no longer dominates. A new paradigm prevails. We would rather be rejected than to exclude or not reach out. We would rather be vulnerable than isolated. In short, anything is better than living without love and compassion. Once we trust and experience love's genuine all-inclusive nature, we become courageous and believe in ourselves. Acceptance dominates fear, when we acknowledge that all Life is worthy of love, concern and consideration. We begin to understand that extending love is not dependent upon the perfection or usefulness of another; rather, it depends upon our level of acceptance, trust and compassion. We must reach this point for the sake of all.

INTENTION

If I view change as meaningful, as something constructive, I can transform my life in a positive way. I intend to learn from others who live in a compassionate manner. I will focus and be aware of how this new viewpoint affects my feelings, thoughts and behaviors.

AWARENESS

I will list in my journal three actions that I could take to show my love and compassion on any level to any person.

DAY 220—WISDOM

"But I do not want people to call me a fool and if my head stays stuffed with straw instead of brains, as yours is, how am I ever to know anything?"
Scarecrow, The Wizard of Oz (1900)

PREMISE

The assimilation of humility, gratitude, acceptance and patience into our daily lives evolves and expands into wisdom, love and courage. This may involve years of practice and perseverance. The humility, gratitude, acceptance and patience that you have been practicing, ultimately will serve as the foundation for the next step. At this point, a new dimension of living is experienced. We become more spiritually minded and hence more compassionate, generous and forgiving. Each quality fortifies and flows seamlessly into the other creating a cycle of reciprocal reinforcement. These qualities are inseparable. Each is necessary for the maximum utilization of the other, yet each is unique in its contribution to the whole, like fingers on a hand. With courage, wisdom becomes the intellectual expression and manifestation of love just as love becomes the preeminent emotional expression of wisdom.

INTENTION

As I focus and intend to develop the foundational qualities of humility, gratitude, acceptance and patience, I will understand that my final goal is to live a life filled with wisdom, love and courage.

AWARENESS

I will write in my journal one instance that illustrates how I am changing for the better. I will frame my past and my present in a positive way so that I cannot demean my progress, as is my habit.

DAY 221—COURAGE

"Courage is the thing. All goes if courage goes."
J.M. Barrie (1922)

PREMISE

In our culture, courage is rarely, if ever, associated with humility. Yet, with some thought, we can discover that the two are inextricably intertwined. It takes enormous courage to be humble because to be humble it is to understand our genuine lack of power. To be humble is to have the courage to realize that we are not self-reliant, not in total control, despite what the "child-self" would have us believe. Courage needs humility and yet we cannot develop humility until we have the courage to face the truth. Humility helps us develop courage because it allows us to see the truth about who we are. With courage, we continually discover our limits, foibles and imperfections. To be human is to be flawed; humility sharpens our awareness of this, courage then gets us through the day and transforms weakness to strength.

INTENTION

I will succeed in this task. Courage begets courage as fear begets fear. I can begin moving forward, simply by intending courage and being aware of those situations where it may be expressed.

AWARENESS

I will begin my morning by thinking about how I can express courage, optimism and self-affirmation. Living a happy and contented life is a challenge that I am willing to undertake because I do not like the alternatives.

DAY 222—LOVE

"Love is what we were born with. Fear is what we learned here."
Marianne Williamson (1992)

PREMISE

To express love we must we learn to trust and risk rejection. We must have the strength and courage to be vulnerable. Unfortunately, we would rather be safe than susceptible, exclusive rather than inclusive and rejecting rather than accepting. It is easier to be wrapped in a blanket of defensiveness than to reach out to show caring and respect for another. We prefer standing and watching, waiting for another to take the initiative, so that we can believe, falsely, we are in control and in charge of acceptance and rejection. No risk, no fear; no action, no growth.

INTENTION

I am like a small animal hiding in the bushes from any interaction with another. I want trust, I want to move forward and have a friend or lover but I can't risk rejection. I'm tired of failing. However, I know that just because I have yet to succeed does not mean that I can't succeed. I will look at the fear, consider my reluctance and determine if I should risk. I must move on with my life and that includes confronting my trepidation regarding relationships.

AWARENESS

I will think of one person I would like to approach in a more friendly way. I will construct a strategy, make that approach, and note the results as well as my feelings. I will ponder whether I am being too reckless or if I am being courageous and following the path to progress.

DAY 223—WISDOM

"The perfection of wisdom and the end of true philosophy is to proportion our wants to our possessions, our ambitions to our capacities, we will then be happy and virtuous people."
Mark Twain (1885)

PREMISE

The synergism of experience, love and courage results in wisdom. Wisdom notes when to move ahead and when to retreat, what to include and what to omit, what we control and what we do not. It knows proportion and distinguishes "wants" from "needs." It feels gratitude; grateful for the moment, grateful for friends, grateful for all we have. It focuses far less on the past or future, what we lack, moments lost or times betrayed. Wisdom embraces "what is" and moves ever forward in strength, love and acceptance. Wisdom "knows" that it doesn't know and that it can learn anytime from anyone.

INTENTION

I will develop the wisdom to love and the love to be wise. I will look at the "big picture," so I get a sense of proportion, appreciating what I have and treasuring the moment for what it is. I will make a point to thank a friend, gaze humbly at nature and view the present as an opportunity to learn.

AWARENESS

I will note and write down how I demonstrate wisdom by living a perspective of the "now". I will also write one instance where I expressed gratitude today.

DAY 224—COURAGE

"Growth demands a temporary surrender of security."
Gail Sheehy (1962)

PREMISE

We need courage to grow because growth requires adapting to change and change is unpredictable both, as to cause and in to effect. Courage allows us to loosen the shackles of the child-self and confront the obvious, as we move beyond the self-imposed limits of bias and comfort. Courage is the muscle of life; it is the little engine that can. It is necessary to realize and protect our ideals. Courage is also necessary to preserve relationships, to cede control (surrender), to love and to accept. It takes as much courage, maybe more, to acknowledge our strengths and assets, as it does to wallow in our weakness and deficits.

INTENTION

I will trust today. I will trust in the beneficence of the Universe and the goodwill of my fellow journeyers. This thought, fills me with dread, as though I were jumping into a turbulent ocean with no one to save me. But I can and I will swim. I will pray and I will grow.

AWARENESS

Today I will risk rejection. I will also risk not achieving my expectations and I will just try to practice perseverance. I will not be intimidated by impediments and I will not hide from frustration. I will focus on advancement, enlightenment and transformation.

DAY 225—LOVE

"Love is the energy of the soul."
Gary Zukov (1999)

PREMISE

Humility, gratitude, patience and acceptance, generate love and in turn are reinforced by love. They are part of your personality repertoire and therefore an integral component of your being. Love is a powerful connection to others and it is a force that is generated by self-acceptance. It grows by daily use. It can never be depleted only strengthened. The more you manifest (giveaway), the more you get back; each time, a little stronger, a bit more intense.

INTENTION

I can, with intent and awareness, determine situations where I have control and where I don't. I understand that I have little, if no control, over most things external to me. But I do control my intent and I can intend to do the next good thing. I will focus on this at the beginning of each day and reflect on my successes at night.

AWARENESS

I will write about one situation where I was aware of choice and how I chose to be loving, accepting or understanding.

DAY 226—WISDOM

"Within each experience of pain or negativity is the opportunity to challenge the perception that lies behind it, and to choose to learn with wisdom."
Gary Zukov (1999)

PREMISE

A significant part of wisdom is thinking about our thinking processes, our biases and our habits. Wisdom is an awareness of internal and external stimuli, our interpretation of that stimuli and the impulse to react in a specific manner. It is awareness of feelings and the external circumstances in which we find ourselves. Wisdom has the courage to scrutinize, to question, to show ignorance and to bow and say, "Teach me." It is a harmony and acceptance of the self, while ever striving to improve. It is the realization that we must embrace change and that repeating the same patterns of behavior will lead only to the same results.

INTENTION

I can rise above the negativity that descends upon me, unpredictably yet unrelentingly. I can prevent this from overpowering me and dominating my mood by choosing to reject the accompanying self-pity and to take the responsibility to remember the Good, the joyful and the effective. I can exercise choice and I can choose the positive, loving and inclusive.

AWARENESS

I will note three instances, today, where I behaved positively or at least non-destructively. I will especially note situations where I triumphed (continued in my determination to pursue the "good') despite frustration and demoralization.

DAY 227—COURAGE

"It is never too late to be what you might have been."
George Elliott (1849)

PREMISE

Be courageous. Achieve your destiny and become all that you were created to become. This is your responsibility. To avoid it is to become disempowered and imprisoned by fear, doubt and ineffectiveness. It takes exceptional courage to assume responsibility and to move forward, confronting change, impediments and frustrations. To progress, as is our destiny, it is necessary to accept the power of the Cosmos (God's plan) and it is crucial that we embrace those aspects of ourselves that we can control while we surrender those aspects of life that we can't.

INTENTION

I can empower myself by taking responsibility for my thoughts, feelings and behaviors. I can develop the awareness of a participant/observer and the intent of a compassionate, affirmative human being. I intend to actualize this goal and to be aware of the changes that it generates in my attitude and relationships. I will be patient in my pursuit and courageous in my attempts. I am responsible for creating the happiness that I seek and for attaining my goals.

AWARENESS

I will list at least three personality traits (e.g. perseverance, integrity, gratitude, etc.) that I now have and are crucial to my evolution and progression. I will delineate those qualities in terms that enable able me to use them in my interactions and daily life. I will write these definitions in my journal.

DAY 228—LOVE

"Love is the force of the soul, it is what heals the personality."
Gary Zukov (1999)

PREMISE

Love is power. It is omnipresent and at our disposal whenever we choose to manifest it. But we must "use it or lose it," because the countervailing force, the child-self, is also extremely powerful and fights for domination. This child-self (the vestige from our past) fears trust, acceptance, humility and gratitude. It resists forgiveness and patience. The child-self will deny and destroy everything that generates love as well as each inclination to be compassionate, unselfish and empathic. This is the struggle that is the human condition. This is why we need to focus awareness by thinking about our thinking and energizing intent by expanding love and propagating tenderness and mercy.

INTENTION

I can teach myself to pause, breathe and think before I react to emotionally charged situations. In moments of provocation, I can learn to step-back, depersonalize and distance myself, so that I do not make the situation worse by reinforcing negative energy. These are skills and they can be learned like any skill, if I am willing (intending) to observe, listen and change.

AWARENESS

I will list and recite three specific things I can control. This is important because it facilitates self-affirmation and empowerment.

DAY 229—WISDOM

"It is impossible to live pleasurably without living wisely and justly."
Epicurus (262 B.C.E.)

PREMISE

If we are to consider a new situation in terms of its effects on others, we must strive, each day, to circumvent the perspective of the personal and immediate. This is the compassionate side of wisdom. Such a viewpoint includes patience and trust. Similar to love, this is generated from humility and acceptance. The wise use wisdom in all things and understand that they have just begun to learn. Judgment and comparison cease to exist when love and wisdom dominate our perspective. "I" becomes "we", immediacy submits to patience and fear is replaced by trust.

INTENTION

I have the power to make a difference. I can extend good into the world with each interaction, each moment of my life. With courage, I can open my heart and allow the wisdom of love to flow. I was born with an innate potential. My destiny is to fulfill that potential. My guidance is wisdom and humility. I will ask for help any time of the day through a simple prayer.

AWARENESS

Today, I will write in my journal one instance of positive learning and one situation that confirms I am on the right path to growth and maturation. I understand that it is critical to my development to note my progress, so that in times of anxiety, distress and frustration I am able to move ahead instead of retreating in fear.

DAY 230—COURAGE

"Courage is to feel the daily daggers of relentless steel and to keep on living."
Douglas Mallock (1928)

PREMISE

Courage is a necessary factor in our spiritual, emotional and behavioral quest for renewal and contentment. Courage both empowers and motivates, as we discover our strengths and vulnerabilities. If we are to succeed, we must have the courage and trust to let go of our self-limiting and disparaging past and embrace all that we can be. Be humble and learn. Watch and listen. There is a plan greater than ourselves, devised by a beneficent power whose goodness and wisdom are beyond imagination. We have a purpose and we have the capacity to achieve that purpose.

INTENTION

Courage is confidence and perseverance proceeding with one step at a time during periods of crisis. I can develop such patience and persistence as I slowly achieve my goals. I can have the courage of focus and the determination to achieve. I can re-evaluate, re-strategize and re-assert, as I continue my journey towards compassion and contentment.

AWARENESS

I will note, today, what I attract into my life as I pursue acceptance, compassion and kindness. I will ponder the perspective that has brought me to where I am and note the difference this has made in my life and in the lives of those I love.

DAY 231—LOVE

"Your task is not to seek love, but merely to seek and find all the barriers within yourself that you have built against love."
Jalal Ud-Din Rumi (1268 C.E.)

PREMISE

We must expand our vision in order to recognize the blessings before us. We must magnify our awareness beyond the barriers of past preconceptions and perceive the promise of our future, revealed in the present. We are like children; cowering as we cover our eyes to deny the creature we created, the one that is lurking in the dark unknown. We are afraid and we don't want to see what is clearly before us because we fear change. Change presents challenges and the effects of change are unknown. As we cling to the familiar (no matter how destructive) and defer action and growth, we slowly die, resigned and smug in sameness. The tragedy of our lives is not the mistakes we make but the times we never try. We refuse to see, to trust and to grow. We remain in our prisons, unhappy and unable to move, looking elsewhere for our freedom. The key as always is within. Love can be the vehicle to liberate us, if only we will risk.

INTENTION

I can learn to look honestly at myself and acknowledge the barriers I have created to trust and care. I can learn to articulate what that "little voice" is saying to me, as I am confronted with situations where I must choose inclusion over separation, love over fear and compassion over anger.

AWARENESS

I will list and recite three specific things over which I have no control. I will ponder what I can do to regain control. Is it action or loving acceptance?

DAY 232—WISDOM

"Wisdom is being able to see beyond the activities of the personality to the force of the immortal soul."
Gary Zukov (1999)

PREMISE

Wisdom considers the greater good as opposed to the child-self's "good." Wisdom clarifies our perceptions, assessments and reactions to situations through lenses of love, compassion and understanding. It requires a substantial reorientation of a worldview from "what's in it for me?" to "how can I help?" Wisdom assists in this reorientation by inclining us towards unity instead of division, gratitude instead of arrogance and trust instead of fear. This necessitates intent, awareness, perseverance and self-control.

INTENTION

I am able to refine my previous view of people, places and things that was based on the biases and perspectives of my past. I can now look to the future while solidly in the present. I can see how my past influenced me without my future being similarly predetermined. I can move forward in wisdom as I let go of resentment, victimhood and myth. I can face truth and I am free to choose the life I want to live.

AWARENESS

In my journal, I will list two choices I made today with positive intent. I will note the results of these choices and how they are different from past outcomes.

DAY 233—COURAGE

"Courage is the price that life exacts for granting peace."
Amelia Earhart (1932)

PREMISE

In order to achieve wellness, in addition to freedom and growth, courage must permeate all aspects of our lives. To face the challenges and changes encountered in our daily travails, we need the courage to express and manifest humility, gratitude, patience and acceptance. Courage is the cost of being wise and loving. Courage suppresses the child-self as it elevates the spiritual-self. To have the courage to be joyous, to take risks with the purpose of evolving and expanding, are the goals of a well-lived life. Courage is not only necessary but also vital to this pursuit.

INTENTION

I will manifest courage today. I will be "me" and if I don't know who I am at that moment; courage will help me determine it. I have a natural tendency to fear, to remember the bad and to shy away from change. I will try to alter that tendency today, just a little bit. That will be my intent. The goal for today is to open my heart and have the courage to be patient and to love. I can choose to have the courage to see what is before me, and to be true to myself, whoever I am, in the moment.

AWARENESS

I will note my fear and how I circumvented it today. I will note in my journal one instance where I faced my fear, hesitation and anxiety. I will also document the "self-talk" that I applied to accomplish this.

DAY 234—LOVE

*"Love and compassion are necessities not luxuries.
Without them, humanity cannot survive."*
The Dali Lama (1998)

PREMISE

Again and again we are offered love. Now is the time to accept. Risk and be vulnerable. The rewards are far greater than the consequences but we must confront our demon-based fear. Awareness and intent will guide us. As we choose, we empower ourselves and reinforce the Spirit that unites us all. Through such choice, we make the decision to loosen the child-self's grip and to live a life of contentment and peace. Today is the day and now is the time to commit to love and freedom or remain in a self-protective shell creating an existence of isolation, self-absorption and delusional control. Just as we are taught what makes us laugh and what offends, what is beautiful and what is beastly, we can learn how to serve and how to love without being submissive or subordinate.

INTENTION

I can learn and progress. Each day I'm learning and improving on assimilating humility, gratitude, acceptance and patience into my life. Progress is slow but I am patient. I trust that I am on the right path. I'm happier and more content as I move forward.

AWARENESS

I will write in my journal with no editing or hesitation, one thing I learned about loving from my past. I will also try to remember and note who taught me this valuable lesson.

DAY 235—WISDOM

"Wisdom is being able to see the role of responsible choice and choosing accordingly in each moment."
Gary Zukov (1999)

PREMISE

Wisdom allows us to move beyond the obvious and into the spiritual realm of existence. It reminds us that we are primarily a spiritual entity inhabiting a physical body. This physical container of our spirit will soon die and decay but our spirit will live forever. That soul, that spiritual-self, is united with the force of life that is expressed in all things. With wisdom we are better able to channel and constrain impulsive responses and as such, self-mastery is more attainable. Instead of panic, we can distance, objectify and assess, thereby increasing self-control and contentment, peace and serenity. These feelings are the result of our ascendant spirit.

INTENTION

I am strong enough to see beyond the physical. I can feel the strength and wisdom of my spiritual-self so I am no longer limited by physical constraints and biological predilections. I have the courage to accept this and to love. I can move forward with empathy, kindness and compassion. This is how wisdom releases the potential of my spirit.

AWARENESS

Today, I will stop and consider all the choices before me at this moment. I will pause and ponder this three times today and document my observations in my journal.

DAY 236—COURAGE

"Courage is resistance to fear, mastery of fear—not absence of fear."
Mark Twain (1894)

PREMISE

It takes courage to live our daily lives. Courage is more than external and obvious brave deeds (saving someone from a burning building etc.). Courage is living each day to the fullest by pursuing our destiny and actualizing our ideals. Don't regret what "could have been" or complain about what is. The change you may need begins by looking in the mirror. So confront change. Choose the freedom of choice. Face the truth, take responsibility, empower yourself and move forward. It takes courage to cherish ourselves and to cherish others. It takes courage to learn and to teach. If we are to achieve our destiny, make a unique contribution and fully participate in life, we must intend and manifest courage.

INTENTION

I can do this. I can confront my fear and the deceit, denial and delusion that have me stuck where I no longer want to be. I can move forward with bravery, integrity and conviction. I can teach and I can learn. Others can be helped from my missteps and misjudgments. I will let no mistake be wasted.

AWARENESS

I will note in my journal two occasions where I took a risk today. I will note the Good aspects of this changed behavior and the motivation and reasoning behind my decisions. I will be aware of the positive self-talk that has enabled me to confront my fear and manifest courage.

DAY 237—LOVE

"Love is what heals the personality."
Gary Zukov (1999)

PREMISE

Although the practice of awareness and intent is necessary as we transact our daily routines and proceed with the business of life, a more permanent perspective of all encompassing love-mindedness is necessary to consistently achieve contentment. We must assimilate an attitude of love as part of our very being. The power of love has no limits and it is vital that we choose to participate in that power if we are to fully realize our destiny. As Plato writes: "Love is . . . the helper and the healer of all ills that stand in the way of human happiness."

INTENTION

I must keep reminding myself that power is behind my eyes and not in front of them. It is natural that I fear the unknown and change is the unknown, so it is natural that I fear change. However, I know that I have the power to grow and evolve and I can set a courageous course to accept compassion in my life and infuse generosity in my behavior. I know this and I can do this. I can choose the loving over the fearful.

AWAREN4ESS

How can love heal me? I will document, in my journal, one instance where, during the day, I behaved in a loving way as opposed to being fearful, rejecting or judgmental. I will also note the outcome and my impressions of this new course of behavior.

DAY 238—WISDOM

"Wise people internally understand how to regulate their emotions, body, and intellect."
Lama Surya Das (2007)

PREMISE

Wisdom gives meaning to our lives and to our interactions. It lifts us beyond self-involvement. We become more than we would be, because we are involved with more than self-interest. As we expand our compassion, so indeed our spirit expands. As we nurture, we grow; just as when we teach we learn, give and then receive etc. Wisdom knows that true happiness is found in serving. It helps us manifest self-control and separates us from selfishness. We must give it away to keep it. This paradox becomes startlingly apparent as we gain wisdom. When we mature and grow, wisdom dominates and the child-self diminishes. What confused us in the past becomes clear in the present and we confidently smile as we move into the future. These are the effects of wisdom on our lives.

INTENTION

I can choose wisdom to enter my life. I can regulate my emotions through my loving intent and intellectual awareness. I will neither suppress nor discharge emotion without consideration for others and the future. The insight developed by wisdom has enhanced foresight, such that I feel confident in confronting the daily challenges of life.

AWARENESS

I will make a special effort and intention to direct my reactions today with consideration and concern for others.

DAY 239—COURAGE

". . . the secret to happiness is freedom and the secret to freedom is courage."
Thucydides (431 B.C.E.)

PREMISE

There is no greater gift that you can choose to give yourself than manifesting the courage to be you. Who you are, your identity, is a process and an evolving event, ever changing as we gain more information and experience. Discovering yourself is not like finding America, although it may take as long. It is a life long process of trial and error, victory and defeat, loving and losing. This process requires courage. Every day we choose to show courage by taking responsibility for our life and our choices. Free yourself from the opinion of others, both the praise and the scorn. As you do, you will create the life you were meant to have by a benevolent Universe. Live in courage and you will experience freedom as never before.

INTENTION

I can and I will take responsibility for my choices and the results of those choices. I will intend love, acceptance, understanding and compassion. I will win a few, lose a few and a few will be "rained out." But I will develop, grow, evolve as I continue to manifest courage in every event and interaction in my daily life.

AWARENESS

Today I will pray for courage in the morning and tonight, I will be grateful for those instances in which I showed courage. I will document one such instance and give thanks for my new awareness.

DAY 240—LOVE

"Love is not idealization, it is acceptance."
Deepak Chopra (1997)

PREMISE

As we deliberate the question of our appeal and desirability, ultimately we will come to a point of humble and grateful self-acceptance. This is not complacency or conceit, nor does it end the quest to initiate or respond to love. Rather, it is a quiet, tranquil sensation that embraces "being" rather than "becoming." Love embraces the present rather than the future, trust rather than fear and patience rather than impulsivity. It is an appreciation of the "now". Advancing an awareness of love and unity will eventually encompass a more inclusive and compassionate perspective. This is a function of time, motivation and intent. It is a process that will evolve in its own manner and tempo, as we progress on our journey and begin to genuinely love and accept ourselves.

INTENTION

I know that my thoughts and my interpretation of events determine how I respond to a situation. I also know that other people respond, in turn, to my reactions. Therefore, if I begin with the intent of loving-kindness, eventually the fruits of my intent will blossom.

AWARENESS

Today, I will attempt to get in contact with my spiritual side, through either prayer or purposeful thought. Each time I begin to feel any destructive or self-sabotaging impulse I will pause, breathe and think of my higher purpose.

DAY 241—WISDOM

"Sometimes wisdom consists of knowing what to focus on and what to ignore."
Lama Surya Das (2007)

PREMISE

Change is ever occurring and ever present. We can easily become overwhelmed, if we don't focus on what we can control. The key is awareness. Thinking about our thinking and intending the next good thing for the benefit of all will keep us on the path to positive evolution. Wisdom helps us with the transition from self to others. It also strengthens and self-reinforces because each step away from our past is a step towards a new self and a beneficent destiny. Wisdom understands that the past is a transition not a jail; life is a process and we must continue growing if we are to be content. It is all cyclical and it is all for the Good. Enjoy the ride. Your attitude is about the only thing that you can control so be positive and stay strong and loving.

INTENTION

I can focus on my loving intent and use wisdom to filter all of my incoming impressions. Wisdom will allow that sacred pause between emotional impression and behavioral reaction so that I may choose in the best interests of all.

AWARENESS

I will renew my goals for the day as I rise and before I leave my home. I will review my level of achievement and note it tonight in my journal.

DAY 242—COURAGE

"Sometimes even to live is an act of courage."
Seneca (1st century, C.E.)

PREMISE

Courage is not aggressive, it is not obnoxious and it is not loud. It IS determination, trust, belief and patience. It is facing the challenge of change and choice while resisting the lassitude of the status quo. It is internal before it is external. It is feeling and intent before it is impulse and action. It is trust before belief. It is not force but it is power. It is love not hate and forgiveness not revenge. It lies in all of our hearts, just waiting to be called upon.

INTENTION

Each day is an opportunity to express courage. I don't have to throw myself in front of a bus, face enemy fire or be pummeled for my beliefs. I can get out of bed; perform my daily tasks and return to rest. I can do so with love, humility, acceptance and compassion. This is courage and this I can to.

AWARENESS

Today I will call upon courage. I will make a special effort with a special intent to feel the power of my spiritual self.

DAY 243—LOVE

"If you truly love yourself, you will never hurt another."
Buddha (523 B.C.E.)

PREMISE

Self-love and self-acceptance are an all-encompassing sense of soul serenity. You will have no anger towards yourself, no hate, no regret because you are now exactly where you should be despite miscalculations and misjudgments. Therefore, you have no energy left for anger to propel either inward, towards you, or outward, in the form of resentment and retribution, towards another. In this state, you have a feeling and a knowing that you are where you should be, as a unique participant in a process much greater than yourself. You are a single yet significant part of a divine whole. Like a solitary brick in a Gothic Cathedral, you are singular and small but essential to the entire structure. We know that we are lovable and we feel the love that encompasses us.

INTENTION

What I am searching for is a feeling, and feelings can be elusive and confusing. Yet I know how I feel when I am doing right and I know how I feel when I'm not. It is as palpable as a cold breeze on a summer's night. I know that I am afraid of losing myself when I have such strong feelings of unity and intimacy, but I can do this, a step at the time. I just need to intend love and focus on the next good thing.

AWARENESS

I will set my objective on clarifying and completing the next good thing to do. I will note in my journal two instances where I forced myself to reassess and reorganize.

DAY 244—WISDOM

"The art of being wise is the art of knowing what to overlook."
William James (1877)

PREMISE

One of the few certainties in life is change. As we become older, our perspective and our life goals transform. We begin to refine our reality as we create and re-create ourselves, in an ever-evolving cycle. As we age, we feel our bodies lose the strength, endurance and flexibility they once had. We begin to view our friends, both present and past, differently. Our goals, our past and our future, are each viewed through a different lens. If we have practiced humility, gratitude, acceptance and patience in our youth, we will achieve the contentment of the wise. Wisdom is serene, and approaches this significant transformation of our identity with a calm assurance and trust that our purpose and destiny are being fulfilled. All is, as it should be. This is the joy of wisdom.

INTENTION

I can face change with the certainty that with loving intent I will use such change to enhance my growth and evolution. I will see change through wisdom's filter and not through fear. Change is my Higher Power's message to move forward, despite its challenges and frustrations.

AWARENESS

I will seek a chance to confront change in a loving and reasonable manner. I will see change as an occasion to transcend not as an opportunity to avoid, delay or deny.

DAY 245—COURAGE

"You have plenty of courage, I am sure, answered Oz. All you need is confidence in yourself."
Oz to the Cowardly Lion, The Wizard of OZ (1900)

PREMISE

Where does courage come from? How do we attain the motivation and confidence to confront that which we've always avoided, excused, rationalized or dismissed? It can be generated from patience and trust in the goodness of the Universe as well as the self-confidence that we are becoming who we were meant to be. At other times when circumstances are not ideal, those times when all else fails and all the attempts at avoidance, deception and delay flounder; our Higher Power intervenes, gives us a good shake and forces us to choose what is best.

INTENTION

I will be proactive today in gaining courage. I will not let my situation get to a point where I must rely on the "gift of desperation." If I renew my intent each morning to live fully and I have the desire to face disappointment, frustration and other impediments, I will develop the courage to face facts. One step at a time, moment by moment, I will get better by doing better.

AWARENESS

What can I do? What can I do well? Do I do it? Today, I will ponder this and note my thoughts in my journal. I will begin to develop the outline of a strategy, so that I may make the most of my talents and be the most effective I can be, as I pursue my goals.

DAY 246—LOVE

"What makes you happy is not the love that other people feel for you, but the love you feel for other people."
Don Miguel Ruiz (2004)

PREMISE

As we grow and mature, we begin to recognize that it is not in our power to control another, no matter how intense or intimate the interconnection may be. This is frightening at first, because we feel our vulnerability. We have chosen to give love to another and that individual can choose whatever they wish to do with our precious gift. The more personal/intimate the relationship and the more dependent we are, the more the issue of control becomes restrictive to love and caring. Control is a function of fear and causes the other to resist. Like grasping at a slick object, the tighter we grip the easier it escapes. So let love happen. Infuse the other with respect, acceptance and gratitude as you receive the same.

INTENTION

I can be strong AND loving. I can give the precious gift of love and expect nothing in return. I can do this without being self-destructive because I understand that love has many expressions. I will give it freely without expectations, remuneration or recompense. I will respect and love myself foremost.

AWARENESS

Today, I will note the different expressions and forms of love. I will be more aware of my feelings of vulnerability and desire for control when I experience love.

DAY 247—WISDOM

"'I feel wise indeed' he answered earnestly. 'When I get used to my brains I shall know everything.'"
Scarecrow, The Wizard of Oz, (1900)

PREMISE

Life and growth require change and change is stressful. When you finish reading this passage, your body, and your friends and loved ones, as well as the world in general, will have changed in many ways. Cells die, more are created; wars end, wars begin; there is birth and then death; this is the life cycle; this is change. We can choose how to encounter and frame (perceive) the stress of these moments, as we experience our journey and the tasks of growth. As we ". . . get used to . . . brains", we adapt; we begin to make decisions consistent with our objectives and our well-being. Wisdom knows that we shall not "know" everything nor shall we always make the "best" decisions. However, wisdom also "knows" that we can learn and therefore do better, with each step and in every interaction. Wisdom also "knows" that this is as it "should" be, because we practice acceptance, gratitude, patience and trust.

INTENTION

I understand that wisdom is in the moment. It is not something that will come in the future without awareness. I can focus on the moment, engage my spiritual self and assess any circumstance with both head and heart. Reason can combine with compassion and I will be assured of making the best decision at that moment. Wisdom is an amalgam of qualities, actualized in the moment with compassion and viewed through the lens of experience.

AWARENESS

I will be alert to opportunities that help me explore my new sense of self.

DAY 248—COURAGE

"Courage is a kind of salvation."
Plato (4th century B.C.E.)

PREMISE

With courage we begin to take responsibility for our essential goodness. We learn to embrace and cherish ourselves because there is a reason and purpose to our existence. Courage assists in revealing that purpose and motivates us to fulfill our destiny. It is, indeed, our salvation. With courage, we will always do our best because we fear neither failure nor criticism. "Success is going from failure to failure without loss of enthusiasm"; Winston Churchill famously said. As we move forward, we realize there is no real defeat, only occasions to learn. Yes, courage is a "kind of salvation."

INTENTION

If I am to be truly free, to feel that no one and no thing can control me, to believe that no desire can rule me; I must have the courage to face truth, to create change and to effectively assess results. If I am to be master of my fate, I must accept this challenge and have the humility to seek strength, reassurance and direction.

AWARENESS

What does courage feel like? How did I express it today? I will note this tonight. I will describe what courage is to me and I will detail how I manifested it today.

DAY 249—LOVE

"Try to treat with equal love all people with whom you have relations. Thus the abyss between 'myself' and 'yourself' will be filled in . . ."
Sri Anandamayi Ma (1968 C.E.)

PREMISE

As we begin to realize the goal of our journey towards self-love and self-acceptance, we see our similarities rather than differences, we find agreement rather then discord and we actualize acceptance rather than exclusion. We discover ourselves in others and we realize that by serving them, we are served. By expressing love, we receive it. We understand and live by the belief that every encounter is sacred and an opportunity to bring forth love and peace. Again, the power of unity and of reciprocity is realized. As our love, respect and compassion for humanity intensifies, so it does for us. This, in turn, generates more love and caring. Such is the cycle of love to which we aspire.

INTENTION

I am one with all and no amount of consumer propaganda can make me deny this fact. During my best times, I can feel this union, the interconnection, the strength, the acceptance and the love. I will try to cultivate that feeling and re-create it during times of stress.

AWARENESS

I will note, one time today, where I overcame the feeling of stress and isolation and instead, I will create, in myself, a feeling of unity, belonging, and wellness.

DAY 250—WISDOM

"Blessed is the man who finds wisdom, who gains understanding; for he is more profitable than silver and yields better returns than gold."
Proverbs 3:13

PREMISE

Wisdom reminds us that the "external" can always be controlled by the "internal." Reality lies behind the eyes not in front of them. We are in control, so the feeling of vulnerability that is created by desire is abated. Wisdom soothes and offers solace. Practicing awareness, focusing on the moment and actualizing inclusive, compassionate perspectives are strategies of the wise and the empowered. A wise person understands that change is not to be feared; it is the routine and invariant that stops growth and the cessation of growth equals death. Therefore, we must keep moving and growing. Change is to be embraced and encouraged.

INTENTION

I can focus inwardly and I can put forth the necessary effort to see truth and to free myself from the myths of the past. I can empower myself by determining what I can control, acting on it and moving forward. I am able to do this, and I was created to do this.

AWARENESS

I will note three things that I genuinely control. I will also note five things that I do not control. I will create a short prayer of acceptance for that which I don't control and recite it as needed.

DAY 251—COURAGE

"You must do the thing you think you cannot do."
Eleanor Roosevelt (1949)

PREMISE

Develop the courage to examine, re-examine and examine yet again, your thoughts, the feelings associated with those thoughts and the actions/reactions resulting from those thoughts and feelings. How do they apply to today? How have they shaped you to where you are at this moment? In order to become empowered and to take responsibility for your life, you must delineate and articulate your thought process (think about thinking) and take full responsibility for those thoughts and their subsequent feelings and behaviors. What has been learned can be changed; new habits and patterns of thought can be created as you access your spiritual-self and vanquish your child-self.

INTENTION

I can review my assumptions and expectations as well as all I was taught about change, control, my strengths and my weaknesses. I can ponder my perspective to discover those thoughts that predispose me to an avoidance that eventually leads to confrontation. I can focus on this task despite my child-self's noise and distraction. I will succeed. I will embrace truth because the ultimate truth is that I am good and I am loved.

AWARENESS

What are my most dominant fears; failure, embarrassment, success, physical illness? Each is a fear most people have to some degree. I will choose which is most significant in preventing growth and which is most powerful in contributing to avoidance.

DAY 252—LOVE

"When you find love you find yourself."
Deepak Chopra (2004)

PREMISE

It is also said that you must accept and love yourself before you can find love in another. It is often our own self-imposed hatred and insecurity that urges us to control others instead of letting them grow and evolve. The fact is, if love is to flourish on any level of intimacy, from "hello" to a sexual relationship, we must accept the other "as is" and relinquish the need to confine, change or control. Love is not about managing or improving the other. It is about acceptance and appreciation. The friend/lover in front of you can be your greatest teacher and chooses to be with you at this time, in this place. Appreciate this and your relationship will flourish.

INTENTION

I understand that acceptance is crucial to loving others as well as myself. Although I can't change what is outside of me, I can change my attitude towards love, my behavioral reaction to it and my feelings about it. I finally accept that I can't control the world, or those who inhabit it. Knowing what I can and can't control is essential to my development and my achieving satisfying relationships.

AWARENESS

I will note in my journal one situation and one opportunity where I decided upon love over fear. I will also note the effects of this decision and whether I will continue this strategy in the future.

DAY 253—WISDOM

". . . but you may come with me, if you like. If Oz will not give you any brains, you will be no worse off than you are now."
The Wizard of Oz (1900)

PREMISE

Be aware. Be aware of each moment and every interaction. To be aware is to create choice and to become empowered. Do not go through life anesthetized, immobilized and uninformed. Have the courage to feel, act and know. Question what is and ask why not? No matter how trivial the emotion, action or thought may seem to be, awareness will make it meaningful. It will allow you to make a difference. It will give meaning to your life and meaning to your travails. You will no longer toil for naught. You will have the experience AND the meaning. Seize the "Now". Live in the moment and learn. Feel the Spirit; it is and always will be within you. But you must reach AND grasp it. You must trust in yourself and your destiny. Try and you will succeed.

INTENTION

I can be brave; I can risk and confront change because right now I am certain of my spiritual-self. I am certain that life is not as good as I can make it. I can be happy and more content with my friends, the world and myself in general, if I just let wisdom be my guide.

AWARENESS

I will be silent on three different occasions today when I am tempted to speak, control or advise. I will find a place of quiet to sit, and focus on breathing as I strive to experience and appreciate my spiritual-self.

DAY 254—COURAGE

"This is courage in man:/to bear unflinchingly what heaven sends."
Euripides (422 B.C.E.)

PREMISE

We can bear any external event, if we avoid the child-self's cry of victimization, blame and irresponsibility. If we accept our history and our present as opportunities to learn, we will be manifesting courage. Now, we can begin to plan the actions required to confront a problem. We can move beyond our "comfort zone" and initiate action on creating a new beginning. With the confidence bestowed by courage, we can sharpen awareness and energize intent, so that we monitor our thoughts and comprehend the patterns that emerge. We can begin to receive the signals from the spiritual-self and ignore the incessant blather of the child-self.

INTENTION

I know I am never given problems that I can't solve. I know that, at any moment, I have all I need to overcome the obstacles impeding success. I know but sometimes I don't feel. Sometimes I feel scared, tired and uncertain. I will remind myself that feelings are not facts and that I can move forward. Sometimes the solution to my distress is simply accepting my situation and moving on to what I can control.

AWARENESS

I will list my five strongest stressors, both self-imposed and those imposed from the outside. I will assign a relative numerical value from 1 (least) to 5 (strongest). I will then create a strategy to minimize the distress from each, a step at a time. I will begin with the least intense and slowly work my way to the more difficult situations.

DAY 255—LOVE

"Love seeketh not itself to please,/ Nor for itself hath any care;/ But for another gives it's ease/ And builds a Heaven in Hell's despair."
William Blake (1820)

PREMISE

When we live in love, we do not judge or compare, rather we focus on acceptance, tolerance and inclusion. This focus will increase our satisfaction, contentment and serenity. The person next to us is a spiritual gift who can teach us to grow. We must listen and try to understand, as well as to accept what is said, even though we may disagree. Learn to listen so that you can listen to learn. Ultimate transformation emerges from the change that is generated, as a relationship evolves and matures. The person in front of us personifies love because they freely choose to be there. Our goal, when we are living love, is to cherish what we see and to be grateful for those who share the journey of Life with us.

INTENTION

I know it takes courage to quiet the "child-self" and to care about another. The child-self constantly says, "what about me?" "Take care of me, if you don't you will die." But I know better. I know St. Francis was correct. Let me be more concerned about giving love than being loved.

AWARENESS

I will note in my journal one instance where my child-self cries out, "what about me?" and where I ignored it and served another despite my fear and reluctance.

DATE 256—WISDOM

"Knowing others is knowledge. Knowing one's self is wisdom."
Lao Tzu (6th century B.C.E.)

PREMISE

Wisdom is knowledge that every moment of every day presents an occasion to give and express love, kindness and compassion. This is how we achieve a contented life. Wisdom is the intellectual control center, but it is only effective when it channels love and humility so that we accept the self, others and current circumstances. Wisdom is accepting what you can't control and taking responsibility for what you can (Serenity Prayer). Be responsible for your own development, not anyone else's. You control your thoughts, actions and feelings. Intend to love and leave the rest to your Higher Power. There is no wisdom without love and no love without wisdom.

INTENTION

I have been given the strategy; the practical knowledge and now I will intend the strength and motivation to face my current situation with wisdom and courage. I can confront my strengths and weaknesses, my dreams and my perspectives. I am able to do this because this is my destiny and I will strive to fulfill it.

AWARENESS

I must be silent to know who I am. I must focus on the signals from my spiritual-self and ignore the external noise of greed and anger, as well as the internal noise of the child-self. I will describe in my journal three different roles I play each day (as a friend, child and student), as I begin the first small step to discover who I really am and whom I believe I can become.

DAY 257—COURAGE

"But my people have worn green glasses on their eyes so long that most of them think it really is an Emerald City."
The Wizard of Oz (1900)

PREMISE

Have the courage to remove those glasses. Those lenses have you seeing the world and yourself in a manner that is false and needs to be changed. Courage will help you 1. Energize the intent to find the falsehoods of your life, 2. Have the wisdom to actually find them and the courage to confront them, 3. Change them, and 4. Sharpen awareness so that you see the genuine nature of your actions. Rediscover yourself. Break the barriers that limit your field of vision. See beyond yourself. Begin to search for truth and satisfaction within yourself and shun the external and superficial. To become empowered, you must take responsibility first, for your thoughts, then for the feelings that result from those thoughts, and finally for the actions that you take as a culmination of this entire process.

INTENTION

Am I wearing "green glasses"? Am I deluding myself? If so, are these delusions as much about what I "can't" do, as about what I "can"? I must review my life each day, with each interaction and note my strengths as well as my weaknesses. How can I use my innate skills and strengths for the Good of all?

AWARENESS

I will note three acts that I can do today to help others (for example, show respect, be polite, be kind etc.). I will manifest one of them.

DAY 258—LOVE

"I pray you give me a heart that I may be as other men are."
Woodman, The Wizard of OZ (1900)

PREMISE

Our goal is to attain a style and manner of living, such that all of our thoughts, feelings and behaviors are motivated and dominated by a consolidation of courage, love and wisdom. This becomes our primary perspective as we adapt, adjust and strategize with each new encounter and every event. At this level, love becomes the emotional embodiment of wisdom, expressed and energized by courage. Therefore, love can have the synergistic power to unify the most potent forces in the Universe. Knowing this presents an opportunity to view love from a different perspective and to use this positive power to achieve our goals.

INTENTION

I know change is inevitable, yet I resist. As I resist change, I resist my destiny and the love and unity that accompany it. I know that if I am to live a life of contentment, I must accept change and I must develop the wisdom to learn from it and the courage to embrace it. Without change I cannot grow. I must and I will find the courage to confront fear and live the life I was meant to live.

AWARENESS

I will note, today, how I resist change. I will write in my journal what specific fearful thoughts I entertain as I face the challenge of change. I will attempt to be an objective participant/observer as I document my thoughts, feelings and reactions. I hope to learn from this exercise so that I construct effective strategies to overcome my opposition to transition.

DAY 259—WISDOM

"We must become the wise ones and the visionary leaders we wish to see in the world today."
Surya Das (2007)

PREMISE

Wisdom allows us to accept that there are many things over which we have no control. Wisdom mitigates the fear of being powerless by replacing it with the belief that our Higher Power and our spiritual-self can resolve and overcome any impediment to our destiny. Self-acceptance is also a necessary condition to attain contentment. We are as God created us, perfect, yet we do need to modify some of the tendencies from our child-self that are no longer appropriate or effective to live in our current world. We have all that we need to be content, right here, right now. To achieve the full benefit of wisdom, we must open our eyes, increase our awareness, and become humble, grateful and patient.

INTENTION

I can achieve in myself the change I want to see. I am able to alter my destructive habits (child-self) so that I evolve into the Good person I want to see in others. I can accept myself, not based on what I own, how I look or whom I know, but based on who I am. I am a creation of the Universe and a participant in its lifecycle of growth and evolution. I can embrace my unique role in life and appreciate the significance of my actions on others.

AWARENESS

I will notice today, that what I criticize in others is in reality something I hate about myself. I will note in my journal one observation to this effect.

DAY 260—COURAGE

"Have the courage to be wise."
Virgil (40 B.C.E.)

PREMISE

Let caution go "a little." Get out of the "comfort zone." Move from the status quo and into the business that is life. It is scary, inconvenient and at times uncomfortable but ultimately you and those you love will benefit as the transcendent replaces the fleeting. The Serenity Prayer requests that we have the courage to change that which we can control. Look for control internally. Don't try to control, blame or manipulate others, rather direct your energy on becoming the change you want to see in them. With each action, reaction and interaction we can master our thoughts, behavior and feelings, if we so choose. So choose!

INTENTION

Yes, it is a paradox that I must strive to understand; give it away to keep it. Let me stop being "brave" and self-protective, as I rationalize and justify the status quo so that I avoid encountering what is before me. Like Dorothy in The Wizard of Oz, I must leave myself so that I may discover myself and come home. I must achieve the courage to face my familiar beliefs and myself so that I am finally able to flee the prison of the past and become what I was created to be.

AWARENESS

I will talk to a friend about what "courage" means and how someone "achieves" it. I will note the important points from this discussion in order to re-assess and re-energize my strategy for achieving courage, wisdom and love in all my interactions.

DAY 261—LOVE

"Love isn't love until it's 'unconditional.'"
Marianne Williamson (1997)

PREMISE

There is a vital interconnection between love and energy, each reinforcing the other as we grow and evolve. When we achieve self-acceptance, we develop a more subtle and powerful form of love that transcends physical needs and desires. We begin to accept our unity and connection with others as we simultaneously experience our own individuality and value. At the same time, we become humbled to be part of such an incomprehensible plan; we take pride in our power to contribute to this grand design and to make a positive difference as part of the totality. Love has transformed us into a more refined level of being.

INTENTION

I will delineate and deliberate those issues, feelings and actions that impede my progress as I continue on my journey. Through this process, my goals will become clarified and achievable. As my heart opens and I become less defensive, I will discover meaning, love and caring in each of my actions and interactions. If I appreciate the talents I have and I accept myself, both good and bad, it is more likely that I will accept another unconditionally. This will transpire because I will feel strong enough to improve and not shirk from my responsibilities by judging or comparing myself with any other.

AWARENESS

I will make a brief list of what I like and don't like about a close friend. I will then choose to accept and not attempt to change or control those qualities that I find annoying. I will look beyond those traits and attempt to discover a lesson from them.

DAY 262—WISDOM

Wisdom is a knowledge that ". . . everything we do affects all that lives and that our own seemingly individual existence is inextricably linked with countless other lives."
Surya Das (2007)

PREMISE

Wisdom facilitates the process of accepting ourselves, our loved ones and our world with all the perceived frailties, faults and flaws. It promotes and embraces an all-inclusive world-view. Wisdom is both a cause and effect of acceptance. Like so many qualities mentioned in this book, wisdom creates a self-perpetuating, self-reinforcing cycle of growth and contentment. It inspires us to be optimistic and patient despite discouragement, disappointment and dilemma. As we evolve, wisdom and acceptance activate love and construct a world-view that is all encompassing, unified and beneficent. A calmness and contentment pervade the self and all defensiveness is defused. We bask in oneness, trust and serenity.

INTENTION

Everything I do has a much larger effect than I had believed. I might not see it and I may not feel it but I know that my acts are important and that I have choices. Which shall I select; good or evil, life or death, love or fear? Each moment, in every circumstance, these choices are my responsibility and I pray to choose the "good".

AWARENESS

I will note in my journal how one of my actions can affect many people beyond myself. For example, I smile at a stranger, they then become less fearful and are more likely to smile at another, who in turn smiles at others etc.

DAY 263—COURAGE

"Courage means facing what we can't change."
Keep It Simple, Hazleton (1989)

PREMISE

Acceptance takes courage. It also requires patience and trust. Our destiny is to be on a path that allows life to be filled with satisfaction and contentment. However, we must first gain courage to face the challenge of change and the impediments that obstruct our way and distract our attention. The next step is to determine what we can do about the change that has occurred. We must have the courage to act on this knowledge and let the rest go. Both action and passivity can require courage. It depends on the situation. It is needed when we have to encounter truth and restrain impulse. It can also be required for doing good when we desire to do harm. To manifest courage is to have moderation and rationality rule when excess and impulse vie for dominance.

INTENTION

I will succeed one step, one day, at a time by facing what I can't control. I do this by accepting my vulnerability and the fear that arises from this acceptance. I will develop, slowly but surely, the courage to "let it go" and to allow vulnerability and fear to pass through me.

AWARENESS

Today, I will list two things that I cannot control as well as the strategies and self-affirmations that I use to move forward. With trust in my Higher Power and myself, I will view my circumstances as learning opportunities to grow and expand in love. All will be well when the Universe is in charge.

DAY 264—LOVE

"I am a Woodman, and made of tin. Therefore, I have no heart and cannot love."
Woodman, The Wizard of Oz (1900)

PREMISE

The closer we are to our goal of genuine spiritual love (this being the pinnacle of personal growth), the stronger and more powerful the child-self becomes, kicking and screaming as is resists its own demise. If we are to achieve our primary spiritual mission and experience the essence of serenity, we must extend and expand love in others and ourselves. Our sacred objective is to serve and decrease suffering with that service. Our ultimate purpose on Earth is to promote mutually loving, compassionate relationships, as well as to enhance respect, caring and empathy for those we encounter during this journey.

INTENTION

Each moment, I can choose to quiet the child-self, confront change and use it as an opportunity to learn and grow or I can run back into the arms of the status quo. I must focus and persevere. I realize that this is not easy but just because I have not attained these goals does not mean I can't attain them. I am not helpless and I am not ignorant. I know what I want and I know I have the power get it.

AWARENESS

Today, I will make a list of three things that I can achieve so that genuine spiritual love is strengthened. For example, I will be polite and respectful in all of my interactions and I will tell someone close how I feel. I will also strive to be generous and compassionate.

DAY 265—WISDOM

"As a rock remains unmoved by a stone, so the wise man remains unmoved by praise or blame."
The Dhammapada

PREMISE

What others think about us is none of our business. We have one judge and that is our Higher Power who created us and everything else we see. We simply need to "be" and allow others the same privilege. A very wise man once said; "live and let live." Wisdom helps us distance ourselves from the shackles of sameness as it mitigates the submissive urge for praise. We accept whom we are and view flaws as necessary for growth. Our progress must originate from the inside because that is all we control. Our thoughts as well as our subsequent feelings and actions can be channeled and comprehended by our spiritual-self. Ignore the fearful cries of the child-self as it struggles to prevent such positive growth. Let wisdom and love dominate your life.

INTENTION

I can ignore the intense need to be approved, loved and praised by those who know me, don't know me or will know me. I need to please only my Higher Power and to be strong in my principles. I know that I am now and always will be a work in progress. Who I "am" at any moment is who I know myself to be in that moment. Wisdom will guide me as long as I have the courage to allow it and the intent to do the next right thing.

AWARENESS

I will write in my journal by five adjectives that describe who I am at this very moment and three adjectives that describe whom I want to become.

DAY 266—COURAGE

"Courage is fear that has said its prayers."
Dorothy Bernard

PREMISE

If we are aware of the peril in a current situation, courage and humility can guide us as to what may be in our control but beyond our comfort zone. Therefore, we must respond to the challenge. Perhaps, it is time to ask for help. This is a form of prayer and an acknowledgement that although we have behaved in certain ways, this time the familiar response is no longer effective or appropriate. Awareness provides such a guide because it leads to wisdom. Awareness of the self, its weaknesses and strengths requires courage. We must recognize our biases as well as the patterns of behavior keeping us chained to the status quo. With this knowledge and the strength of courage, we can begin to choose correctly. A brief prayer, connecting us to our spiritual-self, will benefit this decision-making process.

INTENTION

I can achieve the courage to ask for help both from those near me and from my Higher Power. This will reinforce my spiritual-self, the source of all courage. I can develop and practice courage only if I acknowledge fear and the change that generates it.

AWARENESS

I will make note today of fear inducing situations and when I pray for help during times of distress. I will attempt to create an effective strategy so that I become more effective in conquering my hesitancies.

DAY 267—LOVE

"To fear love is to fear life and those who fear life are already three parts dead."
Bertrand Russell (1947)

PREMISE

Fear is at the core of dysfunction and the most severe impediment to advancement. We must loosen the shackles of the "I" so that "we" becomes the most significant aspect of our identity. When this happens and we mature emotionally, we become less fearful of trusting others because we are confident in our core and spiritual selves. We conquer the illusory independence of the child-self and celebrate the unity that is life. Rejection, fear and hatred (for ourselves and others) dissipate. Do not deny yourself this experience of love, rather cherish and feel its multiple flavors and colors. Embrace its fragrance and caress its intimate melody. This is a dance of discovery and tenderness.

INTENTION

If I continue to develop the traits of humility, gratitude, acceptance and patience, I know that I will begin to respond to changes and challenges with confidence. I will be more in contact with, and aware of, my spiritual-self and I will trust in the power and benevolence of my destiny. I will face fear and embrace others as the true "family" members that they are.

AWARENESS

I will note three acts of kindness in my journal for today. I will further record the circumstances that brought these acts about and the responses of those involved including myself. How do I feel about my progress towards compassion and kindness so far?

DAY 268—WISDOM

"What wisdom can you find that is greater than kindness?"
Jean Jacques Russo (1747)

PREMISE

To be wise is to seek peace and contentment, to contemplate the moment while being aware of future's promise and past's influence. It is to intend compassion. Wisdom detaches from the child-self and courageously embraces the spiritual-self. It desires to serve rather than be served. Wisdom is inclusion, love and nurturance even as the child-self screams to exclude, hate and attack. Wisdom is the knowledge that happiness lies in supporting and assisting another. This is our purpose, our destiny. We are one with all and any person can be our teacher, keeping us on wisdom's path.

INTENTION

I am able to be wise and not limited by past definitions or past mistakes. I can be wise enough to be kind and build on what I have, who I am and what I have achieved, instead of being weakened by what I lack, who I am not and why I have failed. I can be wise, independent and courageous enough to be positive towards others, my future and myself.

AWARENESS

I will make an effort learn about myself by writing a brief letter to a fictional stranger whom I am about to meet. I will describe myself physically as well as my likes and dislikes. I will save the letter for future reference.

DAY 269—COURAGE

"Courage is not simply one of the virtues but the form of every virtue at the testing points . . ."
C. S. Lewis (1949)

PREMISE

Courage is the reality that channels behavior so that our intent is put into action. This behavior generated by courage can be directed through a heightened awareness based on personal history and more recent spirit mindedness. In this way courage frames experience so that it is more consistent with the positive growth that has recently occurred in our personality. With awareness piloting our courage, our thoughts have life-affirming direction and our impulses are harnessed. Awareness provides us with a moment of reflection to pause and better evaluate our actions. Courage supports awareness because it gives us the incentive and energy to do what we believe to be the "good" and the determination to resist alternative paths that we've frequented in the past.

INTENTION

I will put my hopes, trust and prayers into action by confronting what I tend to avoid. In this way, I will learn and grow, one confrontation at a time. I can create the courage to face fear, identify and isolate its causes and choose an effective plan of confrontation and resolution. Taking just one step at the time and keeping my plan as simple as possible, prevents me from being overwhelmed and facilitates forward progression.

AWARENESS

I will compose a brief, personal prayer to use throughout the day.

DAY 270—LOVE

*"Where there is patience and humility,
there is neither anger nor vexation."*
Francis of Assisi (1225 C.E.)

PREMISE

Patience and humility are the archenemies of the child-self. If we are to succeed in achieving peace and contentment, we must reduce the power of the child-self by allowing love and trust to enter our hearts. Courage is the solution. Surrender and acceptance are the means. The child-self spawns fear. Fear serves stagnation and, in turn generates isolation, arrogance, aggression, envy and apathy. Each is unique but each is based on fear's many forms and guises. Fear is constantly morphed by our own rationalizations and self-deceptions. It hampers movement and growth thereby, impeding progress and love. We must become aware of this and have the intent and courage to defeat it. Love conquers all. Fear is the opposite of love not hate, so let's attain courage and proceed with love.

INTENTION

I know now that I have choices. I can choose love or I can choose fear. If I am aware of these choices, and aware that I have the spiritual power to make them, I will proceed in the direction of my destiny and I will enhance the lives of those I encounter.

AWARENESS

I will note in my journal one stressful instance where I manifested love and patience. I will include specific details of this situation. I will document what else I could have done and why I chose to behave with love and patience.

DAY 271—WISDOM

"Just as a bird with unfledged wings cannot fly up into the sky, so without the power of wisdom we cannot work for the Good of others."
Atisa (1023 C.E.)

PREMISE

Wisdom teaches us to focus on others so that we break the self-destructive cycle of narcissistic obsession. We learn and accept that we are not the center of the Universe and that feelings are fleeting and patience is the key to success. "All is change" and moods, both positive and negative, will ebb and flow like the tides. With the development of wisdom, our lives stop being filled with external delusions that serve only to frustrate. We become empowered, effective and compassionate. We develop a knowledge that we can never give more than we get. Wisdom helps us transform into spiritual beings, as we discard self-interest and silence the child-self.

INTENTION

I am wise is enough, right now, to know that excessive self-interest, self-love and self-involvement is SELF-DESTRUCTIVE. I know that a lifelong goal develops slowly. I also understand that success is composed of one good deed at a time and this perspective involves using my unique strengths to reinforce love and compassion with each interaction.

AWARENESS

I will make an effort today, a special effort; to extend love and respect to each person I meet. I will take small but achievable steps to actualize my objectives and I will focus on progress not perfection.

DAY 272—COURAGE

"Never undertake anything for which you wouldn't have the courage to ask the blessings of heaven."
G. C. Lichtenberg (1790 C.E.)

PREMISE

The courage that fuels humility is the courage to ask for help. The personal quality of courage is a crucial component throughout the problem solving process and effective problem solving is essential if one is to learn and grow. Frequently, identifying and articulating discomfort, distress or malaise is itself a generator of fruitful living because generally we attempt to ignore pain and its antecedent problems rather than confront them. So the first step in problem solving is to eviscerate any denial and to focus on our goal of internal wellness. Once we accept the fact that all is not well and that we have a responsibility to remedy the situation, we may begin to determine and delineate the core issues and subsequently formulate a productive strategy.

INTENTION

I will always be ready to have both the humility and the courage to ask for help.

AWARENESS

I will note the steps I take in the problem solving process and list in my journal each decision and deed from idea, to strategy, to action and result. For example: 1. Identify problem 2. Dissect into steps 3. Identify action 4. Take smallest action and 5. Assess results. If necessary, I will then begin at step one if I have not achieved my desired outcome.

DAY 273—LOVE

"Denying love is the only problem, and embracing it, is the only answer."
A Course in Miracles (1976)

PREMISE

Envy, arrogance and pride are each culturally inculcated. We learn status, stratum and discrimination through the persistent assault of advertising and tutelage by even well-meaning peers and mentors. We become what we possess and we demean others if they don't have the same things. We will never be satisfied because we focus on fabricated and illusory externals. These are predicated upon manufactured (in every sense of the word) "wants" and not on true need. We perceive only yearning and feel only frustration, as we seek the latest "cure" or prize. We create our own jails, as we curse our self-constructed imprisonment. The call from the culture is "happiness is close at hand; just jump a little higher, crawl a little longer." "Easy solutions." "No credit necessary."

INTENTION

I must continually remind myself that all power lies within me, in the potential of my spiritual self. I must also remind myself that to seek false hope in external solutions and to aspire to gratify bogus needs is to live in perpetual frustration and isolation. I know how far I've progressed in respecting the spiritual side of others, as well as my own, but also, I know that I must keep striving to trust in the goodness that is at my core.

AWARENESS

Today, I will think about how important love is in my life and how I tend to take those I love for granted. I will make a special effort to show my gratitude to at least one specific person who has supported me during stressful times.

DAY 274—WISDOM

"Experience is the only thing that brings knowledge, and the longer you are on earth the more experience you are sure to get."
Wizard to Scarecrow, The Wizard of Oz (1900)

PREMISE

With experience, comes knowledge and combined with a perspective of love and compassion, wisdom will emerge. Wisdom is the highest form of knowledge as it merges with intelligence, because it is the culmination of interdependent interactions between and among humility, gratitude, acceptance/forgiveness, as well as patience/trust. Wisdom and love are inseparable as is love and acceptance. With each and every apprehension, thought and emotion, the spiritually evolved individual, living a life of contentment, will blend and express these dispositions. The proportions and dynamics of the deeds will change based on circumstances but the totality of the intent will remain; wisdom will dominate and love will arise.

INTENTION

I will learn from my actions and the reactions of others. If I view these from a perspective of love and acceptance, I will continue to develop wisdom. My choice is to fight in order to stay the same (fear/flight response) or to change and grow (love/approach response).

AWARENESS

I will frame my actions and reactions so that I respond to my experience as lessons that help me grow. I will be a true participant/observer of my own life as I attempt to advance and change. I will make a special effort to forgive and not assume the misjudgments of others to be personal affronts.

DAY 275—COURAGE

"Now I am anxious for a chance to show other beasts how courageous I have grown."
Lion, The Wizard of Oz (1900)

PREMISE

Courage is not alleviation of anxiety; rather, it is overcoming and subordinating anxiety through acceptance, trust and perseverance. Courage is understanding that anxiety is unpleasant but not something to avoid, delay or distort. Not all discomfort must be eluded, denied or circumvented. In fact, discomfort should be acknowledged, assessed and overcome. Malaise, anxiety and vexation can be indicators that we are attaining growth, precisely because a specific thought, feeling or goal is out of our comfort zone (prison?). Subsequent to this wisdom and the lessons gained from our assessment, courage emerges to give us the "heart" (determination) to proceed in a new way so as to learn, grow and love.

INTENTION

Like the Lion in Oz, I am also eager to prove myself. I can feel the courage welling up in me. I'm tired of avoidance, denial and delusion. I can face truth and with the help of those I love and my Higher Power, I can conquer the childish fear that has so restricted my development and happiness.

AWARENESS

I will note today, one specific act of courage. One instance where, after determining this was an action for growth and self-affirmation, I moved forward despite discomfort. I will note my progress in facing my fears of change and how far I have progressed since I began this task.

DAY 276—LOVE

"Love looks through a telescope, envy through a microscope."
Josh Billups (1875)

PREMISE

Love, wisdom and courage can expand our perspective and free us from the clutches of the child-self. This spiritual, intellectual and emotional triumvirate can emancipate us and motivate us to move forward in our goal to become who we were born to be. These three qualities can lead us out of self-imposed physical and psychological limits, to a state of objective observation and impersonal interpretation (the "participant/observer" perspective). We can develop the courage to embrace truth, the love to conquer fear and the wisdom to see beyond ourselves. This requires time and diligence but it can be achieved and it is worth the effort.

INTENTION

I must continue to expand my viewpoint and cease judging and comparing. I strive for acceptance yet I judge and compare. Such thinking leads only to isolation, fear, aggression and hatred. Criticism is simply my child-self crying for attention as it strives to be special yet wanting to be like everyone else. Comparing is permitting the child-self to demand that its needs come first ("if they have it, so must I etc."), that it must be satisfied while it holds the contradictory belief that it is all powerful and independent. Despite all this conflict and turmoil, I can move on and ignore these distractions.

AWARENESS

I will note in my journal one obvious instance of the child-self screaming to be heard and what I did about it. Specifically, I will write what the message was.

DAY 277—WISDOM

"Each of us must learn to work not just for his or her own self, family or nation, but for the benefit of all mankind."
Dali Lama (1998)

PREMISE

As we evoke and assimilate the foundational traits of humility, gratitude, acceptance and trust, a more inclusive worldview will develop to focus our perspective as it shapes our thoughts, feelings and actions. Love and wisdom, wisdom and love will saturate our viewpoints and dominate our decision-making. We will begin to develop a sense of universal responsibility. Our feelings of connectedness will extend beyond those people we know, to all living things. The importance of our planet and ecosystem will be comprehended anew and we will gradually feel responsible for making change and helping others.

INTENTION

I know that I am part of a larger existence, a larger force, a power far greater than I can imagine. I know that I am able to harness that force as part of my spiritual-self and I know that my spiritual-self defines my destiny as beyond my physical boundaries and limits. Now I can feel part of the grand and dynamic unity that is Life.

AWARENESS

Today, I will intend to notice, acknowledge and sense my unity with all living things. I will document in my journal how this feels and what I saw that inspired (in-spirit) these thoughts and feelings.

DAY 278—COURAGE

"Courage is rightly esteemed the first human quality because it is the quality which guarantees all others."
Winston Churchill (1938)

PREMISE

Courage gets us to act, to confront the truth, and to move beyond complacency, rationalization and zones of comfort. The child-self will try to impede this motivation through denial, delay, or deceit. Denial is especially potent and brutish. It becomes an obstacle to success because it renounces responsibility for both creating a problem (by blaming another) and for solving that problem ("I can't", "It's too soon", "There is no solution"). Frequently, denial can be so blinding as to ignore a problem totally (despite feelings in our "heart"), as though the problem did not exist. Courage crashes through these areas (walls) that imprison us. If we choose courage, it will say, "there it is," "I must do this," and, ultimately "I will do this."

INTENTION

I am afraid to acquire courage and express it in my life because if I do, I will have to move forward and take responsibility for both success and failure. I know I can overcome this fear and reluctance, one step, one decision, at a time. There are problems (I can feel them), but I can solve them (I know it), I just have to begin . . . now . . . with one foot in front of the other.

AWARENESS

I will note today, in my journal, one instance where I changed my reaction to a familiar but destructive situation. This is one small positive step for growth and I thank my Higher Power for giving me the courage to move forward.

DAY 279—LOVE

"Humans have not woven the web of life.
We are but one thread within it."
Chief Seattle (1858)

PREMISE

We are taught to think in terms of dichotomies. Love verses hate, "us" versus "them", success versus failure etc. In the spiritual realm of unity, there are no such separations or conflicts. All is one. We are part of a supreme entity that is perfect (it is self-sustaining and continually growing). Each piece seamlessly merges with the other in unison. There is no "me" there is only "all." Therefore, what good we do for others we do for ourselves. The love we give away is the love we get back. Similarly, if we give hatred, suspicion and rejection to the world that is what we will receive. Fear is what we learned and we must overcome this emotion from the child-self so that we understand our mission in life and experience the fullness of unity.

INTENTION

I will continue to fight my temptation to think in terms of extremes. This was the easy path that I chose in the past so that I may justify avoiding change and growth. Instead, I will choose to reflect, to pause and to ponder. For the child-self, the overarching perspective becomes "my way or the highway," but for my spiritual-self I must understand, accept and tolerate. I know what is good because when I do good, I feel good.

AWARENESS

Today I will note in my journal three good deeds that I have chosen to do. I will describe the action and the results as well as how I feel.

DAY 280—WISDOM

"For this is wisdom, to love to live, to accept and to take what fate, or the Gods, may give."
Laurence Hope (1901)

PREMISE

Wisdom blends each of the spiritual faculties (gratitude, humility, acceptance and patience) into an essential world-view that emanates an aura of love and tolerance. Wisdom is the executive, the great organizer, channeling the all-encompassing feelings that mold love into a comprehensible and palpable source of energy manifesting in courage. The ideal and the real now combine, as we feel stronger and more certain than ever. Wisdom mitigates fear of the unknown and allows us to view change as a challenge that can be encountered and controlled. Wisdom imparts the strength of acceptance because it generates confidence in ourselves and trust in a Higher Power motivating us to risk and advance.

INTENTION

I have the courage to change, to be changed and to embrace change. This is both a cause and effect of the wisdom that dominates my perspective. I also have the courage to accept that which I cannot change. I know that at any moment I can choose to embrace my spiritual-self, to unleash the courage in my soul and to trust in my Higher Power.

AWARENESS

I will note in my journal, for today, three instances where I manifested acceptance instead of attempting to control, manage or resist.

DAY 281—COURAGE

"Denial is refusal to see the obvious. It is the child-self covering up its eyes to what is before it."
W. T. Watts, Ph.D. (2010)

PREMISE

If we are to manifest courage in our daily lives and thereby move forward in pursuit of our growth, goals and destiny, we must neutralize denial. You may ask: "How can I identify and then strategize to solve a problem if I don't see the problem?" The first step is to be aware. Denial is a classic psychological "defense mechanism" that can be called upon unconsciously (without our awareness) anytime the child-self feels frightened or threatened from the outside. Identifying this process is crucial to success. EVERYONE uses denial in varying degrees but it can burgeon beyond our control and the only hint is discomfort in familiar situations, unhappiness that occurs only at certain times and/or anxiety that prevents us from doing something that we know (in our "heart") is the "right" thing to do. Again, awareness is the key and intent is the means.

INTENTION

I refuse to close my eyes to challenge and change. I refuse to run and hide, deny and delay. The time is now for me to stop my usual response of procrastinating. Now is the time to act and to begin a new life of freedom and courage.

AWARENESS

I will confront an old habit that I have been postponing for far too long. I will identify the behavior and moderate the actions in small, achievable steps. I will document my successes <u>and</u> failures in my journal.

DAY 282—LOVE

"'I shall take the heart', the Tin Woodsman said, 'for brains do not make one happy, and happiness is the best thing in the world.'"
The Wizard Of Oz (1900)

PREMISE

Receiving and accepting love from others is awkward, if not impossible, if we have not yet learned to love ourselves. Once again, this is an instance of fear dominating, as the child-self asserts its power. There is no room for another because our needs become insatiable. When we fail to love ourselves, when we feel unworthy of love, we begin to doubt our worth and to ask questions that only we can answer. Who would love me? What would they want? Why would they love me? And my favorite: what is wrong with them? Self-hate, self-doubt and the lack self-confidence prevent progress and growth because we isolate, languish and fester in victimhood and self-pity rather than risk and reach out. There are many reasons to reject love and only one reason to accept, namely, to fulfill our destiny and become who we were born to be.

INTENTION

I can and I will continue to trust myself and in the goodness that is at my center. This is my spiritual-self and this is the voice that I must follow, if I am to conquer the fabricated needs of the child-self. I must do this to advance. With prayer and guidance, I will succeed.

AWARENESS

I will note one instance where, in the course of the day, trust dominated fear. I will document the event where I chose to trust rather than to avoid or attack.

DAY 283—WISDOM

"Wisdom rises upon the ruins of folly."
Thomas Fuller, M. D. (1732)

PREMISE

As Dr. Fuller states, we must learn from our errors so they do not become mistakes. Wisdom is possible because it knows and accepts what it can't control. Wisdom is patient because it understands that things happen when the Universe decides, not when we decide. Wisdom is grateful because it acknowledges how many gifts have been freely bestowed on us. Wisdom accepts because it comprehends that we are one and each of us uniquely enhances all life and each of us has a significant role to play in the life of another. Wisdom is a gift that is earned as a result of trial an error, toil and tumult. Wisdom gives life meaning and purpose.

INTENTION

I will admit to mistakes and I will apologize promptly for misjudgments and misunderstandings. I am now able to do this and, therefore, I will learn and evolve in a positive manner. I realize that learning requires mistakes and growth requires learning. However, natural, human error is of no value if I deny it, ignore it or refuse to admit it. Instead, I must have the courage and wisdom to identify my errors and learn from them. Learning is change and wisdom is learned. I can do this with the guidance of my spiritual-self.

AWARENESS

I will seek to identify and admit to another at least two mistakes I make in the course of the day. I know that I will make many more and that's okay.

DAY 284—COURAGE

"Courage allows us to face the fear of change."
W.T. Watts, Ph.D. (2010)

PREMISE

As we persevere, evaluate and assess our progress and objectives, we will continue to benefit from courage because it will focus intensely on our intent and loving compassionate purpose despite fear, denial and hesitation. The self-indulgent distortions that would divert us from successful solutions will be minimized. When necessary, courage will aid us in modifying our plans, expectations and goals, as we continue efforts towards resolution of conflicts and impediments. Consequently, courage plays a significant role in each stage of problem solving by the dissolving the defense mechanism of denial and allowing us to face the fear of change and the self-deceptive, self-sabotaging belief that minimal effort will create maximum results.

INTENTION

Success is a slow process. It requires the courage of patience and perseverance. Because I haven't met expectations does not mean that I can't or I must stop trying; rather it means reevaluation, reassessment and renewal. Patience and perseverance results in success. If I stay focused and trust in the benevolence of the Universe as well as the power of my support and the beneficent guidance that surrounds me, I will succeed.

AWARENESS

I will I reflect and discuss with a friend my hesitations and anxieties about confronting change and growth. I realize this is an essential step towards maturation and that it will take courage. I also understand that courage begets courage. I will pray for guidance.

DAY 285—LOVE

"Love brings a different way of being in the world. It brings harmony and an active interest in the well-being of others."
Gary Zukov (1999)

PREMISE

In our world of the physical, we live in a perspective of dichotomy, conflict and contradiction. There is love versus hate, inclusion versus exclusion, success versus failure. We are taught to be cautious in giving love and we are suspicious about who offers it to us. We are taught that love is earned; one must be worthy. Such caution serves only to confine and confuse our personal perspective that needs to evolve into generosity, acceptance and trust. When love reaches out, we should not reflexively recoil. When we want to love, we must not allow fear and inhibition to restrict us. We must cease questioning why someone would love us and whether we are worthy of love. God loves us, we were created to love and be loved. Love is our destiny and our only path, if we are to achieve contentment.

INTENTION

I know that I am constantly changing, as is the world around me. My choice is to accept change or submit to my child-self's demands of sameness. I must change, if I am to grow, and I must grow, if I am to achieve my destiny and be content. Most importantly, I must face the fear of loving and being loved, if I am to live life as destined.

AWARENESS

Today, I will think about changes, what they mean, how I'm resisting them and what I must do tomorrow. Perhaps the greatest change will be my perspective regarding love.

DAY 286—WISDOM

"The fool doth think he is wise, but the wise man knows himself to be a fool."
William Shakespeare (1599)

PREMISE

Wisdom is having the patience to realize that many events occur at times during which we have no control. Wisdom is accepting the level of mastery we do have at that time and focusing on that. Under such circumstances, it is far better to simply observe than to fruitlessly attempt to manage and command. Acceptance helps wisdom emerge and wisdom itself reinforces acceptance. It is said that acceptance is passive and in many circumstances, especially those over which we have no control, a passive response is the correct response.

INTENTION

I am able to acknowledge that I don't know. I will allow myself to ponder, question and to request an answer. I will continue to learn by watching and listening rather than acting and speaking. I can ask and I can follow advice. This is the essence of manifesting wisdom each day. I will be wise enough to understand that while the questions are eternal the answers are often transitory.

AWARENESS

Today, I will make a special effort to listen to someone rather than to assert my opinion or assessment. When necessary I will repeat what I believe I heard. This will help me clarify and to expand the discussion.

DAY 287—COURAGE

"A particularly poisonous form of denial is the denial of our strengths and assets, causing us to feel and believe that we cannot act when we must."
W. T. Watts, Ph.D. (2010)

PREMISE

Denial hampers progress and impedes courage because it obscures the wide variety of genuine solutions that are available to us any moment in time. In addition to complicating the solution, denial also masks, camouflages and disguises problems. When confronted with change we often feel overwhelmed, powerless, confused and anxious. This is courage being neutralized by the child-self. When fear and distrust overwhelm and bewilder perspective, we are inclined to reflexively and routinely repeat past behaviors, despite our experience that they are ineffective. Sometimes, we hope for a different result. Under any circumstances, courage is necessary to identify and overcome this tendency so that the cycle of self-sabotage ceases.

INTENTION

I will take responsibility for my strengths. I will use them for love, compassion and acceptance. I will have the courage to feel the unity that exists within all living things and I will develop determination and perseverance from that thought.

AWARENESS

I will list five strengths that I manifested today and I will reflect on my competence and abilities as opposed to my weaknesses and flaws.

DAY 288—LOVE

"Where there is hatred let me sow love . . ."
Francis of Assisi (1220 C.E.)

PREMISE

Self-hate, self-destruction, low self-esteem, depression, whatever the label you choose to describe that feeling of alienation, isolation and/or resentment, it is just another negative mindset used to separate us from our spiritual essence. How can you cultivate love in the soil of self-hate? Love, must be given if it is to expand and you can't give what you don't have and you can't have what you don't feel. If you are taught that you are deficient, deprived and disabled and if you never challenge and change these teachings, you will be unable to perceive the abundance, the benevolence and the kindness that encompasses every moment of every day.

INTENTION

If there is hatred in my heart for others, I must harbor hatred for myself. This is a spiritual cancer that I must destroy and it can be destroyed only by intending to help others and accepting myself as a creation that contributes in a unique way to the growth and evolution of the Cosmos.

AWARENESS

I will make a list of three resentments I have and a list of three people whom I dislike. I will then review the lists and counter the bases of these negative assumptions with positive statements.

DAY 289—COURAGE

"One doesn't discover new lands without consenting to lose sight of the shore for a very long time."
Andre Gide (1935)

PREMISE

Facing change and discovering new ways to think, feel and behave is indeed frightening. Courage is necessary if we are to overcome the fear and impediments that accompany growth. It is a fundamental temperament that inspires ("in spirit") action in all areas of living. Courage is indispensable for the expression of each spiritual quality that constitutes a life of serenity. It is crucial to daily living, spiritual growth and the Grand Plan that is our destiny. Courage gives us options in life and living, as it expands our perspectives and helps us break the habits that restrain our progress. Courage will motivate us to move in directions that we know, in our spirit, we must pursue but which we've delayed, denied and avoided due to fear.

INTENTION

I am able and I have strength that I've not used. Each day I become more aware of my abilities and more effective in defeating my deficits. I realize that I bear the responsibility for my reality and the life that I create. I pray for the endurance to fulfill my destiny and to achieve my objectives.

AWARENESS

Today, I will make a special effort to take responsibility for whatever happens to me.

DAY 290—WISDOM

"The seat of knowledge is in the head; of wisdom, the heart."
William Hazlitt (1823)

PREMISE

Arrogance is a mask we wear to hide the fear of vulnerability and self-discovery. Arrogance restricts any attempt to defeat the forces of stagnation and self-satisfaction. It is a manifestation of the frightened child-self, defending the status quo as a necessary and good situation. If we are to strive for advancement and achieve our destiny, we must face the unpleasant truth of our current situation. If we were truly content, we would not be reading these words at this time. We must look with courage at the face in the mirror. We must not hide behind blame, resentment, self-pity or guilt. We must be responsible, for the "now", and to pursue the Good, admit mistakes, learn, move forward and evolve, in love and compassion.

INTENTION

Wisdom is the ultimate merging of head and heart. It uses the knowledge of experience for the Good of all. Wisdom is being aware, perceptive and discerning as it understands, accepts and commiserates. Only through such heart/head unification will we achieve dignity and serenity.

AWARENESS

I will make a special effort today to note how many decisions I make with the head/heart combination. I will document one such decision in my journal noting the specific logic and empathic aspects of this process.

DAY 291—LOVE

"For my part I will bear all the unhappiness without a murmur, if you will give me a heart."
Tin Man to the Wizard, The Wizard of Oz (1900)

PREMISE

God makes no mistakes. You were created with feelings and a heart. Therefore, they are good and necessary for living a life of contentment. They can be guides to the soul or they can deceive and become enemies to growth and fulfillment. Each day, in every way, we can choose to be better and to be less swayed by our physical environment. We can enhance our goal of spiritual mindedness, if we intend to do so and make that intention explicit. Each day we must review our long and short-term objectives. Each day we must strive to fulfill our destiny, to be all we can and to overpower self-imposed barriers. So reach out to others, celebrate who you are and embrace life!

INTENTION

I understand that a significant part of not finding love is not loving myself and therefore feeling unworthy of respect and appreciation. When we find someone who loves us, we often wonder why, what's wrong with them that they would love me. My mission then becomes discovering what IS wrong with them, thereby sabotaging the relationship and the potential for love and sharing. I can overcome this, if I just accept myself.

AWARENESS

I will note in my journal, my intention to view the "ordinary" and mundane aspects of my daily existence through a spiritual lens. Tonight I will elaborate on one instance that stands out. I will begin to view myself as being both loving and loveable. I will list in my journal five things that make me attractive.

DAY 292—WISDOM

"The only wisdom we can hope to acquire is the wisdom of humility."
T.S. Eliot (1940)

PREMISE

With humility and courage we can overpower the child-self and attain wisdom. Humility is a catalyst to wisdom's development because it mitigates the natural but self-destructive tendencies of arrogance and complacency. These are rooted in a self-protective narcissism. Humility is the basis of all the life-enhancing ideals that propel us to maturation and serenity. It is the foundation of growth, the soil of virtue. Arrogance emerges from the child-self's insecurity. However, we must shed this skin and emerge, evolve and expand into a wise, loving and courageous person.

INTENTION

I will have the humility and courage to admit, as much as possible, to my confusion and the lack of knowledge. Hopefully, through this process, I will begin "to know what I don't know." Wisdom is focusing on the internal. Wisdom can apologize and therefore requires humility. Wisdom does not vaunt its knowledge rather it highlights its ignorance in an effort to learn and grow. I can do this. I can admit my weaknesses so they may become my strengths. I can develop the wisdom not only to accept but also to embrace who I am.

AWARENESS

I will make myself aware of the need to be precise and factual at the expense of others. I will also make myself aware of my need to control and direct discussions rather than listening and learning. These destructive habits will cease.

DAY 293—COURAGE

"Courage is reckoned the greatest of all virtues because unless a man has that virtue, he has no security for preserving any other."
Samuel Johnson (1747)

PREMISE

Courage is fundamental to progress and advancement precisely because it gives us the motivation to move forward, to become extricated from the status quo and instead to move towards growth and self-affirmation. Courage emboldens us to face self-deceit and delusion while giving us the freedom to act in a manner independent of both the Good and bad opinions of others. Courage assists in the challenge of self-discovery and improves problem solving, as we face "truth" and discover new confidence and optimism. It empowers us to confront daily frustrations with love and acceptance. Most importantly, courage arouses and galvanizes our spirit to conquer all impediments as we move foreword to achieve our objectives.

INTENTION

I can feel courage in my heart whenever I so desire. I can call on strength, practice perseverance and manifest fortitude anytime I intend. Each day I see evidence of my progress and at any moment I can accept all of the spiritual qualities necessary to overcome all impediments. I have everything I need, at any moment, if I trust and maintain an open heart.

AWARENESS

I will make a special effort to feel that courage in my spirit and in my heart. I will describe in detail this experience in my journal so that I may be aware, in the future, of this sensation of strength, unity and love.

DAY 294—LOVE

"Love is, above all, the gift of oneself."
Jean Anouilh (1948)

PREMISE

Love is the third goal of ideal spiritual living. The other two are wisdom and courage. Love is the emotional reflection and expression of wisdom. Love and wisdom, although independent and separate, operate such that they converge, coalesce and combine to generate the gift and perspective of "love mindedness." This perspective gives us the strength and insight to react and interact in a manner that generates joy, compassion and benevolence.

INTENTION

I am able to focus on my goals and with planning and awareness, I will reach those goals slowly, one step at a time. I can develop a comprehensive perspective of "love mindedness" which means that when I'm faced with conflict my first questions are what can I learn? How can I help and how can I express kindness? I must stop asking; "what's in it for me?" Change is progress as long as I change for the better, living with a more loving, selfless, approach to life and its tribulations. This perspective runs counter to the consumer culture and all the messages that shout: "I must have" or "I must win and be best." I know that I can do this with the help of my Higher Power and all of my friends but I must pray and ask for help when necessary.

AWARENESS

I will make a list of five things that I can do to express a genuine and all-encompassing perspective of love.

DAY 295—WISDOM

"The growth of wisdom may be gauged exactly by the diminution of ill-temper."
Frederick Nietzsche (1875)

PREMISE

Arrogance is fear's grand disguise. Arrogance is the person who whistles past the graveyard. When fear says, "I can't," "I'm doomed," "I am a victim," arrogance says, "I deserve," "I'm better than," "bring it to me." However, both fear and arrogance generate stagnation, isolation and distortion. Wisdom mitigates this tendency. It sees change as a challenge and choice, an opportunity to learn and evolve, an occasion to discern who we really are and to embrace our unique role in a larger, grander plan. Wisdom transforms fear and inaction into challenge, enemies into friends and avoidance into confrontation.

INTENTION

As I grow in wisdom, as well as in the other qualities, I notice that I am calmer and more content with my world and myself. Increasingly, I am able to accept what I can't control and to change what I can. I am developing the wisdom to know the difference, the courage to act on that knowledge and the intention to manifest love throughout the process.

AWARENESS

I will pray today for the contentment and acceptance as well as the forgiveness and understanding, necessary to achieve the objectives fundamental to living a life dominated by wisdom, love and courage.

DAY 296—COURAGE

"Have the courage to act instead of react."
Earlene Larson Jenks

PREMISE

Courage must not be confused with recklessness or impulsivity. Courage comes from a mixture of love and wisdom. When courageous, we act after appropriate consideration and assessment, as well as, with an intention of love and compassion. Courage, love and wisdom are the three supreme qualities that dominate a self-actualized individual. Recklessness, impulsivity and self-indulgence are the trademarks of the child-self. Courage is the behavioral expression and the emotional conduit to our ultimate goal of living in wisdom and love. While courage is the behavioral foundation for all the spiritual characteristics to which we aspire, it is also essential in the evolution of self-discovery and self-actualization.

INTENTION

I am good but negative self-statements and self-sabotaging actions have hidden much of my goodness. Whether these were learned or inborn does not matter. I must be aware, when they appear, so that I may silence them with positive counter statements.

AWARENESS

I will make a list of five things that I can do to express and to manifest a genuine and all-encompassing perspective of love as well as a positive view of myself.

DAY 297—LOVE

"In order to love simply, it is necessary to know how to show love."
Fyodor Dostoyevsky (1895)

PREMISE

Our destiny in life is self-fulfillment; to become who we were created to be. As a flower must blossom, so we must become. As we release ourselves from fear and the status quo, we begin the journey of discovering who we are and what is our authentic purpose. The catalysts for this process are forgiveness, humility, gratitude and patience. Each is an active choice, a decision made in the present and primed through intent. The opportunities to manifest each of these are limited only by our lack of willpower and commitment. We must increase our awareness of such occasions and constantly renew our intent. We must make this happen. The change we want to see in others must begin with us.

INTENTION

I am so afraid to show love and caring. I am afraid to be kind and to make myself vulnerable. I feel that I'll look foolish or get rejected etc. etc. Please Lord, help me to overcome this. It's in Your hands. If I am to achieve my objectives and be all that I can, I must face my fear of loving and open my heart to kindness and benevolence.

AWARENESS

I will demonstrate and manifest a compassionate, caring attitude today to a random person and I will note the event, including the precipitating circumstances, my feelings and the results of this action. I will note briefly my evaluation of my own progress.

DAY 298—WISDOM

"Wisdom is ofttimes nearer when we stoop/than when we soar."
William Wordsworth (1814)

PREMISE

Arrogance is another component of our child-self that impedes intelligence from evolving into wisdom, love, humility and authentic pride. Arrogance is pride polluted by the child-self. Pride is a natural and self-rewarding feeling of worth and efficacy that results from achievement, competence and kindness. Arrogance is a feeling of superiority and entitlement that completely annihilates the "we" for the "I." Wisdom, by definition, considers everyone and repels narcissism as a wasteful love that can never be satisfied. Wisdom merges past, present and future, "we" and "me", "each" and "all" in a comprehensive culmination of growth and good.

INTENTION

I am able to distinguish arrogance from pride and healthy self-esteem. As I remove, or at least, diminish the ancient voice of my child-self, fear also diminishes and wisdom appears. As I see myself through wise eyes, I can appreciate that I am a creation of God with a unique destiny and my differences from others are positive aspects of myself that I can use to help all.

AWARENESS

I will document the ways in which I am unique and I will write in my journal why this is good and how I can use my idiosyncrasies to serve the needs of my fellow travelers.

DAY 299—COURAGE

"Courage is necessary if we are to learn from our misjudgments and misperceptions. If we are to grow and achieve our goals we must exercise courage."
W. T. Watts, Ph.D. (2011)

PREMISE

Courage is a transcendental goal assuring that each interaction, thought, feeling and reaction is grounded in love and wisdom. Courage quiets the constant self-involvement of the child-self and urges the spiritual-self to express acceptance and to reject judging, comparing or disparaging. The "I" subserves the "we" and the "they." Unity is no longer a frightening concept; rather, through courage it is embraced and becomes a source of comfort and strength. As we to toil in our own garden, we begin to share experience, strength and hope with our fellows and we comprehend the notion that we are "one of many who are one." It is from this perspective that we fulfill our destiny and live as we were created to live. Courage is the catalyst that materializes this ideal.

INTENTION

I can energize my spiritual-self. This is the dwelling place of all courage. I can become aware of the strength generated by my thoughts of unity with all life. I am indeed one of the many who are one and I can grow in love and peace if I intend to do so.

AWARENESS

I will take special note today of my similarities with others . . . especially when I find them annoying. I will write this in my journal and ponder why that which annoys me most about others are traits that are also essential to me.

DAY 300—LOVE

"Words have no language which can utter the secrets of love . . ."
Andre Gide (1947)

PREMISE

There is only one "love" but it comes in many forms depending on the level of sexual attraction and subsequent intimacy. However, all love is consists of four components. These components are humility, gratitude, acceptance and patience. Humility requires that we be humble before others in order to allow mutual respect. Humility is a simple acknowledgment of empathy, equality and compassion. It is neither submissive nor obsequious. It is an acknowledgment of respect from one traveler to another. Gratitude is necessary because it is an extension of respect, a recognition that another has chosen to be with us and to offer their love, companionship and camaraderie in exchange for our company, empathy and trust. Acceptance is allowing the other into our space without qualification or demand. Finally, patience is the process of learning from another about who we are and how "to be with" someone else. It is acknowledging and accepting that events as well as the actions of others occur in God's time not ours.

INTENTION

I can summon the courage to be vulnerable, to trust and to reach out. I know in my heart that I am a better person to have this other person in my life.

AWARENESS

I will document in my journal the first person that comes to mind when I think of friendship. I will include three things that attract me to this person.

DAY 301—WISDOM

"Wisdom is the answer, the antidote, the single medicine that relieves all ills and afflictions."
Surya Das (2007)

PREMISE

Wisdom promotes an ever evolving spiritual, loving, accepting and understanding perspective. It is the final dethroning of the child-self, although it will always loudly tantrum as it stays in its room. With wisdom the light pierces the clouds; we become "enlightened" as we allow knowledge, spirit and compassion to mold our assumptions. Our lives and actions achieve meaning, as we progress into awareness and altruism. Wisdom gives us direction and definition; distinguishing wants from needs, love from desire and acceptance from complacency. It gives us hope that we can achieve our goals because we are better able to focus on what we can control.

INTENTION

As I grow in humility, gratitude, patience and acceptance, I know that wisdom will emerge. I know that I am capable of building the foundation for love, courage and wisdom with each act and each intention as I manifest compassion, acceptance and understanding. I can do this and I am now wise enough to realize that my child-self is all that blocks my way.

AWARENESS

I will think today about how my first reaction to any circumstance is frequently a reflection of my child-self. Rather than having an open mind to new experience; in my fear I immediately frame what is happening in terms of bias, and my past history. I will be especially alert to that today.

DAY 302—COURAGE

"Courage empowers us to look inside and become free from the self-limiting thoughts generated from our own past and reinforced as we grew."
W. T. Watts, Ph.D. (2011)

PREMISE

The audacity to question the self-sabotaging and self-limiting myths of the past is fueled by courage. Who am I? What can I do to make my life lovingly meaningful? These questions and many more like them are raised and acknowledged because love and wisdom have merged to create courage. Such bravery motivates us to separate our perceived faults and strengths from the mix that is our life story. Courage requires that we confront these myths, handed down and generated from others, who harbor their own inherited myths (misinformation). We must confront the self-destructive ideas that chain us to the past with the positive affirmations in the present. We can choose to rediscover ourselves through trial and error so that each day slightly reshapes who we are as we allow change, challenge and choice to move us forward towards our destiny.

INTENTION

I will summon the courage today, to be me. I will attempt something new, some new attitude, new perspective or new behavior that distances me from my past and begins to sever an old habit. It will do something that I have been meaning to do but have delayed because I fear change. I can do this. I am a work in progress and not a final product. May this always be so. The journey is crucial; the destination is in God's hands.

AWARENESS

I will note in my journal one act of difference, its results and my reactions to these results.

PART FIVE

LOVE, WISDOM, COURAGE (PART 2)

DAYS 303—365

ENDING TO BEGIN

Dear Reader:

You have reached the final stages of this part of the journey. You have begun to assimilate humility, gratitude, acceptance and patience into your life on a daily basis and this has served as a spiritual foundation such that your new worldview encompasses actions motivated by courage and framed in wisdom and love.

You have learned to take the perspective of "participant/ observer" and as your awareness has increased, you have assessed and reassessed, evaluated and reevaluated your strategies for achieving your objectives. Now is the time to reinforce these lessons.

You must continue to challenge old beliefs from your past and to confront the fear that prevents you from moving forward. You must persevere in order to achieve the strength to be vulnerable and the courage to fail. Develop special patience for the virtues of love and inclusion; they are the most difficult to master. You have come a long way and, as always, there is a long way to go. However, throughout this last period of time you have worked hard, learned lessons and energized your fortitude so that you can be certain of the path and the intent that will keep you on that path.

It is now time to put these lessons to work as only you can. It is time to create meaningful experiences as you encounter life and use courage to define who you are and what you will achieve.

God bless, Namaste and be well. You will always be in my thoughts and prayers.

W. T. Watts, Ph.D.

DAY 303—LOVE

"The love we give away is the only love we keep."
Elbert Hubbard, The Note Book (1927)

PREMISE

Do not take love, kindness or friendship for granted. This is a significant impediment to greater intimacy and a common mistake we often make. Frequently, it is only after we have alienated or dismissed a loved one that we feel our loss and comprehend our grief. This can be avoided if each day we get back to basics and foster the gratitude, patience, acceptance and humility necessary to appreciate the fact that friendship, love and intimacy are gifts, freely given by another. Such gifts are blessings and must be treasured.

INTENTION

The essence of growth is taking responsibility for my choices and moving on to the next event. It is so easy to shirk responsibility. We live in a culture of victimhood and dependence. It is far easier to submit to the child-self's "I didn't do it" or "I can't do it" than to take responsibility for our behavior, feelings and thoughts. I acknowledge and accept my accountability for each aspect of my behavior and all of my choices as well as each step in the process of assessment, evaluation and strategizing. My thoughts create feelings and I create and choose my thoughts. With awareness and intent, I can adjust my thoughts in a positive direction and target my behavior towards service.

AWARENESS

I will make a list of three destructive thoughts I had today and I will begin to notice a pattern. I will document counter-thoughts to each of these so that I begin to construct a cognitive strategy to mitigate self-defeat.

DAY 304—WISDOM

"Cultivating wisdom trains us away from the destructive habits of thinking, speaking and behaving. It's a remedy for overcoming not only selfishness, stupidity and unfairness, but also feelings of confusion and meaninglessness."
Surya Das (2007)

PREMISE

Wisdom facilitates objectivity and provides emotional control It therefore instills empowerment. Wisdom helps us maintain the necessary emotional and intellectual distance so that we perpetuate a participant/observer perspective in those intense situations that present themselves in our daily life. With wisdom we become sufficiently empowered to frame quotidian conflicts in magnanimous terms, as life's challenges and changes are prioritized and organized into an appropriate and effective frame of reference.

INTENTION

I am capable of disavowing self-destructive thoughts, strategies and feelings. I no longer need this negativity in my life. I have the wisdom and courage to denounce blame, resentment and victimhood and to take responsibility for my everyday thoughts, feelings and conclusions. I can create empowerment within myself and I can manifest the necessary courage to preserve and celebrate my individuality and integrity.

AWARENESS

Today, I will note in my journal three instances in which I stood up for myself where previously I would have remained silent and possibly bitter. I will also document and consider one instance where I did not do this, much to my disappointment.

DAY 305—COURAGE

"One man with courage makes a majority."
Andrew Jackson (1832)

PREMISE

We can and we do make a difference. Our lives have meaning and we have power that is hidden but waiting to be discovered through courage. Courage invigorates and elucidates our understanding of who we are and what is our role in life for today. Courage activates the incentive and intensity to pursue our goals and objectives. Courage gives us the strength and certainty to follow through and persevere in a commitment. Courage will also tell us when it is time to reflect and recede. Like the tides, life has its ebb and flows, so, we must be aware, attend and decide when and when not to set sail.

INTENTION

I have been frightened of my power and the responsibility it incurs. I have hidden from accountability, competence and effectiveness. I am unnerved by change, progress and uncertainty. So much is unknown and so much seems risky. But if I believe that I am unique and that I have a purpose, I will summon the courage to confront change and accept challenge. I can do this if I trust that there is a meaning to my life and that the Universe is all wise and benevolent.

AWARENESS

Today, I will think about the potential that I have to do good deeds as well as to do evil. I will choose the "good" and note this in my journal. I will perform tasks that benefit the lives of others, even to a small degree and describe them as well as the decision making process that resulted in them.

DAY 306—LOVE

"True love seeks to make someone happy rather than to become happy."
Samuel Johnson (1779)

PREMISE

Love is service. It is to place the self, second and the other first. Love seeks to please but should never be subservient. Each day, with every interaction we must intend to respond with love and caring, otherwise love will wither and die. Love must be active; it must be protected and enriched so that it remains new and exciting. No one has ever grown tired of hearing "I love you" from a loved one. Love is the manifestation of our Higher Power. We are the tools of God and our expression of love is part of our sacred mission. Only through manifesting and receiving love, will we achieve a life of contentment and fulfillment.

INTENTION

I will not look to others to find myself. I will not look to others to satisfy me, to characterize me or to make me feel secure. I will empower myself by giving away what I have so freely been given. I will look to please without sacrificing who I am. I will look to help, to bolster and support without bending, and to enrich without impoverishing. In short, I will look to serve others and thereby strengthen myself. I will freely express and receive love.

AWARENESS

I will note one specific act of kindness and determine whether I demeaned or enhanced myself. I will determine if I am fulfilled and strong rather than deficient and subservient. I will exhibit kindness with no thought of reciprocation or expectation of recompense. I will give because that is the way of contentment.

DAY 307—WISDOM

"Common sense suits itself to the ways of the world. Wisdom tries to conform to the ways of heaven."
Joseph Joubert (1842)

PREMISE

Throughout the ages, wisdom has been so admired precisely because it is extremely difficult to achieve. It is a combination and assimilation, of the best of head and heart, experience and love, action and desire. Attainment of wisdom is contingent upon rising above the child-self and achieving a perspective that blends the basic transformative traits (humility, gratitude, acceptance and patience) with the selfless expressions of service and benevolence. Wisdom fuses with experience and manifests itself through acts of loving-kindness. It emerges from a life filled with good work and service.

INTENTION

Wisdom is the ability to see beyond the "horizon", to feel with more than your fingers and to "know" with your heart. I can develop this ability. I have the perseverance within my spiritual-self to learn from the ordinary so that it is transformed to the "extraordinary." I have the power within; I have the courage and experience to actualize it. With the help of my Higher Power, I can invigorate my focus and intention as I transform each act into a spiritual achievement.

AWARENESS

Today, I will discover a "lesson" in the ordinary and I will allow myself to feel the wonder of oneness with the Universe. I will describe both this feeling and the behavior that lead to this in my journal.

DAY 308—COURAGE

"It's courage that gets you up when you are down. It is courage that discovers meaning in helplessness and gives "heart" to the "disheartened."
W. T. Watts, Ph.D. (2011)

PREMISE

Courage is the capacity to re-create, to rise above so as to reassemble the pieces of broken expectations. Courage is necessary to forge a new path and form a new perspective as we learn and evolve. New strategies suddenly come to mind and the fortitude and conviction to use those strategies motivate our inner core. Courage creates and empowers this independence. It is essential for spiritual growth and physical energy. It gives us the creativity and determination to make the most of failure and to capitalize on strengths.

INTENTION

No matter how many mistakes I have made and no matter how badly I have behaved, if I choose change, if I choose to live a life of humility, gratitude, acceptance and patience, all of those misjudgments, misinterpretations and misdeeds can be used to help others. I will not regret my past as long as I appreciate my present and understand that it is my past encounters (both positive and negative) that have put me where I am. By sharing my history, and my beliefs, I can help others to discover the courage to begin anew and to face their own challenges to fulfillment.

AWARENESS

What does it mean to "take responsibility" for both the Good and bad? I will write at least one paragraph to better define this issue and to clarify my thinking. How is this related to empowerment and self-esteem?

DAY 309—LOVE

"Love is an act of endless forgiveness . . ."
Peter Ustinov (1958)

PREMISE

Intimacy requires acceptance and tolerance. We cannot and should not attempt to change anyone but ourselves and this applies especially to those we love. It is better to leave the relationship than to go through the endless frustration of attempting to control the uncontrollable. Intimacy and loving, mutually fulfilling, interpersonal relations are crucial to maintaining sound emotional health. To love, to play, to plan and to work are goals that involve others and that we achieve when we function as mentally healthy individuals. Intimacy is not dependency. It is the ability to be sufficiently courageous and independent so as to share your deepest, most private feelings with the confidence that such honesty will be treasured. Intimacy requires the self-possession and self-discipline to be sufficiently vulnerable to trust another without sacrificing the self.

INTENTION

I understand that if I am to develop an intimate relationship, I must accept many aspects of the person that I would ordinarily reject providing that these negative aspects are not destructive to either of us. I must trust and resist the temptation to find fault, blame or resentment for minor irritations.

AWARENESS

I will note six aspects of a person who is very close to me. I will list three characteristics that I like and three that I don't. I will consider if those I do not like are destructive to myself or the other person and if not I will move on with the relationship and accept that which I cannot change.

DAY 310—COURAGE

"Courage is doing what you're afraid to do."
Eddie Rickenbacker

PREMISE

Courage is facing, embracing and preventing fear from hampering our journey of self-discovery, evolution and contentment. This is the crucial point; embrace fear do NOT to deny, defer or deflect it. It is an opportunity to learn despite its unpleasantness. Change is constant, so the sooner we face this truth the sooner we begin our journey to self-actualization. Don't let the status quo justify inaction. We inadvertently embrace the familiar, the routine, and the predictable as we become complacent. We do this because we resist change and the responsibility that accompanies growth and transition. We fear the unknown because we cannot control it and lack of control raises feelings of vulnerability. So face reality. Be confident and move forward.

INTENTION

I can "bite the bullet" and confront change. I will pray for courage and I will seek the challenging, the novel and the untested. There are so many things I can do if I will only free myself from fear and avoidance. I have come so far and I must never forget how far. I must not hide behind weakness or past failures. I can, I must and I will achieve my objectives and thereby attain my destiny and become all that I was created to be.

AWARENESS

What is success? I will ponder this today and take notes. In my journal I will define what I must do to be "successful". I will also describe how I it would feel to consider myself a "success".

DAY 311—WISDOM

"The beginning of wisdom is found in doubt; by doubting we come to the question, and by seeking we may come upon the truth."
Pierre Abelard (1135 C.E.)

PREMISE

We must question and doubt, if we are to discover the truth about who we are and the nature of our place in the world. As we gain wisdom, we gain acceptance and in turn, acceptance reinforces wisdom. We begin to see change and growth and we cease to battle the inevitable. We begin to live with others and realistically (with no expectations) embark upon all social and interactive experience. We maintain our ideals but accept limits. We are now living intently but not complacently. We are realizing and experiencing genuine inner peace.

INTENTION

I no longer need to accept what I learned from others at face value or what I am told without challenging those perceptions with thoughts and reflections. I respect others, their view of the world and their intent. However, I have the courage to find my own way and the humility to learn from others. I will decide the right course and path that suits me after deliberating and considering all viewpoints. I will make a determination with a loving heart and a wise vision.

AWARENESS

I will note in my journal a situation in which I hesitate before accepting an "opinion" as definitive. This will be done with respect and appreciation. I will listen to learn but I will evaluate what I am told and put it in a perspective of my past experience. When in doubt I will pray and ask for guidance from my Higher Power.

DAY 312—LOVE

"To be emotionally committed to somebody is very difficult, but to be alone is impossible."
Stephen Sondheim (1965)

PREMISE

Emotional commitment is difficult because when we finally decide that we wish to expand a relationship, we become vulnerable and therefore, frightened. Sometimes in reaction to this fear, we attempt to find fault with another or react in negative ways such that there is a severing of the emotional connection. Groucho Marx famously stated that he would never join a club that would have him as a member. This attitude is similar to one that many share: "if he/she likes/loves me what's wrong with them?" Then in order to mitigate our fear and satisfy our curiosity we tend to look under a microscope to find an answer to that question. This is a variant to that musical comedy theme of: "I love you, you're perfect, now change." Be aware and forewarned, this has destroyed many relationships and is caused by self-deprecation and attempting intimacy while being defensive. So be open and loving while realizing that "trusting but verifying" may also be necessary.

INTENTION

I do fear loneliness but I do not fear being alone. Although I would prefer to share my life more intimately with someone, I realize that some relationships are special and rare. "Healthy" relationships enhance both partners and I know that I need to teach the other how I wish to be treated in order to avoid misunderstandings. I will move forward with courage, optimism and caution but with an open heart and a willing mind.

AWARENESS

What do you hate about being alone? Make a list of three things that are good about solitude and three things that are destructive about it.

DAY 313—WISDOM

"It is characteristic of wisdom not to do desperate things."
Henry David Thoreau (1847)

PREMISE

A wise person realizes and accepts that change is essential to life. Change is constant, unrelenting and it is inescapable. It is integral to life and essential for growth. So it is not in the nature of the wise to react extra-ordinarily when challenged by change. It is in the nature of the wise to adapt the viewpoint of the "participant/observer", to be in the world but not of the world, to distance oneself from distress, anxiety and aggression and to observe and assess rather than react with impulse and abandon. This is the ideal manner of evaluating external circumstances. Be wise, be prudent, take a breath and understand that stress and happiness will come and go, go and come. Emotions are transitory. The most difficult aspect of painful emotions is the delusion that they will never end. Under stressful circumstances, think of your experiences and realize that good and bad always visit but then depart.

INTENTION

Wisdom knows harmony and I can bring harmony and balance to my daily living, if I chose to do so. I have the knowledge, the will, the intent and the courage to choose change and choose it consistently. I am responsible for the reality that I create. I am accountable for my decisions and their results. I celebrate this power because I intend always to select the Good, the kind, and the benevolent. Thusly, I live in wisdom.

AWARENESS

Today, I will note how wisdom and kindness are reflected in my ordinary relationships. I will document two instances where I paused, reflected and resisted my first impulse to react in the "usual" matter. I will document the specific actions that manifested kindness and wisdom. I will also make note of how this made me feel.

DAY 314—COURAGE

"Behind them was the dark forest they had passed safely through, although they had suffered many discouragements; but before them was a lovely, sunny country that seemed to beckon them on to the Emerald City."
The Wizard of Oz (1900)

PREMISE

The past is behind us, and although the future is unknown it can become "sunny" if we choose to make it so. There is one certainty. If we are to live a contented and fulfilling life, we must make change manageable by taking control of what we can. Courage is the ultimate expression of assurance, creativity and trust. Courage is the "life force." It rises to proclaim life and love as the proven powers of the Universe. With courage, we inherit the fortitude to support and cherish the downtrodden, to defend the weak and to oppose the popular. We gain the strength, boldness and motivation to fulfill our destiny. When we live in courage, love and wisdom, we will search, pursue, and discover that "lovely, sunny country that seemed to beckon . . ."

INTENTION

I have passed through a "dark forest" and I'm certain that there are more to come. I will remember that my Higher Power never gives me more than I can conquer. If I have faith, I will find a way. I always have what I need to overcome any impediments to my objectives. I will become all that I was created to be. I will use my unique strengths to help others and to generate love, inclusion and acceptance in all my activities and challenges.

AWARENESS

I will think about how far I have come. Where have I improved most? What do I need to work on now? I will note these in my journal and I will create a strategy to confront and solve such questions.

DAY 315—LOVE

"We cannot love others as others unless
we possess sufficient self love . . ."
Judith Viorst (1986)

PREMISE

Self-love is a necessary condition for a healthy relationship. Self-love expands acceptance to the beloved with no demands, conditions, expectations or power plays other than mutual respect. As humans, we frequently try to control friends and loved ones in areas where we cannot control ourselves. Self-love decreases this tendency as it reinforces self-acceptance. If we can answer the key questions of life, namely, are we lovable and are we loved, in the affirmative, all of our relations with others will be more satisfactory and joyful. We will focus on managing ourselves and allow our Higher Power to worry about everyone else. In order to love another successfully in a positive, life-affirming manner, we must first look internally and see the goodness of our spirit. From this point, the love that perpetually surrounds us will become apparent. We can then proceed to the task and pleasure of loving another.

INTENTION

Sometimes, I get so confused. I know that I want someone to share intimate moments and life goals but at the same time, I am afraid of trusting and being hurt. I know but I will continue to remind myself that I must risk if I am to reap a reward.

AWARENESS

Today, I will note in my journal why I resist love. I will be as honest and courageous with myself as possible in order to determine why I am afraid of acceptance, inclusion and, on occasion, passion. I realize that I should not just give my love without caution but I believe I have been excessively guarded and withdrawn.

DAY 316—WISDOM

*"We do not receive wisdom, we must discover it for ourselves,
after a long journey through the wilderness which
no one else can make for us . . ."*
Marcel Proust (1915)

PREMISE

The synergism of life experience, love and humility results in wisdom. For many spiritual scholars, wisdom is more than knowledge and learning; it is seeing the "Big Picture." Wisdom fuses "us" and "them", "me" and "thee", past and future. It is the perfect combination of practicality and idealism, active and passive behavior, acceptance and forgiveness. Wisdom allows us to see the uniqueness of the individual while not missing the power of the whole. We perceive both the trees and the forest with trust and patience. This is wisdom. This is the merging as well as the assimilation of contradiction and paradox, reality and imagination. It is the result of living life with the intent to serve and learn.

INTENTION

Wisdom requires equal amounts of deeds and deliberation, teaching and learning, expectation and resolution. In some ways, wisdom is a paradox, an ambiguous yet conclusive concept that must be discovered. Yes, it is complex and confusing, but if I cultivate my spiritual-self and merge head with heart, I will get the feeling, knowledge, certainty and contentment that wisdom offers.

AWARENESS

I will attempt to define what wisdom is, as it relates to my daily living. I will create a practical definition such that I will know when I am acting in a "wise" manner.

DAY 317—COURAGE

"Oh God, give us the courage to change what should be changed."
Reinhold Niebuhr (1934)

PREMISE

Courage is the quality that allows us to cope with life as we use our spiritual perspective to nurture and to reinforce humility, gratitude, acceptance and patience. Courage empowers us to accept the changeless (that which we can't change) and to change the changeable. It provides energy to incite and revitalize the spiritual qualities necessary to function effectively and to achieve fulfillment. To have courage is to have contentment because it is to live without fear.

INTENTION

I want to be free from fear and I realize that I must face fear to lose fear. The surest way to be stuck is to avoid what you need to confront. Fear comes with change and they are both inescapable. So to be free, I must risk the comfort of certainty and challenge the status quo. I must also accept change and move forward in love and learning by courageously enduring the immutable.

AWARENESS

I will write one instance of determination that I manifested today. I will note how I felt, why I chose that particular moment and what happened as a result of my decision. I will also document how I feel about my progress in pursuing courage and attempting to practice it in my daily living.

DAY 318—LOVE

"Love dies only when growth stops."
Pearl S. Buck (1967)

PREMISE

If we love the "other" out of "need" rather than needing the other because we love them, we begin the relationship with a critical vulnerability. "Need" as the dominant emotion is frequently confused with "want" and it emerges from a place in us where fears, as well as feelings of inadequacy, reside. We "need"/"want" someone because we fear . . . (You fill in the space). Our biggest fear is being alone. Being alone and being "lonely" are frequently considered to be synonymous. However, this is an erroneous and self-sabotaging thought ("solitude revives; isolation kills", Roux, 1886). The point is that a love or an attraction that originates from a belief that we are unable or inadequate to fulfill our needs is doomed. Expectations dominate acceptance; "what can I get?" trumps "what can I give?" It becomes about "me" not about "we." To experience relationships of substance and depth, requires a commitment and devotion to the "other" as well as a security in the "self" that allows for sharing, acceptance and trust.

INTENTION

I want to love, I want to risk and become unguarded because I know that I have the strength to withstand any potential loss and I know that I must learn to love and risk, if I am to grow. With every risk there is an opportunity. I will be strong and move forward.

AWARENESS

In my journal I will list three reasons why I am lovable. I will also list three reasons why I would benefit from an intimate relationship. Finally, I will list three things that make me hesitate from committing to a more intimate relationship.

DAY 319—WISDOM

". . . Our wisdom is the point of view from which we come at last to regard the world."
Marcel Proust (1915)

PREMISE

Evolving as a loving spirit is both the cause and result of self-acceptance. Ultimately, this blossoms into a world-view embracing others and trusting in a plan beyond our comprehension. Wisdom is the highest form of knowledge and intelligence. It is a culmination of the reciprocal interactions between and among all the basic transformative attributes that would lead to self-actualization. Wisdom blends each spiritual faculty (humility, gratitude, acceptance and patience) into a fundamental perspective that generates love and acceptance.

INTENTION

I am constantly changing my perspective as I live life with awareness and intent. I choose, and then learn from the consequences of my choices so that I may reassess, re-evaluate and re-strategize. In this way, I bring to each new situation a unique, more experienced and wiser perspective. Next, I move forward and progress, learning from all the inconveniences and frustrations that constitute growth and maturation. As I change, everything around me changes as well. In turn, there is an adjustment, a new decision and a new day begins created by a new me. This is life lived with wisdom; and I give thanks.

AWARENESS

Today, I will note how wisdom has changed me for the better. I will note one new routine, habit or relationship that has been generated by the intention to be wise.

DAY 320—COURAGE

"Never stop because you are afraid: you are never so likely to be wrong."
Fridtjot Nansen (1921)

PREMISE

A certainty in life, one of the few, is that if you make a decision based on fear you will most likely make the wrong decision. Fear cannot be avoided but it can be diminished and moderated by confrontation. Courage gives us that ability. Courage is the ability to confront fear, especially the fear generated by change. Either you will succeed, that is, meet your expectations or you won't. If you do accomplish your goals and expectations, a feeling of temporary satisfaction can be enjoyed. Contrariwise, if your hopes are impeded, it serves no purpose to blame, resent or condemn, rather it behooves us to reassess, reevaluate and re-strategize. There is acceptance and there is relinquishment of responsibility. Wisdom gained through prayer and guidance will help us make that distinction.

INTENTION

I can face truth, reality and change. All of these can generate fear and anxiety. When such distress strikes, these distinctions disappear as I run and hide, avoid and defer or delay and deny. If I can't see you, you don't exist says my child-self.

AWARENESS

I will make a special note today when I yield to fear. I will describe the feelings and the circumstances in my journal as well as my efforts to flee from responsibility and to attribute blame, create resentment or otherwise embrace victimhood.

DAY 321—LOVE

"Immature love says: 'I love you because I need you'. Mature love says: 'I need you because I love you.'"
Erich Fromm (1962)

PREMISE

We frequently confuse love and lust, need and want, humility and humiliation. In the spiritual realm, there is only one dichotomy, love and fear. As Marianne Williamson says: "love is what we are born with, fear is what we learn." All beings share the same source and are one in a sacred union. We participate in a changeless life force that is special and crucial throughout the Universe; an incomprehensible force that flows throughout our bodies and the bodies of all living things. All positive emotions are reflections of this love. Love is their origin. All negative emotions are born of fear. Fear is a rejection of love and a source of evil throughout the world.

INTENTION

I can acquire and access the power that is my spiritual-self, so that my thoughts focus on the positive. I can intend humility, acceptance, patience and gratitude, so that my reactions reflect love, wisdom and courage. I can obliterate fear by being aware of its power and its weakness. Simple awareness and acknowledgment will help me move on. The light of love, the brightness of self-confidence and the incandescence of courage, will overcome fear and show me the way. I can move forward, develop and achieve my objectives with a trust and confidence that love and compassion conquer fear and arrogance.

AWARENESS

I will document two dichotomies that I encountered today and I will refute them choosing the middle path. If I am to achieve my objectives and live contentedly, I must confront and reconcile all dichotomies so that I may focus on the path to self-fulfillment.

DAY 322—WISDOM

"Knowledge is merely brilliance in the organization of ideas. It is not true wisdom. The truly wise go beyond knowledge."
Confucius (500 B.C.E.)

PREMISE

Wisdom is understanding and accepting what happens because we know it is part of a greater plan. Wisdom is a belief and a "knowing", that the Universe and the events presented to us are exactly as they should be. Wisdom is an awareness that we must learn from and embrace choice and that we must not run from challenge. Wisdom is acceptance of the "self "as well as the "other" with a comprehension of the perfection of each and an acknowledgment of the commonality of purpose that we all share. That purpose is mutual well-being and growth.

INTENTION

I know that wisdom is more than facts and I know that it will take patience, acceptance, humility AND gratitude to attain wisdom and to assimilate it into my life. I am working on this and I am a work in progress. I am improving and part of my new wisdom is to realize that I will never reach "perfection." But, I am able to "perfectly" try to be "perfectly" me. Wisdom is knowledge of what you can control and accepting what you can't. Courage is acting on this knowledge and love is doing so with compassionate concern for the effects of your actions on others.

AWARENESS

I will pray for "wisdom" today, in the morning, at night, and "as needed" throughout the day.

DAY 323—COURAGE

"There is no such thing as bravery; only degrees of fear."
John Wainwright

PREMISE

Courage (the heart) and bravery (the act) are not without fear. It is withstanding fear, learning from fear, assessing and concluding to move forward despite fear that is courage. It is never absence of fear. Fear must be understood for both its protective and destructive qualities. It is neither "bad" nor "good". It simply "is" and it is part of life, change and choice. Therefore, if we experience fear, it does not mean that we should run (either away from or towards), rather it means pause, breathe, assess, strategize, and then act. The more accepting we are of fear and all feelings, the better our internal guidance for action. The "participant/observer" acknowledges, evaluates, accepts and then acts on its assessment rather than reflexively reacting to an emotional impulse that may or may not be based on a false premise or a misperception.

INTENTION

I will not fear-fear, neither will I be depressed about depression nor anxious about anxiety. I will become aware of my feelings and use my skills as a participant/observer so that I am alert to those internal signals that are so vital for my growth and direction. I will listen and determine to my best ability, at that time, what I will do. I will make every effort to choose the next best thing and strive with all my resources to remain on the path of the "good".

AWARENESS

I will note two feelings (for example anger and depression) and write in my journal exactly what are the sensations that accompanied them. (Hint: just write down, do not edit, all images and thoughts that come to mind).

DAY 324—LOVE

"There is no fear in love; but perfect love casteth out fear."
1 John 4:18

PREMISE

The main purpose of fear in modern times is to keep us isolated and stagnant. It is the child-self's wish to remain a child, remain in the status quo, justify and rationalize indoctrinated beliefs as it wallows in conceit, complacence and inertia. Fear is manifested in many ways; anger, abuse, criticism, addiction, and many other hostile emotions and self-destructive behaviors. In many ways, it is easier to avoid the responsibility of developing our God given gifts and to fail. It is easier to feel sorry for ourselves and embrace blame, resentment and victimhood than to maximize the "hand" we were given. It is easier to dig a deeper hole than to move forward, grow, evolve and mature. In many ways, it's easier to repel our destiny but in so many ways this will create unhappiness, isolation, dissatisfaction, resentment. So the lesson is to stop resisting, embrace life and allow the goodness of the Universe to energize you as it expands your unique skills for the Good of all.

INTENTION

I can rise above self-imposed negativity. I can strive for goals and face failure and imperfection. I can embrace who I am and be gratified for what I have. In sum, I can have the courage and love to be myself as part of a greater whole.

AWARENESS

I will ponder my fears. What am I afraid of? I will list in my journal three things that make me hesitate to move forward when I know that I should. I will also think about, document and distinguish between fear of failure and fear of success.

DAY 325—WISDOM

"Knowledge is proud that he has learned so much;
wisdom is humble that he knows no more."
William Cow (1785)

PREMISE

When we fulfill our destiny and gain wisdom, we also achieve contentment and self-actualization. As love and wisdom combine, they interact and influence all aspects of our lives, making positive change inevitable for those we encounter and ourselves. When this occurs, all of our thoughts, feelings and actions are suffused with humility, gratitude, acceptance and patience. They are directed by a head-heart combination and fueled by courage. Such experiences occur at the peak of our functioning and are the epitome of physical and spiritual development. This is the consumation of our efforts and the realization of our blessings.

INTENTION

I have the strength, the courage and the wisdom to be humble. At the same time, humility reinforces and generates wisdom. Such positive reciprocity is the cycle of life and I am grateful to be a small, but significant, part of such a wondrous design.

AWARENESS

I will stop several times today to think about the miracle that is life. I will note and document in my journal two things that I have discovered today about how small yet significant I am in the Grand Plan that is the Universe. I will give thanks for all that I am, all that I have and all that I have yet to discover.

DAY 326—COURAGE

"We fail only if we fail to act. We succeed when we learn. Therefore, there are no mistakes, only lessons to be grasped."
W. T. Watts, Ph.D. (2011)

PREMISE

Courage empowers us to reach new dimensions in personal and spiritual development. It helps us to become free from both the Good and the bad opinions of others, so that as we listen to outside input, we stay focused and true to our nature. Courage helps us choose to what degree we hesitate and to what degree we move forward when faced with fear, anxiety and doubt. We are neither blinded nor pushed but rather guided by the qualities of acceptance, patience, gratitude and humility. We cease being afraid of truth and we do not fear asking for help, nor are we afraid to fail (that is not to meet expectations). We fear only inaction and ignoring truth and destiny.

INTENTION

I have the integrity and the responsibility to be the best that I can be at any given moment. If I am to refine my strengths and talents, I must truly acknowledge them and not hide behind my weaknesses and my fear of empowerment, responsibility, and success. I will be grateful for my strengths and utilize them for the Good of all, as I move ahead.

AWARENESS

Today, I will note and write in my journal two strengths that I use to solve problems. I will be specific as to the situation and as to the talents and abilities that I used. Did I benefit others?

DAY 327—LOVE

"O divine Master, grant that I may not so much be loved, as to love."
St. Francis of Assisi (1220 C.E.)

PREMISE

The goal is to love and to be loved. To comprehend that you are lovable and to be aware that you are loved for yourself and possibly, even better, in spite of yourself, is a gift from heaven and the result of practicing the basic qualities of humility, gratitude, acceptance and patience. Love is not love if it is conditional. Therefore, we must give our love freely. This is a courageous act that involves risk, trust and self-acceptance, for you cannot offer another what you don't possess. Trust in our Higher Power and trust that we have the resiliency to endure any rejection, disappointment or disillusionment are necessary conditions to offer love without expectation of recompense. So, to return to the Good Francis, it is a wise choice and a genuine gift simply to have the ability to love, to serve and to be unselfish rather than to fear and to isolate.

INTENTION

I can learn to view interpersonal relations as an opportunity to learn about myself, if I simply let go of my fear and defensiveness. I will pray for the courage to embrace another with affirmation and compassion.

AWARENESS

I will write a brief opinion in my journal as to why it is better to love than to be loved. I will also ponder and note what is the nature of "love" for me. Does ALL love involve risk? Must ALL love lead to intimacy? Must I always be vulnerable when I extend love? Finally, what is the nature of "rejection"? How do I define it and how do I tolerate it? Can I reject, rejection?

DAY 328—WISDOM

"The only problem is that our wisdom is obscured like the sun behind a cloud."
Tulka Rinpocher (1980)

PREMISE

This metaphor is so apropos. Clouds do, in fact, block wisdom. Clouds of doubt and clouds of fear prevent us from moving forward. These obstructions, bred of expectation and delusion, chain us to the dark of our past indoctrination, as we grope and stumble throughout our life tasks. Slowly, as we develop the other traits (humility, gratitude, acceptance and patience), wisdom will be realized and manifested in our daily lives. Wisdom is the pinnacle of intellectual development because it combines our "thinking" selves with our "feeling" selves. This results in a head-heart combination that maximizes our potential for virtue.

INTENTION

I will not fear or defer courage, I will develop the will to break through the clouds of doubt and allow the light of acceptance, love and gratitude to shine through. My awareness will increase and this light will energize my intent.

AWARENESS

Today, I will note three impediments that hamper my experiencing truth. I will especially focus on my resistance to new thoughts and new feelings as well as my resistance to approaching familiar obstacles with novel solutions.

DAY 329—COURAGE

"Fear is only as deep as the mind allows."
Japanese Proverb

PREMISE

Courage is risking "failure" (not meeting expectations). It is also perseverance (getting up when knocked down) and patience (realizing that it's not ineffectiveness or inability that frustrates results but impatience). Finally, gratitude (appreciation for what you have and how far you've come) contributes to successful and contented living by empowering us to acknowledge the wonder and benefits of what we have rather than feeling the frustration and deprivation of what we don't. All of these qualities comprise what is generally called "courage." Remember, every ending is the parent of a beginning, should we so choose. The choice is, do I move on and embrace change or do I remain mired and stuck in the status quo. Success and lack thereof, is part of effective and courageous living. Goals and objectives, ideals and expectations are simply part of the greater process that we pursue when we embrace our destiny.

INTENTION

What can be worse than hiding? What can be worse than denying who you are and what you can do? A major life issue that I will face today is, should I remain comfortably with the status quo, as I delay, deny or defer positive, life-affirming action, or should I move forward and confront change and the distressful choices that accompany change?

AWARENESS

I will act today, even in some small way, to face a fear. I will confront a person or situation that I have avoided and I will note in my journal what I did and how I overcame my fear. I will take special note of the physical sensations that precede and follow my encounter.

DAY 330—LOVE

"Love is all we have, the only way that each can help the other."
Euripides (408 B.C.E.)

PREMISE

We need each other, we need to express love and have love expressed to us. In Indian yoga, human relationships are viewed as arenas for spiritual practice, classrooms for the sacred. If we respect another and trust them such that we let our defenses down and listen, we can learn far more about ourselves than through simple introspection. Whatever the message; praise, annoyance, compassion, or rejection, we can learn and grow. The person who chooses to be with us is potentially the best teacher about who we are. This doesn't mean that everything said must be accepted but for our own benefit, it should be considered. Acceptance, gratitude and mutual respect are fundamental to a productive relationship.

INTENTION

Inter-dependence is the beginning of relating, inclusion and communication, not dependence or independence. I understand that all of the positive emotions; love, compassion, empathy, sympathy etc. involve variations of merging "me" with "you" to form a "we." The child-self fears this because it irrationally believes that it will die if it becomes independent yet paradoxically and destructively it yearns for the power that independence brings.

AWARENESS

I will strive to trust another today by being kind. I will rethink my fears about being close to someone and consider the reality of becoming "vulnerable." What does being "vulnerable" mean? Is it something that must be avoided like the flu or is it something that must be overpowered if I am to progress?

DAY 331—WISDOM

"Experience is not what happens to you; it is what you do with what happens to you."
Aldous Huxley (1956)

PREMISE

Experience is the result of action, action involves assessment (ideally) and assessment involves choices. Therefore, each day we must decide, act and learn when choice and change are presented to us. If we choose from a wise and a loving perspective, the result can always be beneficial. If we do not choose wisely, we can at least learn from that choice, so that we may still mature and advance. When we are wise, we embrace mistakes as opportunities to learn and move forward. Wisdom gives us integrity because we empower ourselves to benefit from error and we know and comprehend that as we learn, these specific "mistakes" will occur only once. Integrity involves perceiving and responding to change from a central and consistent core in our being. We feel fulfilled and contented because we are self-possessed, firm but flexible in the knowledge of who we are and what we can do to achieve our life objectives.

INTENTION

I am able to make my experiences meaningful. I can learn from triumphs as well as mistakes, from serendipity as well as tribulation. I can and will view my Higher Power's hand in everything that transpires. I will move forward and evolve, always intending kindness, expressing respect and feeling compassion.

AWARENESS

I will note one circumstance, action or feeling that is exceptional and I will write what I learned about it and how it will expand my behavior, perspective and awareness.

DAY 332—COURAGE

"I am one of many who are one; I am small and I am large,
my job, my fate is to be as perfect as I can be and as imperfect as I am.
I must love, accept, learn and progress in order to
create the 'me' that I am meant to be."
This is the mantra of courage.
W. T. Watts, Ph.D. (2011)

PREMISE

Courage reminds us that what lies ahead is what is meant to be and that we will learn and grow as we confront change and uncertainty. The greatest challenge is to learn who we are and what is our role in this unity called Life. There is no greater mission, nor greater reward than achieving the state of freedom that results from embracing this task. Courage is a necessary condition to achieve this state.

INTENTION

I don't have to be "prepared." I don't have to project all of the terrible things that MAY happen if I rouse myself from this slumber of complacency. I can move forward today with trust and assurance that I am able to surmount every impediment to achieving my objectives.

AWARENESS

What is my biggest fear? I will write about how this makes me unhappy and how I can reverse the cycle of avoidance and stagnation.

DAY 333—LOVE

"To fall in love is to create a religion that has a fallible God."
Jorge Luis Borges (1952)

PREMISE

How can we expect to love another when we can't love ourselves? When we focus on who we are not, what we can't offer, how we are defective, deprived or deficient, how can we expect another to embrace, accept or respect us? No one can fill all the holes in our soul that we have chosen to create or maintain. Understand, we are perfect, as God has made us. Part of this perfection is having the humility to acknowledge that there is an obligation to manifest our many talents for the enrichment of our own lives as well as the lives of those we encounter. Therefore, we must learn about ourselves as we relate to others and to our culture. In this way, we can be better in adapting and overcoming the circumstances that we are given. We can expect to have a fulfilling relationship once we accept ourselves and focus on serving the needs of the "other."

INTENTION

I will make a special effort to moderate my projections, fears and expectations of others. I will monitor my thoughts and feelings, so that I am aware of the strong emotions associated with intimacy. I feel confident enough to move slowly but steadily towards my goal. The central objective is to develop a positive and mutually beneficial relationship with another, governed by respect, acceptance and compassion.

AWARENESS

Today, I will note in my journal three objectives that I would like to achieve in a relationship with another. I must focus on these in order to overcome my fears of vulnerability and rejection. In this way, I will succeed in creating a connection that enhances not only myself but also another.

DAY 334—WISDOM

"To the wise, nothing is alien or remote."
Antisthenes (385 B.C.E.)

PREMISE

Wisdom is openness to new experience and information, as it condenses and assimilates the past. It is the culmination of history and memories reviewed, considered and accepted with love and gratitude. Wisdom includes courage because it creates truth. It is acceptance because we get the strength to observe and not manage. We no longer futilely attempt to control that which is beyond us, yet we strive, with the greatest conviction and determination, to achieve what is just beyond our usual grasp. We take small steps with grand design. We are humble yet possess a positive sense of self and a sturdy self-worth. Wisdom is humble in knowing its limits and grateful to know its power.

INTENTION

As I expand my perspective through wisdom, situations, actions and reactions that I previously thought impossible now become imaginable and even attainable. I find new and better ways to do things that formerly perplexed me. I now advocate for myself and face challenges that I would have previously avoided. In sum, the attainment of wisdom has given me courage and patience. I will persevere in the face of frustration and embrace the new and untried.

AWARENESS

Today, I will strive to do something new, to attempt something different or to do an old thing in a new way. My goal is to pursue innovative and imaginative solutions for old problems and to avoid the reflexive reactions that have kept me chained to the past.

DAY 335—COURAGE

"Whatever you do, you need courage. Whatever course you decide upon, there is always someone to tell you that you are wrong."
Ralph Waldo Emerson (1850)

PREMISE

Moving forward, listening and learning as we focus on our goals, is a necessary condition for success and is generated by courage. When we encounter new experiences or embark upon daily routines, obstacles and challenges abound, as we attempt to assimilate courage with love and wisdom. Such adjustment is impeded by the usual images from a culture that promotes fear, deficiency and incompetence. But remember, these impediments also can generate courage if we choose to view obstacles as lessons or guideposts rather than just more frustration and oppressions that will overwhelm us and confine us to the status quo. It's all in our attitude and we can control that.

INTENTION

It is so difficult at times to ignore those voices that say, "I can't" and do not want me to grow and achieve. It is so easy to believe that they are correct. It's easy to say to myself, "I've never done it so I will never do it" and then sit back and ponder how terrible life is. But how does that feel? Am I not forfeiting a part of myself? The essential, spiritual part of me, pushes towards my destiny and says, "You can!" I must intend to be in touch with that part of myself. I must nurture it and revel in it because I was created for a reason and only I can fulfill that true purpose.

AWARENESS

Can I? I will write one paragraph answering this question and exposing the self-talk phrases that say I'm deprived, defective or deficient.

DAY 336—LOVE

"It is not our purpose to become each other; it is to recognize each other, to learn to see the other and to respect them for what they are."
Hermann Hess (1955)

PREMISE

"I love you" is no longer an unconditional declaration. It has become the norm to qualify this statement, to make conditions or enumerate expectations. We tend to demand certain favors, gifts or rewards before professing our love. "I love you" becomes "I love you if . . ." Our assumption is that the other will provide something that we have been unable to provide for ourselves. Our hopes are high that they will love us, fix us, and make us feel good about who we are. Such a relationship is composed of two "ME's" instead of one "we." The potential for merging these "ME's" into a viable "we" is small, especially if each partner looks only to how much their needs are fulfilled and sees the other exclusively as a vehicle for further acquisitions. At best, the other becomes simply a partner in the quest for more "stuff" and if this goal is not attained, they become useless.

INTENTION

I always want to change things, to be in control, to manage anyone else but myself. This has ruined many relationships, particularly intimate relations. I intend to let go, to accept, and to understand that another's way of doing things is just as valid and worthy of respect as my way.

AWARENESS

I will resist the temptation to advise and to judge, for today. Instead, I will make a special effort to accept and be grateful for those who choose to share my life. I will write in my journal the names of two important people and three reasons why they play such a crucial role in my growth.

DAY 337—WISDOM

"A wise man will make more opportunities than he finds."
Francis Bacon (1625)

PREMISE

Wisdom is a seismic change of perspective that becomes permanently blended into our daily life. We actually see things differently. We now acknowledge a meaning, purpose and goodness to our existence where before there was an empty randomness and indifference. This is one of the goals of practicing humility, gratitude, acceptance and patience. Wisdom is a result of our awareness and intent to live a good life and to be of service to others. This sensation becomes more than a sum of its parts. As we become stronger individuals, we simultaneously strengthen the feeling of unity to our physical world through the development of our spiritual selves. We inhabit the world but the world does not have to inhabit us. We understand that we are primarily spiritual beings with a physical shell, not physical beings sheltering the spiritual. Wisdom is an all encompassing, inclusive perspective that creates a new mindset and understanding, thereby changing the remainder of our life.

INTENTION

Wisdom embraces joy and innovation thereby expanding alternatives and opportunity. With choice I become empowered. With wisdom, I can extend my options because I fear so little and I have a strong desire to grow. Wisdom widens my vista, it accepts challenge with confidence and is creative and perseverant in its search for resolutions. Wisdom gladly tackles the challenges of life that I previously avoided.

AWARENESS

Today, I will note what I am doing differently to solve familiar problems and to tolerate frustration. I will decide what I can do to improve tomorrow.

DAY 338—COURAGE

"What doesn't destroy us, makes us stronger."
Friedrich Nietzsche (1880)

PREMISE

Courage is often generated despite our best efforts to avoid it. The very fear that we first attempted to suppress, deny or avoid through complacency, arrogance and grandiosity actually creates courage because we are inevitably forced to confront that which we avoided. The basic, child-self defenses against fear eventually fail. Out of self-preservation, when all other alternatives are depleted, we find courage. It is the last option of our immature, fearful selves. There is nothing left to do but to face this challenge even though our child-self continues to protest, scream and thrash about. Change cannot be avoided, fear cannot be evaded, and we cannot be less than we were meant to be without sacrificing contentment, serenity and self-esteem. Therefore, we can run but we cannot hide from change, challenge or circumstance.

INTENTION

I will increase my efforts to confront change and overcome challenge because, ultimately, it is the best, most effective way, to savor life and achieve my objectives. I will not wait to become motivated by the negative energy of self-hate, inadequacy and vulnerability that accompany the avoidance, delay or denial of growth. Now is the time to begin.

AWARENESS

Today, I will pray for courage so that I may overcome my reluctance to encounter obstacles and inconveniences. I can face distress and I can persevere through obstruction even if it is self-imposed. With support from those I know and my Higher Power, I will fulfill my destiny.

DAY 339—LOVE

"Love is what you've been through with somebody."
James Thurber (1948)

PREMISE

Each relationship, casual to intimate, gives us an opportunity not only to learn more about ourselves but also to create a new self-image as we reassess, evolve and experience the world in a new way. Relationships are our spiritual classroom but it is crucial to remember that each step in this process of construction, confronts past preconceptions, habits and biases. Our tendency to comfortably categorize new experiences based on former assumptions must be challenged if we are to progress. Because we are changing, our perspective is changing and we must shed the skins of past distortions. Each moment presents opportunities to start anew, therefore, don't use them to confirm the old. Don't smother the chance to discover in favor of the comfort of confirmation, the smugness of certainty or the myopia of intransigence.

INTENTION

I can be resilient and not controlling. I can learn without teaching and listen without speaking. In other words, I can be a good friend, partner and lover. Today, I will make an extra effort to express my respect, appreciation and caring for those close to me.

AWARENESS

I will make a point of listening and repeating what I heard for clarification, not judgment. I will take special notice and be particularly aware of my tendencies to interrupt or "shut out" someone when I feel tense or threatened. For today I will practice listening rather than discoursing or sermonizing.

DAY 340—WISDOM

"Knowledge can be communicated but not wisdom."
Hermann Hesse (1945)

PREMISE

Wisdom is not simply knowledge, intelligence, or experience. Wisdom is a changed perspective, a new you, a novel and courageous way of viewing the world and your place in it. You see, act and feel differently. You "know" that you don't "know" but you are hopeful that you are learning each day as you mature and progress. You begin to feel like an integral part of a larger plan. There emerges a head/heart comprehension that pervades your being. You are, indeed, part of a larger whole, in the right place at the right time. You appreciate that you have a purpose and you are pursuing it in a manner that only you can create. You begin to act with love and awareness, caring for others and yourself as you evolve. Wisdom, like gratitude, is elusive. You must take the steps and work hard to defeat or subjugate the child-self as you pursue a life aspiring to humility, gratitude, acceptance/forgiveness and patience/trust. It then happens and you feel with your "head/heart" and know that this is the path you will continue to travel.

INTENTION

Wisdom, like feelings, should not be limited by words. Both must be experienced to understand their true meaning. They should not be confined, shaped or distorted by preconceptions or expressions. They must be felt with both head and heart. There is a "knowing" that I have when things are "right." This feeling is composed of acceptance, love and confidence. Wisdom is being where I should be and that is where I am.

AWARENESS

I will write in my journal about the "feeling" of wisdom.

DAY 341—COURAGE

"Fortune assists the brave."
Terence (165 B.C.E.)

PREMISE

Courage will appear when we receive the "gift of desperation." When we have finally failed in our efforts to maintain the status quo, to remain stuck, and to attempt the same solutions hoping for different results, courage will appear. Courage will thwart our attempts to blame every possible person or thing, forcing us to look internally, to take responsibility, to confront that which we avoided, and then to act with intent and purpose. We begin to "do" not to wait. Courage appears as the final strategy, the last effort, to cope with change. Despite the deeply ingrained beliefs that we are incapable of change, that we are helpless and dependent, we find that we must make a decision and that we must act in order to relieve the pain, depression, and the stress. There is no choice; we must begin. At this point, courage comes to the rescue.

INTENTION

"God helps those who helped themselves." I must want to succeed. I must intend to move beyond fear and beyond the status quo. I must take responsibility for the reality I create. I must act with love, acceptance and gratitude as I shed resentment, regret or rebuke. I can and I will do this with the help of my Higher Power.

AWARENESS

I will pray today, for the strength and courage to be me.

DAY 342—LOVE

"Surrender is the door one must pass through to find passion."
Deepak Chopra (2004)

PREMISE

Coping with change and knowing what we can do about it are life-long issues and part of our journey; they are essential to the process of learning and growth yet they are never fully resolved. Our objective is to discover meaning in our existence and to manifest the Good, as we learn precisely what that is. If we focus on love and compassion we cannot stray. This process of Life never ends. However, when we pursue both love and wisdom, we learn to navigate transition and to become more comfortable with surrendering the outcome of events to our Higher Power. We have little option or choice once we genuinely understand the delusion of controlling the external. The fact is we have little, if any control over those things outside of us. The only reasonable alternative is acceptance, and mastery of that which occurs behind the eyes. Appreciate change as a path to mature. Change is a message within the noise, a light in the darkness. Change is more than an inconvenience, alteration or frustration; it is an opportunity to renew perspectives, reassess your life objectives and re-strategize to resolve persistent impediments to fulfillment. Change is growth, trust is the soil that will nourish and energize your subsequent evolution.

INTENTION

I will renounce past bias, myth and misjudgment. I can get out of my way and become who I was created to be. I can listen to learn and learn to listen.

AWARENESS

I will write in my journal three ways that I have changed in recent months. I will take special note of my ability to be more open-minded, inclusive and accepting in my daily interactions.

DAY 343—WISDOM

"Youth is the time to study wisdom; old age is the time practice it."
Jean Jacques Rousseau (1782)

PREMISE

Wisdom is greater than the acquisition and assimilation of simple facts. It is one of the basic qualities that leads to contentment. Wisdom is simultaneously the result and antecedent of a major transformation of thought, feeling and action. It is a perspective and life strategy created by experience, tempered by failure and buoyed by love and tolerance. Wisdom is built by acceptance, gratitude, humility, and patience. These basic qualities are a necessary but not a sufficient condition for the acquisition of a genuine, evolved life style. Our goal is, each day, to practice and expand love, courage and wisdom. Some call it a "spiritual awakening," others a "divine intervention" but however it occurs; one must be grateful for its presence in our lives. Many can work towards this objective but not everyone will achieve it.

INTENTION

I can develop wisdom as I can become all that I was created to be. Wisdom is the culmination of many steps, just as it is the beginning of many more. The journey continues as the destination fades, transforms and re-emerges. With wisdom I know the way and I am eager to learn the way. Such is the paradox. Such is life.

AWARENESS

I will note one example of how I manifested a head-heart solution in any manner that was new and untried. I will approach one interaction from a new perspective emphasizing tolerance, patience and acceptance.

DAY 344—COURAGE

"Courage is knowing what not to fear."
Plato (377 B.C.E.)

PREMISE

Courage is facing truth, acting upon what you can and can't control. Therefore, courage is facing the fear of change and the fear of taking responsibility for our reactions, thoughts and feelings about that change. We can learn not to fear our essence, the person we are at our core. We know that we can confront change, responsibility and success, as well as failure. We no longer need to hide behind resentment, victimhood or inadequacy. We have "a knowing" that we indeed, are capable and that we will fulfill commitments and achieve objectives. We know that we do not have to evade responsibility for our lives, decisions or thoughts, by hiding in pessimism. With courage we can shed denial and therefore despair, as we vanquish thoughts of "can't." We no longer accept ideas or feelings of ineptitude nor do we participate in self-sabotaging actions (expecting different results from customary and comfortable reactions). Courage gives us the incentive to "become" and the serenity to "be."

INTENTION

I can free myself from the familiar, the habitual and the unthinking. I no longer must take comfort in habit and routine. I can attain the courage to look forward, to think of others and to expand my perspective beyond fear and false satisfaction. I can confront, conquer and grow. I can make a difference as I learn and teach others through my example. I can live my life sharing love yet achieving exactly what I need when I need it.

AWARENESS

I will make a special effort to help one person today. I will note what I did and how it made me feel to help another. I realize that all of my experience can benefit others.

DAY 345—LOVE

"Up to the point when they emerged, two lovers walked a separate path. Together, they will create a new path with no past, where every step moves into the unknown . . ."
Deepak Chopra (1997)

PREMISE

Be open to and aware of each moment as an opportunity to learn something new about yourself and your world. Focus on the needs of the other and what you can contribute to the relationship, the "we," the "us." Such behavior will be both informative and productive. To bond positively with another on any level of intimacy, we must subordinate the ego/child-self's needs and wants. For a relationship to flourish, the prime motive becomes to love and serve. "What can I do?" versus "what can I get?"

INTENTION

I will allow myself to be spontaneous, to surrender to the present and be guided by my partner. I can become a "we" without sacrificing the "I" simply by being aware of the moment and reaffirming my strength and flexibility to transform and mature. I will remember that to be strong is to bend, not to be rigid.

AWARENESS

I will make a special effort, with a special intention, to listen to my partner and not to be defensive, demanding or controlling. The idea is to learn as much as possible about myself and how I behave while engaging in a new, more intimate relationship. I will be especially cautious about being subservient and failing to advocate equal respect for myself. This is the dilemma: how much do I give of "me" in order to preserve and generate a more intimate relationship (a "we").

DAY 346—WISDOM

"If you only had your brains in your head you would be as good a man as any of them . . ."
The Wizard Of Oz (1900)

PREMISE

The truth is that we need both heart and mind, combined with experience, as seen through the perspectives of forgiveness and acceptance, if we are to live in wisdom. Wisdom is formed as humility, gratitude, acceptance and patience grow and interact reciprocally. This is a function of time, intent, awareness and assimilation of experience. Many whom are spiritually versed and knowledgeable do not attain wisdom because such qualities are absent from this process of spiritual growth. Wisdom requires an intermixing of understanding, love and compassion such that they blend into a dynamic system while retaining their individual flavors.

INTENTION

I am beginning to develop the necessary "head-heart", "body-spirit", "me-we", attitudes. I feel singular yet united, intelligent yet naive, strong yet vulnerable. I am a work in progress and I am just where I need to be in my evolution. This is because I intend to improve my positive qualities and I am aware of the effects of this intent on my daily life and relationships.

AWARENESS

I will write about three areas of improvement in my journal. I will focus on those areas and circumstances that reflect my growth in humility, acceptance, gratitude and courage because each of these is a building block of wisdom.

DAY 347—COURAGE

"Often, the test of courage is not to die but to live."
Vittorio Alfieri

PREMISE

Low self-esteem is basically a deeply ingrained, delusional and self-destructive belief that we are incapable and/or unworthy of creating self-fulfillment, satisfaction and contentment in our lives. The notion of being responsible and self-empowered fills us with fear and avoidance. It is depressing but it is more comfortable not to act. It is easier but more debilitating to resist change than it is to advance and expand. Unfortunately, when we entertain such thoughts of change, we reflexively recall past failures and current deficits, thereby hurling ourselves into the arms of immobility, dependence and victimhood. We retreat from the responsibility of fulfilling our destiny and maximizing our strengths and uniqueness. We hide rather than confront. We cower in a corner rather than facing our responsibility and creating our reality. Such is our condition and such is the challenge we must confront, if we are to prosper and flourish.

INTENTION

It is easy to escape, defer and delay, but it is also tormenting, depressing and distressful. The more we run, the more frightened we become. We run from our shadow only to find it waiting for us when we tire. We hide our eyes only to stumble and fall. We cover our ears only to hear our inner voice cry, "You must!" Avoidance does not work. Deferring does not defeat. We cannot run from ourselves and we cannot escape our destiny. If we are to transform into whom we were created to be, we must start now. No delays, no excuses. Now!

AWARENESS

For today, I will make every effort to face truth and I will avoid no challenge. I will confront my fear, face my anxiety and move forward in the trust that I am guided by a beneficent power far greater than myself.

DAY 348—LOVE

"Everything that irritates us about others, can lead us to an understanding of ourselves."
Carl Jung (1925)

PREMISE

Don't be afraid to be wrong, misunderstood or misled. Don't fear the criticism or anger of others by being defensive. Listen to learn. Be silent, observe, hear, feel and breathe. Seek commonalities and avoid differences. Attempt to join not separate. Identify don't compare. Aspire and endeavor to emphasize and define the "we" not the "I." Nurture this "we", so that the "I" may grow. During disagreements, the goal should be to understand rather than to be understood, if you wish the relationship to progress and prosper. Opposition does not mean "wrong" or "right," it is simply an alternative perspective with the potential for insight. We are all like the blind describing different parts of the same animal. Listening and learning is a process that will ultimately reveal a synthesis and accommodation where both parties can feel understood, accepted and respected.

INTENTION

Instead of looking for blame, I can have the wisdom to look inward and not to be distracted by externals, prejudices and preconceptions. I will not fear difference and I will not reflexively recoil from opposition. Rather, I will listen and respect. I will strive not to condemn, vilify or deprecate but rather to understand in the moment. What is happening and what I am creating in this instant is my responsibility and subject to my control. If I focus on instilling love, acceptance and understanding and if I banish fear, the moment will flourish.

AWARENESS

I will be keenly aware of my tendency to place blame for an uncomfortable situation. For today I will, instead, strive to perceive what I can control and pray for the will and energy to manifest that control with love and compassion.

DAY 349—WISDOM

"If it be true that a man is rich who wants nothing,
a wise man is a very rich man."
Jean De La Bruyere (1688)

PREMISE

It takes work, intent and awareness to be extricated from this swamp of entitlement, narcissism, arrogance and superficiality, that is the consumer culture. While it has given physical pleasure and comfort to many, it has often done so the expense of spirituality, mutual respect and basic decency. We must, above all else, stop, reflect and acknowledge that there is a problem. Then we must rouse the courage, perseverance and wisdom to delineate the issue and construct a plan of growth.

INTENTION

What is the difference between wants and needs? This is such an important distinction and one that I didn't make, all that long ago. I am getting wise. I am making progress. I can feel the self-confidence, the pride and the hope, as I realize that I have all that I need in this moment. I know each day that I am improving and that as long as I keep trying and I intend to do the next "good" thing, I will remain content and true to my path. Life is good, now.

AWARENESS

What do I truly need? I will answer that today in my journal and I will take special note as I go through my daily routine to acknowledge and identify what I genuinely need and what is unnecessary for my progress and spiritual health.

DAY 350—COURAGE

"Keep your fears to yourself; share your courage with others."
Robert Louis Stevenson (1884)

PREMISE

We do not "have to" submit to fear and helplessness. We do not "have to" continue in the demeaning, insulting and debilitating circumstances of our present situation. We can break free; we can choose liberation over servitude and forge a path of discovery and independence. If we focus and persevere, intend love and compassion and approach obstacles with a willingness to learn, we can realize our destiny, and live life to the fullest.

INTENTION

I am not helpless and I will not accept that I am imprisoned in my own jail. I can and will move forward and ultimately embrace life and change. I must be patient. I must not confuse impediments, frustration and disappointments with inability or ineffectiveness. If I have not yet achieved my goals, it does not mean that I cannot achieve my goals.

AWARENESS

I will note in my journal three things that I CAN do to express courage and I will follow that plan today.

DAY 351—LOVE

"When we have climbed over the wall we shall know what is on the other side."
Dorothy, The Wizard of Oz (1900)

PREMISE

Dorothy's matter-of-fact statement about courage is admirable and courageous. She accepts that frustration and uncertainty is part of the process of attaining her objective but rather than personalize or become offended, she simply accepts impediments as they are and develops a strategy to circumvent them. Such courage is necessary if we are to love and build lasting and fulfilling relationships. We can neither discover nor offer love unless we choose to allow love into our life. If we perceive ourselves to be lovable, it is logical to expect to be loved. If the child-self's criticism, fear and need for control prevents us from appreciating who we are (a reflection of an all-powerful life force) it will be far more difficult to find or give love to another. Surrender your defenses and have the resolve to be vulnerable so as to love. In order to receive love you must give love in every area of your life. Risk, dare and confront the fear so that you may advance yourself and those you encounter.

INTENTION

I can develop the courage of tolerance. I can understand that even though someone is solving a problem in a different manner, it is not necessarily wrong. I will have the courage to watch and learn that love is an opportunity to increase self-understanding. I can prosper from differences. I don't have to be threatened by any other, as I live my life and allow others to live theirs.

AWARENESS

On at least one occasion, I will resist the temptation to interfere, manage and control. Instead, I will "allow." I will document this instance in my journal.

DAY 352—WISDOM

"Wisdom is the principal thing; therefore get wisdom; and with all thy getting get an understanding."
Proverbs 4:7

PREMISE

It takes wisdom to look beyond the illusions of current circumstances. It takes courage to face the truth. All too often, this motivation is spurred by pain, disappointment and desperation, so that there is no choice but to react and break from the status quo. Understand, that the problems you face and the feelings generated by your interpretation of those problems are all created by you, as you battle change and embrace stagnation. Each step is in your control. Strength and power arise from within. A new pill, gadget or relationship will not save you from yourself. Only you can do this and the first step is attaining the courage, wisdom and understanding that you are responsible for the reality you create and the situation in which you find yourself.

INTENTION

I can look for strength and hope inside myself, especially as I connect with my spiritual-self. When I take a moment, stop the world as well as the outside noise and turmoil, I can actually feel the power of my spirit, my essence. I am primarily a spiritual entity and I always will be, no matter the state of my body or the world. My spirit soars and I am grateful.

AWARENESS

I will note today where I showed improvement in confidence and spirit during a particularly difficult circumstance. I will write this in my journal and express, gratitude for all the gifts that I have been given and all the progress that I have made.

DAY 353—COURAGE

"Courage is not the roar going into battle but the quiet voice that gets you out of bed each morning to face the day."
Edward Francis Albee (1922)

PREMISE

Change scares us. It is unsettling, unpredictable and inherently unstable. It is the "great unknown" and the source of much anxiety. It renders us helpless because the unknown cannot he predicted or controlled. It is a wave that we must ride to the beach or become overpowered. Yet we are uncertain as to how to respond. Do we confront change or do we hide, delay and defer? We do not trust our abilities, our vision or ourselves. Instead of acceptance and riding the wave, we avoid and stay out of the water. No matter how hot, how uncomfortable, no matter how ultimately destructive, we stay on shore and watch life from afar. We have resigned and submitted to helplessness, blame and resentment instead of empowerment, acceptance and courage.

INTENTION

I can stop this trend and change my usual way of responding to my usual problems. I can "go into the water" and partake in life. I can risk and confront the unknown and unpredictable. Nothing can be as scary as what I imagine. Nothing can be as debilitating and demoralizing as inaction. I must do this! I must change! I must face truth and enhance my destiny. I can do this . . . a step at a time.

AWARENESS

Today, I will note and commit to one, small, definable step to begin my journey to embrace change and to attain my new objectives.

DAY 354—WISDOM

"Dare to be wise; when you begin you are already halfway there."
Horace (33 B.C.E.)

PREMISE

Wisdom requires courage and patience as maturation, compassion and positive reciprocity slowly advance, a step at a time. It takes courage even to be "halfway" there. But there are constant impediments, frustrations and distractions as we struggle to actualize all of the virtues. The consumer culture impedes spiritual enrichment by inundating us with messages of false deprivation, need and deficiency. We must be aware of these messages and think about our thinking as well as our intentions, or the signal for change will be lost among the noises of greed, fear and arrogance. It takes courage to discover truth and to gain the wisdom to perceive further than the external and the superficial. We must see beyond what we want to see and confront whatever is necessary to achieve contentment.

INTENTION

I have the strength, the ability, the patience and the knowledge to grow in wisdom. Wisdom is a skill, a trait that requires more than intent. Wisdom is also a function of time, experience and introspection. Awareness of our behavior, intent to change and then reassessment of results, time after time, will ultimately produce the necessary outcomes. Be wise, persevere and achieve.

AWARENESS

I will note how I've changed up to this point in my pursuit of wisdom. I will take special care to think about my thinking, to ponder my feelings and to reassess my reactions.

DAY 355—COURAGE

"Heroism is the dazzling and the glorious concentration of courage."
Henri Amiel (1852)

PREMISE

Many of us have been taught to focus on what we are not, how we fall short of the ideal, rather than focusing on whom we are and where we are strong. Therefore, we become haunted by our mistakes and oblivious to our successes. Change ceases to become a challenge; it transforms into a threat because action is riskier and more prone to error than inaction. So we hide, we sit, we watch, we become miserable; yet we don't have the energy to change or the knowledge of how to begin. Courage stops this self-destructive cycle. Rather than flee from fear we begin to confront and manage it. Fear stops being distressful and instead becomes a guide, a piece of information, another signal to help us find our way. We can now live and embrace experience, as we grow.

INTENTION

I can begin today. Each day presents an opportunity. I will learn and I will fail. I will excel and I will falter. I will be who I was created to be today, a step a time, moment-by-moment and interaction-by-interaction. One thing I will not do . . . is hide.

AWARENESS

Who am I now? What should I become? Where shall I put my focus? I will write a paragraph and ponder these thoughts today. I will construct a strategy with renewed goals and objectives.

DAY 356—LOVE

"You can accomplish by kindness what you cannot by force."
Publilius Syrus (66 B.C.E.)

PREMISE

It is truly better to love than to be right. As humans we want to be consistent, predictable and correct in all of our perspectives and perceptions. When encountering another who has the same needs but, being unique, has a somewhat different viewpoint, we often become threatened and therefore, fearful. The level or intensity of this fear is directly proportional to our level of intimacy with this person. It is in the best interests of both to forbid and control the child-self from asserting its needs. The child-self is incapable of either understanding or compassion. It is simply a reflection of the primitive part of ourselves that must be subjugated if we are to mature. Although extremely powerful, the child-self is also extremely vulnerable. Therefore, when another presents an alternative perspective, pause, breathe and listen, for they too deserve respect.

INTENTION

I can resist the temptation to "know it all" and I can resist the temptation to try to convince another of my viewpoint or my reality. Instead, I can be confident of my version of things and the rightness of my cause. I can be a majority of one, yet respectful and compassionate towards another.

AWARENESS

I will note a situation where I could have "proven my case" but instead, I relinquished control rather than engage in conflict. I will write of my thoughts and feelings. Was I subjugating myself or was I trying to understand?

DAY 357—WISDOM

"Wisdom comes alone through suffering."
Aeschylus (480 B.C.E.)

PREMISE

Fear can trample the seeds of wisdom. Wisdom is the "mature adult", the authority, trying to discipline the angry and fearful "child-self." This is the same child-self that cries, "don't look, don't see, hide!" The adult, instead, empowers herself, summons the courage to face change and learns as she advances. Fear and anxiety will unceasingly attempt to impede progress and realistic perception. We are forever tempted to cling to our delusions, distortions and disinformation despite their destructiveness. The child-self demands sameness, ritual and routine. Wisdom repels this so as to break from the comfort of the status quo and to move ever forward towards our destiny.

INTENTION

I am wise enough to know that I will never know enough, but I console myself with the idea that I know more today than yesterday, but less than I will tomorrow. So, my objective is to learn now, to witness my life and to give love.

AWARENESS

I will make a mental note and write in my journal, one thing I learned today that I could apply tomorrow, so as to make my life more joyous.

DAY 358—COURAGE

"If one is forever cautious, can one remain a human being?"
Aleksandr Solzhenitsyn (1968)

PREMISE

Courage gives us the strength, motivation and energy to take risks, chances and challenges. Yet the energy of courage is the energy of direction, consideration and focus. Like a stream that is shaped by the land and filtered by rocks, courage is strong, unrelenting yet directed towards a primary source. Similar to the stream, courage is to be used as needed for the benefit of all. Honesty reflects courage when it guides you to be more truthful with yourself and listen to others as they give you observations and information. You can learn without demeaning or compromising yourself simply by listening, then evaluating, assessing and proceeding with a new outlook and a new disposition. It is important to learn from others, to be open to alternative perspectives without being coerced into conformity. Courage will resist such pressures yet encourage innovation and resiliency.

INTENTION

Each day, in every way, I am flourishing, as I emerge from my self-created prison to enter a world where I am effective and responsible. Each day, it becomes more apparent that I am fulfilling my destiny and with courage and gratitude, I will move forward.

AWARENESS

When angry, anxious or depressed, I will take special care not to judge others, project blame or become resentful of my present circumstances. I will summon the courage to take responsibility and reframe the situation so that I learn and mature.

DAY 359—LOVE

"Love is the joy of the Good, the wonder of the wise, the amazement of the Gods."
Plato (400 B.C.E.)

PREMISE

We are taught the qualities and characteristics of those we should love and of those who should love us. Unfortunately, we are also apprised as to how we are deficient, and how we have disappointed and failed to meet the expectations of others. In our world of the physical, there are many dichotomies; among them are success and failure, love and hate. Some say that we must be careful in giving love and suspicious about receiving it. Love is said to be something earned, to be worthy of. Such caution serves only to confine and confuse. Love for others, for life and for the Good, benefits us. It is a gift that we give ourselves. We are part of a supreme whole that is perfect. Each piece seamlessly merges with the other in unison. Therefore, love, courage and wisdom are the major and most necessary qualities we need if we are to achieve a life of fulfillment and contentment. Now that we are aware, we must do the necessary work to assimilate them into our daily life.

INTENTION

I can resist the routine, the status quo and shed the old ideas and fears that so permeate my life. I will be aware of all the ramifications of such intent. I will begin to live a life of contentment because I can begin not only to accept the need for change but also to embrace it.

AWARENESS

Today, I will take special note in how I approach loving others. I am aware of the different degrees of love and intimacy. I am aware of the importance of loving myself primarily and I am aware that I must reach out, accept others and risk. With trust in God and respect for myself I can and will move forward.

DAY 360—WISDOM

"Do not learn how to react, rather learn how to respond."
The Buddha (c. 500 B.C.E.)

PREMISE

Wisdom is having the patience to realize that events occur at times during which we have no control. The planted seed will grow at its own pace and result in characteristics dictated by nature and its singularity, not based on our demands or desires. We have no effect on the outcome. To accept and acquiesce to this is to win the war against change. This is the only war winnable by raising a flag of surrender. Control and implement what you can and leave the rest to your Higher Power. Wisdom is understanding and accepting that it is far better to be an observer than to be a manager. "Go with the flow" and "ride the wave to the beach." Each cliché urges and reinforces the wisdom of acceptance.

INTENTION

I will develop the wisdom to learn from life, to face my mistakes and to embrace truth. I will develop the wisdom that views disappointment through the lens of acceptance. I will develop the wisdom of self-control and awareness.

AWARENESS

I will note in my journal an instance that occurred today where I transformed a disappointment into a learning experience. I will also note an instance where I chose compassion and understanding over anger and arrogance.

DAY 361—COURAGE

"Bravery is stability, not of legs and arms, but of courage and the soul."
Michel De Montaigne (1580)

PREMISE

When fear and distrust hinder perspective, we tend to myopically repeat past behaviors, despite experience. Consequently, we luxuriate in the complacency of our delusions. Courage will pierce this self-destructive pattern of thought. Courage enables us to honestly determine and delineate a problem, as we pursue novel, more fulfilling resolutions. Courage empowers us to live as we were created to live, to make a difference, to accomplish and to progress in harmony with a transcendent spiritual plan. With courage we abandon the child-self so that we may trust in our Higher Power and accede to the delicate design that is our destiny. We now develop the patience to become participant/observers during various detours, delays and assorted frustrations. Without courage, we can experience neither freedom nor love and we cannot realize our destiny.

INTENTION

I can confront fear and live my life. As I learn about myself, and how I respond to the challenge of change, I will develop and improve my skills to endure and persevere through the stress that accompanies transition and uncertainty. With each encounter, I will slowly evolve in mind, body and spirit. As I progress, my responses will be more controlled and more reflective of tolerance and compassion.

AWARENESS

I will document five areas of strength and skill that I believe reflect my true abilities when encountering change and uncertainty. Am I calm, perseverant, logical and objective or do I impulsively react and panic? I will compose and document a strategy that I can use when first confronting the stress of change and I will implement this throughout the day.

DAY 362—LOVE

"Love is union with somebody or something, outside oneself, under the condition of retaining the separateness and integrity of one's own self."
Erich Fromm (1964)

PREMISE

There are times when love reaches out, yet we recoil. We question who would love us, what do they want? Love from others is awkward when we have yet to learn to love ourselves. Once again, this is fear in disguise. Self-hate and self-disparagement prevent our progress because we isolate, languish and fester rather than risking and reaching out. There are many ways that we express self-hate or self-disappointment but the primary one is to hide behind fear, to let life pass us by as we cower in the shadows. Self-hate, self-destruction, low self-esteem, depression, whatever the label, whatever the reaction; it is just another way to separate ourselves from our spiritual essence and to prevent us from living the attitudes of acceptance, patience, love and gratitude.

INTENTION

I must overcome my fear of loss, rejection and vulnerability. I must think of love so that I express love. What I give to the world I get. If I offer fear, anger and exclusion that is what will permeate my life. If when I confront doubt and hesitation, I offer acceptance, patience and trust, I will receive these from others. I create my reality and I wish my world to become a positive place where growth and progress flourish.

AWARENESS

Today, I will risk by reaching out and manifesting acceptance and inclusion in my life. I will practice kindness, compassion and generosity with no desire for recompense other than the Good feelings I get from service.

DAY 363—WISDOM

"Power without wisdom collapses under its own weight."
Horace (22 B.C.E.)

PREMISE

Wisdom accepts the mundane because it knows that there is a greater force at work. Wisdom is derived from experience as we reassess, recalculate and restrategize. Wisdom incites us to view the past from a perspective of forgiveness. Wisdom understands that resentment, blame and victimhood chain us to destructive memories and hamper advancement and evolution. Each experience is the result of action and action requires thought, if it is to succeed. Wisdom knows that we would have chosen better had we known better and it acknowledges that we have learned and now we do, in fact, know better. If we choose from a wise and loving perspective the results can always be beneficial. If we do not so choose, we can at least learn, then grow and then advance.

INTENTION

I am growing wiser despite my hesitations, fears and distrust. I understand and accept that my betterment depends upon shifting my thoughts and behavior to acts of kindness. If I am to evolve into whom I was created to be, I must become aware of the "now" and the opportunities for growth that it presents. I will train myself to view my experiences through lenses of love, acceptance, gratitude, humility, patience, courage and wisdom. When I intend this, I will begin to recreate myself in a more positive and productive way, as the myths of the past gently fade from memory and the promise of the future shines brightly.

AWARENESS

Today, I will note in my journal two instances of annoyingly familiar circumstances where now I reframe my attitude and approach to that of acceptance and inclusion. In this way, I will change the entire sequence of events for the better.

DAY 364—COURAGE

"Whatever I have tried to do in life,
I have tried with all my heart to do it well."
Charles Dickens (1860)

PREMISE

When we become infused with courage, trust, love acceptance and contentment are created and expressed in everyday living. The perfect ceases to impede the Good. We strive to do our best and we feel satisfied when we complete our task. We no longer must become more than we are. We learn to "be." With courage we begin to comprehend truth. We begin to understand that we create our own problems by choosing to attend to those events, among many, that validate and reinforce our negative preconceptions about ourselves, our relationships and the world we inhabit. Each choice we make generates emotions and behavioral responses initiating a cycle of action and reaction that can either promote growth or maintain the inertia. We choose the "same" devil that we know as we shun change and forgo our responsibility to forge a new path and recreate ourselves with positive and loving thoughts. Courage gives us the ability and fortitude to move forward and to avoid lethargy and paralysis.

INTENTION

I realize that the solution to subjugating past myths and creating a more positive and confident identity lies with awareness of the issue and intent to change. I can do this, as each moment presents new opportunities to react differently to the same situations. As I change my thinking, my feelings and behavior will also change and those around me will respond differently. This is indeed scary but it is the most important thing I can do to affirm my destiny.

AWARENESS

I will take note of my biases and predispositions in familiar circumstances. I will change my pattern of response to two of such incidents and document in my journal the effects of this modification.

DAY 365—LOVE

Submit to love faithfully and it gives a person joy. It creates fragrance in the air, ardor from coldness and it beautifies everything around it."
Leos Janacek (1903)

PREMISE

How can you cultivate love in a field of self-hate? You can't give what you don't have and you don't have what you can't feel. If you are taught that you are deficient, deprived or disabled, you cannot perceive the abundance, benevolence or competence that encompasses you. God makes no mistakes. Each day, in every way, we can choose to get better and stronger. We can choose to pursue our goal of spiritual mindedness and advancement. If we are to be content, we must strive to fulfill our destiny to become who we were created to be and to conquer self-imposed barriers. We must work to renew confidence and to begin the minute steps necessary to reach our goals. We can offer and accept a compliment without qualification or question, be who we were created to be and embrace life.

INTENTION

I realize that each time I "intend", I choose to refocus and to become aware of the present moment. In this manner, I create an opportunity to learn, grow and become more powerful than the destructive external forces that reinforce complacency and the status quo. The internal work of self-acceptance comprises the intention to respond to life's travails with gratitude, patience, courage and humility. As I begin to project a more spiritual persona, I will be viewed and responded to differently, thus beginning a positive cycle of growth and mutual enhancement.

AWARENESS

I will be especially aware of my "will" and my "intent", with each interaction. I will focus on change and spiritual mindedness.

Day 366—WISDOM

"The perfection of wisdom . . . is to proportion our wants to our possessions, our ambitions to our capacities, we will then be a happy and virtuous people."
Mark Twain (1870)

PREMISE

Our culture strongly discourages thinking, so wisdom is not one of the basic objectives the average person pursues. To be inarticulate and uninformed is to be "cool" and carefree. The advertisements spewed through the mass media by corporate America do not want us to think beyond the brief "bumper sticker" message presented on TV. Many politicians believe that our attention span and verbal comprehension do not extend beyond a fleeting, emotionally charged slogan. We are told what is wrong with the world and us and we are told how it will be fixed. No thought or reconsideration is necessary. It is so simple and effortless to passively experience life, certain and secure in our misconceptions, complacent in our misapprehensions. It takes discipline and audacity to question and it takes struggle and courage to achieve a life of contentment.

INTENTION

I now realize that I can achieve all that I need if I focus on success and intend the Good. The power is within and I can harness that power with awareness as I energize and release that energy through intent. I must take responsibility and not wait to be rescued, saved or inspired by the external. The time to act is now and I can do this. I have the knowledge, the will and the physical ability to achieve my objectives and to realize my dreams.

AWARENESS

Today, I will give thanks for all that I have learned over the last year as well as for all that I have and for all I will become.

Appendix A

THIRTEEN CORE PRINCIPLES

1. Our life has meaning. We were born at a specific time, in a particular place, with a unique body, for a significant purpose. We are all, each, a part of a divine, greater whole.

2. All living things are part of a benevolent, grand design and as such deserve our respect, compassion and assistance.

3. We have little control over any external event or individual but we can restrain our own responses by mastering our thoughts, feelings and behavior each moment with each interaction. We can therefore establish a loving, affirming reality.

4. We must resist self-destructive and self-denigrating thoughts in order to become whom we were created to be.

5. The foundation and beginning for all positive personality traits is humility.

6. Of the four basic temperaments, acceptance/forgiveness is most conducive for contentment.

7. The gift of gratitude will either prevent or mitigate depression.

8. Patience/trust will allay anxiety.

9. Relationships are spiritual classrooms that present both challenges and opportunities for growth and self-knowledge.

10. Judgment and compassion are the most insidious qualities spawned by the consumer culture. They will destroy compassion, love, acceptance and unity.

11. Love and wisdom are composed of the same essential traits, namely, humility, gratitude, acceptance/forgiveness, and patience/trust.

12. Love is the emotional expression of wisdom and wisdom is the cognitive expression of love.

13. Courage combines all of the aforementioned traits. It serves to motivate us to interact with others, to confront change and to express wisdom and love.

Bibliography and Suggested Reading

Albom, Mitch. Tuesdays with Morrie. New York: Anchor Books, 1997.

Baum, L. Frank. The Wizard of Oz. London: Puffin Books, 1994.

Boorstein, Sylvia. Pay Attention for Goodness' Sake. New York: Ballantine Books, 2002.

Bowlby, John. Attachment and Love. London: Hogarth Press, 1969.

Buddhist Society (Ed.). 1001 Pearls of Buddhist Wisdom. London: Duncan Baird Publishers, 2006.

Byrne, Rhonda. The Secret. New York: Atria Books, 2006.

Casey, Karen. Daily Meditations for Practicing the Course. San Francisco: Hazelden Foundation, 1995.

Chantrell, Glynnis (Ed.). The Oxford Dictionary of Word Histories. Oxford: Oxford University Press, 2002.

Chopra, Deepak. The Path to Love. New York: Three Rivers Press, 1997.

Chopra, Deepak. The Book of Secrets. New York: Harmony Books, 2004.

Covey, Stephen R. The 7 Habits of Highly Effective People. New York: Simon & Schuster, 1989.

Das, Lama Surya. The Big Questions. United States of America: Holtzbrinck Publishers, 2007.

Das, Lama Surya. Buddha Is as Buddha Does. San Francisco: Harper, 2007.

Dyer, Wayne W. Your Sacred Self. New York: Harper Paperbacks, 1995.

Dyer, Wayne W. Wisdom of the Ages. New York: Harper Collins Publishers, 1998.

Dyer, Wayne W. Manifest Your Destiny. New York: Harper Paperbacks, 1999.

Dyer, Wayne W. There's a Spiritual Solution to Every Problem. New York: Harper Collins Publishers, 2001.

Dyer, Wayne W. You'll See It When You Believe It. New York: Quill, 2001.

Foundation for Inner Peace. A Course in Miracles. Tiburon. CA: Foundation for Inner Peace, 1976.

Fromm, Erich. Escape from Freedom. New York: Holt, Rinehart & Winston, 1941.

Hazelden Foundation. Keep It Simple. San Francisco: Hazelden Foundation, 1989.

Jung, Carl G. Analytical Psychology. New York: Moffat, Yard, 1916.

Jung, Carl G. Modern Man in Search of a Soul. New York: Harcourt, Brace & World, 1933.

Karen, Robert, Ph.D. The Forgiving Self. New York: Doubleday, 2001.

Klauser, Henriette Anne. Write It Down, Make It Happen. New York: Simon & Schuster, 2000.

Ladner, Lorne. The Lost Art of Compassion. New York: Harper Collins Publishers, 2001.

Lama, Dalai and Cutler, Howard C. The Art of Happiness. New York: Penguin Putnam Inc., 1998.

Oliver, Joan Duncan. Good Karma. London: Duncan Baird Publishers, 2006.

Rainer, Tristine. The New Diary. New York: Penguin Putnam, Inc., 1978.

Ray, Veronica. Choosing Happiness: The Art of Living Unconditionally. Hazelden Foundation. San Francisco: Harper, 1991.

Rogers, Carl R. On Becoming a Person. Boston: Houghton Mifflin, 1961.

Ross, David. 1001 Pearls of Wisdom. London: Duncan Baird Publishers, 2006.

Ruiz, Don Miguel. The Voice of Knowledge. San Rafael, CA: Amber-Allen Publishing, 2004.

Ryan, M. J. Attitudes of Gratitude. Boston: Conari Press, 1999.

Ryan, M. J. The Power of Patience. New York: Broadway Books/ Random House, 2003.

Ryan, M. J. Trusting Yourself. New York: Broadway Books, 2004.

Ryan, M. J. The Happiness Makeover. New York: Broadway Books, 2005.

Tolle, Eckhart. The Power of Now. Novato, CA: New World Library, 1999.

Wiener, Philip P. (Ed.). Dictionary of the History of Ideas (Vol. III). New York: Charles Scribner's Sons, 1973.

Williamson, Marianne. A Return to Love. New York: Harper Collins Publishers, 1992.

Williamson, Marianne. Everyday Grace. New York: Riverhead Books, 2002.

Williamson, Marianne. A Gift of Change. New York: Harper Collins Publishers, 2004.

Williamson, Marianne. The Age of Miracles. Carlsbad, CA: Hay House, 2008.

Wolf, Fred Alan. Dr. Quantum's Little Book of Big Ideas. Needham, MA: Moment Point Press, 2005.

Zukav, Gary. The Seat of the Soul. New York: Simon & Schuster, 1999.